Economic, Political, and Legal Solutions to Critical Issues in Urban Education and Implications for Teacher Preparation

A volume in
Contemporary Perspectives on Access, Equity, and Achievement
Chance W. Lewis, *Series Editor*

Contemporary Perspectives on Access, Equity, and Achievement

Chance W. Lewis, *Series Editor*

Priorities of the Professoriate: Engaging Multiple Forms of Scholarship Across Rural and Urban Institutions (2015)
Fred A. Bonner II, Rosa M. Banda, Petra A. Robinson, Chance W. Lewis, and Barbara Lofton

Autoethnography as a Lighthouse: Illuminating Race, Research, and the Politics of Schooling (2015)
Stephen Hancock, Ayana Allen, and Chance W. Lewis

Teacher Education and Black Communities: Implications for Access, Equity and Achievement (2014)
Yolanda Sealey-Ruiz, Chance W. Lewis, and Ivory Toldson

Improving Urban Schools: Equity and Access in K–16 STEM Education (2013)
Mary Margaret Capraro, Robert M. Capraro, and Chance W. Lewis

Black Males in Postsecondary Education: Examining their Experiences in Diverse Institutional Contexts (2012)
Adriel A. Hilton, J. Luke Wood, and Chance W. Lewis

Yes We Can! Improving Urban Schools through Innovative Educational Reform (2011)
Leanne L. Howell, Chance W. Lewis, and Norvella Carter

Economic, Political, and Legal Solutions to Critical Issues in Urban Education and Implications for Teacher Preparation

edited by

Stephanie Thomas
Lenoir-Rhyne University

Shanique J. Lee
The University of North Carolina at Charlotte

Chance W. Lewis
The University of North Carolina at Charlotte

INFORMATION AGE PUBLISHING, INC.
Charlotte, NC • www.infoagepub.com

Library of Congress Cataloging-in-Publication Data

A CIP record for this book is available from the Library of Congress
http://www.loc.gov

ISBN: 978-1-64802-938-7 (Paperback)
        978-1-64802-939-4 (Hardcover)
        978-1-64802-940-0 (E-Book)

CONTENTS

INTRODUCTION

WHAT IS THE PROBLEM AND WHY DO WE NEED SOLUTIONS?

It is difficult to change a person's heart or to change based on moral conviction alone. However, policies and laws can be established that will change a person's behavior. Historically, there was rarely a time where societal changes were the result of a desire to do what was morally right. Doing what is right was contingent upon economic advantages, political motivation, or the threat of litigation. The Montgomery Bus Boycott, Student Nonviolent Coordinating Committee (SNCC), and *Brown v. Board of Education* (1954) are a few examples that reveal incentives to reform as a result of an economic, political, and legal threat. By the mid-1900s, the NAACP had learned a valuable lesson in the South, that litigation or the threat thereof as an effective tool in the quest for educational equality (Douglas, 1995). More recently, the #metoo movement, the Los Angeles teachers' strike, which exposed corrupt behavior and insufficient working environments that have existed for decades, and social justice efforts in the Black Lives Matter movement have catapulted social injustices to the forefront of the world. Even during a global pandemic, educational inequities have become even more obvious, exacerbating the issues that have existed all along in urban schools. One of the many attributes of these movements is that they all present solutions through political, economic, and legal means.

Economic, Political and Legal Solutions to Critical Issues in Urban Education   pages ix–xvii
and Implications for Teacher Preparation
Copyright © 2022 by Information Age Publishing
www.infoagepub.com
ix

LEGAL APPREHENSIONS IN EDUCATION

As it pertains to educating African Americans, there was an ongoing role of servitude in the political economy of the South (Anderson, 1988). This was subsequently disrupted through political, economic, and legal measures during Reconstruction. Racist ideologies and economic advantages were seen through Jim Crow laws (Fremon, 2014) that were again disrupted through political, economic, and legal methods. Education perpetuates our democracy, via institutions that afford citizens the skills and knowledge necessary for political participation (Rury, 2002). Even when legal cases are unsuccessful, such as *Pruitt v. Commissioners of Gaston County* (1886) or *Plessy v. Ferguson* (1896), they can forge the way to successful litigation dismantling racist ideologies that oppress African Americans. Although the Pruitt decision did not remove the processes of discrimination against Black schools, it left intact the legal basis for segregated and unequal education (Douglas, 1995). As citizens, educators, policymakers, and community leaders, it is imperative that we participate in the political process and use our authority to mandate the changes that must happen in urban education.

After the *Brown v. Board of Education* ruling that enforced the integration of public schools, teacher preparation did not immediately change to prepare teachers to address their racism before educating Black students (Kluger, 2011). As a result, there are several unintended consequences this Supreme Court ruling had on teacher preparation and Black students. Primarily, the schools with majority Black students continued to be intentionally underfunded, forcing Black students to learn with insufficient and inadequate materials (Anyon, 2014). Similar inequities exist among pupil expenditures, as the amount of money spent per child is drastically different depending on where the child lives and the race of the child (Kozol, 2012). This perpetuated the opportunity gap that has continuously plagued Black and Latinx students. According to Darling-Hammond (2015) and other scholars, the opportunity gap is the accumulation of differences in access to key educational resources such as highly qualified teachers, educational materials, and a high-quality curriculum (Kluger, 2011; Kozol, 2012). Another devastating change, once students began to integrate, was that Black students' intellectual capacity and overall intelligence were questioned by their new White teachers and administrators (Kluger, 2011). Soon there was widespread acceptance that Black students were intellectually inferior to White students, which ultimately led to devastating socio-emotional consequence for Black students (Haycock & Navarro, 1988). This was followed by lowered academic expectations from White teachers for Black students whom they did not want in their schools in the first place. Ongoing racial harassment from White students, coupled with negativity from racist White teachers, led to Black students underperforming in the areas of literacy and mathematics (Brown, 2015; Kunjufu, 1991; Phillip, 1994). Teachers were not prepared to teach Black students nor address racism, which ultimately had negative influences on the educational outcomes of Black students.

Additionally, the implementation of *Brown v. Board of Education* left a lasting impact on Black teachers. Tens of thousands of Black educators all over the United States experienced massive layoffs between 1954 and 1955 (Hudson & Holmes, 1994; King, 1993; Madkins, 2011). The National Education Association estimated that approximately 5,000, or two-thirds, of Black teachers, would lose their jobs among the 11 Southern states (Tillman, 2004). Black teachers were not prepared to teach White students and were selected for all White schools based on their skin color (Hudson & Holmes, 1994). Fairer skinned teachers and former principals from predominately Black schools were forced into all-White schools and were demoted in pay and position. Additionally, the most effective Black teachers were forced to all-White schools, therefore leaving a huge deficit in the remaining Black teaching population. The public schools with a majority of Black students were then staffed with the less effective Black teachers. Tillman (2004) suggested *Brown v. Board of Education* marked the beginning of Black student underachievement given that they were presented with an inferior education.

The lasting effects of *Brown v. Board* exist today with the widening of the opportunity gap with Black students (Smedley et al., 2001). Smedley et al. argued that the school experiences for Black students in the United States continue to be one of the most unequal in the industrialized world, especially as students receive radically different educational opportunities based on their social status. In contrast, successful school systems around the world's urban centers develop teachers to educate students from different cultural, linguistic, and socioeconomic backgrounds, with success (Darling-Hammond et al., 2017). Even though *Brown v. Board* attempted to provide all students with equal access to educational resources in a diverse school setting, today, schools serving a larger number of students of color have considerably fewer resources than schools serving mostly White students (Smedley et al., 2001) and are also provided with underqualified teachers (Peske & Haycock, 2006). In sum, Black educators were effective and present during the educational equity agenda in the United States given their expansive child-centered perspective, yet these voices were perpetually silenced (Walker, 2013).

POLITICAL AFFAIRS IN EDUCATION

More recently, solutions to issues of urban education have been met with legislation, some of which has failed Black and Brown students. The No Child Left Behind (NCLB) Act of 2001, revised as the Elementary and

Secondary Education Act, mandated that all schools hire highly qualified teachers, including schools in predominately under-resourced communities (Schultz, 2014). According to NCLB, a highly qualified teacher must have (a) a bachelor's degree, (b) full state certification or licensure, and (c) prove that they know each subject they teach (No Child Left Behind Act, 2001). However, schools located in economically disadvantaged communities with Black and Brown students have by and large hired a higher percentage of underqualified teachers (Sass et al., 2012). According to this study, the distribution of highly qualified teachers is disproportionally and negatively influencing historically disadvantaged communities of color.

Furthermore, a school with inexperienced and underqualified teachers, is not only a violation of the NCLB Act (2001), but presents serious academic consequences for Black and Brown students (Dee & Jacob, 2011). As it stands, highly qualified teachers gravitate to advantaged schools (Clotfelter et al., 2006). This and other studies further acknowledge how there is a causal relationship between teachers' credentials and student achievement (Adamson & Darling-Hammond, 2012). Literature also expresses that students are not motivated by the assessment-driven culture of NCLB (Tuck, 2012), but by culturally relevant teaching practices (Ladson-Billings, 1995) which have led to increased student achievement for Black and Brown students.

ECONOMIC DISPUTES IN URBAN EDUCATION

Another issue in urban education is the inequitable distribution of qualified educators to Black and Brown students. This has resulted in out-of-field teaching for educators placed in under-resourced urban schools, despite efforts of NCLB (2001) to recruit high-quality teachers in high needs schools (Adamson & Darling-Hammond, 2012). Out-of-field teaching occurs when the teacher of a core academic class does not have a certification or major in the content area they are teaching. Adamson and Darling-Hammond (2012) revealed in their study that economically disadvantaged students of color are disproportionately taught by teachers out of their field. This study further indicated that teacher qualifications influence the student achievement of low-income students of color due to unsuccessful solutions. Another study indicated that Black students tend to have a first-year teacher in comparison to White students who do not, yet the Black student's teachers are more likely to be uncertified or unlicensed (Kumar & Waymack, 2014). This is often the case in under-resourced schools in Black communities. Having an unqualified teacher can have lasting detrimental effects on students that reach beyond the classroom. Furthermore, another study indicated that districts supporting the most economically disadvantaged students have twice the number of uncertified inexperienced teachers

(Adamson & Darling-Hammond, 2012). Teachers are not being well prepared to teach in urban schools, which influences how teachers perform in these schools (Adamson & Darling-Hammond, 2012). It is clear that injustices within urban education and teacher preparation occur and negatively affect academic outcomes, access to educational opportunities for students, and training for teachers. Essentially, economically disadvantaged students of color appear to not only be in under-resourced schools, but given less qualified teachers, and teachers who are teaching outside of their content area. Poor students and students of color are persistently provided with the weakest teachers but expected to academically perform as well as those who have highly qualified teachers with sufficient resources (Peske & Haycock, 2006; Smedley et al., 2001). This begs the question of what new policies are needed to provide low-income communities and urban schools with highly qualified teachers; conversely, do we need to implement the policies that were initially created to solve this problem with economic or legal action?

Student teaching, also known as clinical experience, can dramatically influence a teachers' perspective of what they will face in the classroom (Kluger, 2011). It is also noted as the key component of teacher preparation (Grossman, 2010). The semester-long process, in traditional settings, can comprise up to 40 hours of classroom practice. It connects the student-teacher to the community in an authentic, comprehensive, and systemic way to prepare them for their actual classroom experience (Seth, 2016). During this time, the student teacher receives critical feedback on their performance in the classroom, including clinical competence, teaching effectiveness, and professionalism. At times there appears to be a disconnect between the student teacher and mentor teacher regarding teaching philosophies (Trede & Smith, 2012). This study suggested using reflective practices to explore ways for mentor teachers and student teachers to communicate. During the clinical training, traditional teachers are not typically compensated for their work. This can create an economic hardship that disproportionately influences the historically marginalized (Grant-Smith et al., 2018). Evan stated that many teachers are compelled to take out student loans to survive this semester-long process. The financial stress on teachers can be potentially detrimental. Teacher preparation programs in other countries have paid clinical teaching, which has led to the competitiveness of the field of teaching (Darling-Hammond et al., 2017). In what ways can economic solutions support new educators and be cost-effective?

SOLUTIONS ARE CRITICAL

In what ways can we solve issues in teacher preparation through economic, political, or legal means? It appears that inexperienced, uncertified teachers are disproportionally affecting majority-minority schools and communities with economically disadvantaged students. Black and Brown students deserve equitable access to a quality education, yet has been systemically denied to them due to racism which has pervaded the power structures that keep poor people poor and rich people rich (Royce, 2009). As such, critical race theory (CRT) reminds us how racism has an integral and permanent place in our society, allowing the least qualified teachers to teach the most vulnerable Black and Brown poor children. Furthermore, African American Pedagogical Excellence (AAPE) reinforces the need to prepare a majority White middle-class monolingual female workforce using techniques best illustrated from their Black counterparts (Acosta et al., 2018). Teacher preparation is a matter of equity and social justice, yet has been Whitewashed to perpetuate systemic racism. The most vulnerable of the population continue receiving the least prepared educators. As a result, Black and Brown economically disadvantaged students are provided with fewer opportunities, hence the opportunity gap widens with every school year the student has with an unqualified, unprepared teacher. This can lead to discipline disproportionality (Blake et al., 2011), school push out (Tuck, 2012), and eventually contribute to the school-to-prison pipeline (Pane & Rocco, 2014). Can federal initiatives provide stronger supports and incentives for equalizing education for all students, especially Black and Brown students? How are we to hold federal and state legislators accountable to urban education reform that is effective and sustainable? No matter what the solution is, it is imperative to believe that every child deserves equitable access to quality education; therefore, an interdisciplinary approach is needed to make sure teachers are prepared not only professionally, but mentally. Identifying economic, political, and legal solutions to some of these major concerns could potentially create an environment where teachers are set up for success and all students gain equitable access to quality education through a qualified teacher.

When theorizing this book, the intent is to provide an interdisciplinary look at solutions to critical issues in urban education through political, economic, and legal avenues. This book seeks to provide an interdisciplinary approach to solving issues in education while connecting them to the implications of teacher preparation. Using historical and recent examples, scholars can piece together solutions that will guide others to political, economic and, legal action necessary to dismantle White supremacist systems in education that have bound Black and Brown children to insufficient access to quality education. We intend to offer innovative yet grounded solutions that can purposefully move the conversation toward actions aimed at solving critical issues in education through political, economic, and legal actions.

REFERENCES

Acosta, M. M., Foster, M., & Houchen, D. F. (2018). "Why seek the living among the dead?" African American pedagogical excellence: Exemplar practice for teacher education. *Journal of Teacher Education, 69*(4), 341–353. https://doi .org/10.1177/0022487118761881

Adamson, F., & Darling-Hammond, L. (2012). Funding disparities and the inequitable distribution of Teachers: Evaluating Sources and Solutions. *Education Policy Analysis Archives, 20*(0), 37. https://doi.org/10.14507/epaa.v20n37.2012

Anderson, J. D. (1988). *The education of Blacks in the South, 1860-1935.* University of North Carolina Press.

Anyon, J. (2014). *Radical possibilities: Public policy, urban education, and a new social Movement.* Routledge.

Blake, J. J., Butler, B. R., Lewis, C. W., & Darensbourg, A. (2011). Unmasking the inequitable discipline experiences of urban Black girls: Implications for urban educational stakeholders. *The Urban Review, 43*(1), 90–106. https://doi .org/10.1007/s11256-009-0148-8

Brown, F. (2015). Educational reform and African American male students after Brown v. Board of Education. *International Journal of Educational Reform, 24*(4), 321–334. https://doi.org/10.1177/105678791502400402

Clotfelter, C., Ladd, H. F., Vigdor, J., & Wheeler, J. (2006). High-poverty schools and the distribution of teachers and principals: What are the mechanisms of high-poverty disadvantages? *North Carolina Law Review, 85*, 1345–1380.

Darling-Hammond, L. (2015). *The flat world and education: How America's commitment to equity will determine our future.* Teachers College Press

Darling-Hammond, L., Burns, D., Campbell, C., Goodwin, A. L., Hammerness, K., Low, E.-L., McIntyre, A., Sato, M., & Zeichner, K. (2017). *Empowered educators: How high-performing systems shape teaching quality around the world.* John Wiley & Sons.

Dee, T. S., & Jacob, B. (2011). The impact of No Child Left Behind on student achievement. *Journal of Policy Analysis and Management, 30*(3), 418–446. https://doi .org/10.1002/pam.20586

Douglas, D. M. (1995). *Reading, writing & race: The desegregation of the Charlotte schools.* UNC Press Books.

Fremon, D. K. (2014). *The Jim Crow laws and racism in United States history.* Enslow Publishing, LLC.

Grant-Smith, D., de Zwaan, L., Chapman, R., & Gillett-Swan, J. (2018). 'It's the worst, but real experience is invaluable': Pre-service teacher perspectives of the costs and benefits of professional experience. In D. Heck & A. Ambrosetti (Eds.), *Teacher education in and for uncertain times* (pp. 15–33). Springer. https://doi .org/10.1007/978-981-10-8648-9_2

Grossman, P. (2010). *Learning to practice: The design of clinical experience in teacher preparation.*

Haycock, K., & Navarro, M. S. (1988). *Unfinished business: Fulfilling our children's promise* (A report from the achievement council). Achievement Council. https:// eric.ed.gov/?id=ED299025

Hudson, M. J., & Holmes, B. J. (1994). Missing teachers, impaired communities: The unanticipated consequences of Brown v. Board of Education on the African American teaching force at the precollegiate level. *The Journal of Negro Education, 63*(3), 388–393. https://doi.org/10.2307/2967189

King, S. H. (1993). The limited presence of African-American teachers. *Review of Educational Research, 63*(2), 115–149. https://doi.org/10.3102/00346543063002115

Kluger, R. (2011). *Simple justice: The history of Brown v. Board of Education and Black America's struggle for equality.* Knopf Doubleday Publishing Group.

Kozol, J. (2012). *Savage inequalities: Children in America's schools.* Crown.

Kumar, S., & Waymack, N. (2014). *Unequal access, unequal results: Equitable teacher distribution in Miami-Dade county public schools.* National Council on Teacher Quality. https://eric.ed.gov/?id=ED556309

Kunjufu, J. (1991). The male academy: In whose interest? *Black Collegian; New Orleans, 22*(2), 44.

Ladson-Billings, G. (1995). Toward a theory of culturally relevant pedagogy. *American Educational Research Journal, 32*(3), 465–491. https://doi.org/10.3102/00028312032003465

Madkins, T. C. (2011). The Black teacher shortage: A literature review of historical and contemporary trends. *The Journal of Negro Education; Washington, 80*(3), 417–427,437.

No Child Left Behind Act of 2001, P.L. 107-110, 20 U.S.C. § 6319 (2002). https://www.congress.gov/bill/107th-congress/house-bill/1

Pane, D. M., & Rocco, T. S. (2014). *Transforming the school-to-prison pipeline: Lessons from the classroom.* Springer Science & Business Media.

Peske, H. G., & Haycock, K. (2006). *Teaching inequality: How poor and minority students are shortchanged on teacher quality: A report and recommendations by the education trust.* Education Trust. https://eric.ed.gov/?id=eD494820

Phillip, M.-C. (1994). Brown at 40: Reassessing the case that changed public education in the United States. *Black Issues in Higher Education, 23*(10), 8–14.

Plessy v. Ferguson, 163 US 537. (1896).

Pruitt v. Commissioners of Gaston County, 94 N.C. 513. (1886).

Royce, E. C. (2009). *Poverty and power: The problem of structural inequality.* Rowman & Littlefield.

Rury, J. L. (2002). *Education and social change: Themes in the history of American schooling.* Taylor & Francis.

Sass, T. R., Hannaway, J., Xu, Z., Figlio, D. N., & Feng, L. (2012). Value added of teachers in high-poverty schools and lower poverty schools. *Journal of Urban Economics, 72*(2), 104–122. https://doi.org/10.1016/j.jue.2012.04.004

Schultz, L. M. (2014). Inequitable dispersion: Mapping the distribution of highly qualified teachers in St. Louis metropolitan elementary schools. *Education Policy Analysis Archives, 22*(90). https://eric.ed.gov/?id=EJ1050052

Seth, A. (2016). Study of mental health and burnout in relation to teacher effectiveness among secondary school teachers. *Indian Journal of Health and Wellbeing; Hisar, 7*(7), 769–773.

Smedley, B. D., Stith, A. Y., Colburn, L., & Evans, C. H. (2001). *Inequality in teaching and schooling: How opportunity is rationed to students of color in America.* National Academies Press. https://www.ncbi.nlm.nih.gov/books/NBK223640/

Tillman, L. C. (2004). (Un)intended consequences? The impact of the *Brown v. Board of Education* decision on the employment status of Black educators. *Education and Urban Society, 36*(3), 280–303. https://doi.org/10.1177/00131245 04264360

Trede, F., & Smith, M. (2012). Teaching reflective practice in practice settings: Students' perceptions of their clinical educators. *Teaching in Higher Education, 17*(5), 615–627. https://doi.org/10.1080/13562517.2012.658558

Tuck, E. (2012). *Urban youth and school pushout: Gateways, get-aways, and the GED.* Routledge.

Walker, V. S. (2013). Ninth annual *Brown* lecture in education research: Black educators as educational advocates in the decades before Brown v. Board of education. *Educational Researcher, 42*(4), 207–222. https://doi.org/10 .3102/0013189X13490140

CHAPTER 1

STUDENT ACHIEVEMENT FOR ALL

Afrocentric Curriculum and Abolitionist Pedagogy to Promote Equity and Excellence in Education

Annette Teasdell
Clark Atlanta University

Greg Wiggan
The University of North Carolina at Charlotte

The way to right wrongs is to turn the light of truth upon them.
—Ida B. Wells

The debate on economic, political, and legal solutions to critical issues in urban education should address the need for curriculum reform and enhance pedagogical practices as a means to improve educational outcomes for all students (Baker, 2017; Hansen et al., 2018; Royce, 2015; Rury, 2016). Since *Brown v. Board of Education* (1954) legally outlawed *de jure* segregation, the nation has been challenged with providing equal access to educational

Economic, Political and Legal Solutions to Critical Issues in Urban Education   pages 1–18
and Implications for Teacher Preparation
Copyright © 2022 by Information Age Publishing
www.infoagepub.com

opportunities for African Americans in particular. Recent litigations such as *Ridley v. State of Georgia (Coweta)* (2006), *Fisher & United States v. Tucson Unified School District* (2013), and *Cowan & United States v. Bolivar County Board of Education No. 4* (2017) suggest the nation's educational system is challenged by inequities and disparities in the treatment of students, and that many teachers are entering the field underprepared to teach the nation's diverse learners. According to the Office of Civil Rights (OCR) and the United States Department of Education, approximately 1,500 lawsuits addressing racialized inequities are currently pending (OCR, n.d.; United States Commission on Civil Rights [USCCR], 2007). For example, legal cases such as Milwaukee Public Schools and Tucson Unified School District have provided pathways to educational reform (Hansen et al., 2018).

This work examines the role of the Afrocentric curriculum and abolitionist pedagogy in mediating racialization and marginalization of African Americans in U.S. public schools. The findings indicate positive effects of Afrocentric curriculum reform and abolitionist pedagogy on student performance, as well as in nurturing greater advocacy surrounding educational equity (Baker, 2017; King, 2018; Watson-Vandiver & Wiggan, 2018). Given that schools are currently sites where minoritized students generally experience injurious practices such as *curriculum violence* which occurs when academic processes are manipulated in ways that compromise the intellectual and psychological well-being of learners (Ighodaro & Wiggan, 2011; King, 2018). Afrocentric curriculum and pedagogy are necessary for school reform. This chapter offers strategies and recommendations for educators to develop curriculum models and teaching practices that promote greater inclusion and abolition democracy. Ultimately, this work provides a blueprint for curriculum reform and pedagogy that places African Americans at the center of their educational experience.

Many teachers are entering the field unqualified and underprepared to teach urban and minoritized students. Moreover, schools are increasingly becoming sites where *spirit murdering* occurs, meaning unjust practices in schools are dehumanizing students (Love, 2014, 2016, 2019; Meiners, 2011; Meiners & Winn, 2010; Stovall, 2018). According to Love (2016), "Spirit murdering within a school context is the denial of inclusion, protection, safety, nurturance, and acceptance because of fixed, yet fluid and moldable, structures of racism" (p. 12). Spirit murdering is the act of sustaining injustices through systemic racism that personally, psychologically, and spiritually undermines students and their humanity (Love, 2019; Meiners, 2011; Meiners & Winn, 2010; Stovall, 2018; Williams, 1987). Relatedly, in the context of this chapter, abolitionist pedagogy refers to teaching practices that promote liberation from oppression and foster social justice (Love, 2019). It is designed to meet the needs of the whole child while "resuscitating and revitalizing the once wounded spirit" (Love, 2019, p. 100). In this sense, abolitionist pedagogy can serve as a mediating force against the racialization of students in schools (Love, 2014, 2019; Meiners, 2011; Meiners & Winn, 2010; Stovall, 2018). To effect change in the education industrial complex (the industry of schooling), more research targeted toward effective curriculum reform is necessary (Love, 2019; Meiners, 2011; Meiners & Winn, 2010; Vann & Kunjufu, 1993; Wiggan et al., 2014). Some studies address high-performing African American schools that use an Afrocentric curriculum (Aston & Graves, 2016; Giddings, 2001; Watson, 2015; Watson-Vandiver & Wiggan, 2018; Wiggan et al., 2014). However, only a few studies examine the need for abolitionist pedagogy as a means to transform schools from places where "spirit murdering" occurs to sites of transformative education for freedom (Love, 2019, 2016, 2014; Meiners, 2011; Stovall, 2018).

Thus, the purpose of this chapter is to examine the role of an Afrocentric curriculum and abolitionist pedagogy in mediating the racialization and marginalization of African Americans in U.S. public schools. A review of litigation involving education disparities and improper treatment of minoritized students provides insights on how the legal system has been—and can continue to be—used to effect change, promote social justice, and act as an instrument of abolition (Douglas, 2012; Hansen et al., 2018). Thus, the guiding research question for this investigation is: What is the role of an Afrocentric curriculum and abolitionist pedagogy in establishing what W. E. B. Du Bois called an abolition-democracy model of education (Du Bois & Lewis, 1992)? More research is needed to develop models of instruction that support the learning needs of African American students and adequately prepare teachers to serve them. The chapter offers strategies and recommendations for educators to develop curriculum models and teaching practices that promote greater inclusion and abolition democracy. Ultimately, this work provides a context for curriculum reform and pedagogy that places African Americans at the center of their educational experience.

URBANIZATION AND ITS SOCIAL, ECONOMIC, AND POLITICAL INFLUENCES

From the Great Migration to the current reverse migration of African Americans to the South (Davis & Wiggan, 2018; Harrison, 1991; Talley-Matthews & Wiggan, 2018; Watson-Vandiver, 2018; Wiggan, 2018), the educational implications of urbanization have had far-reaching social, economic, and political influences. This yields new insights on school reform. Despite the verdict in the 1954 Brown v. Board of Education case, which overturned *Plessy v. Ferguson* (1896) and made separate but equal racial facilities unlawful, U.S. schools are still racially segregated (Hansen et al., 2019; Reardon et al., 2012; USCCR, 2007). During the period from 1916–1970, over six million African Americans left the South in a mass exodus (Davis & Wiggan, 2018; Harrison, 1991; Watson-Vandiver, 2018). This Great Migration was largely due to African Americans' determination to escape the racial injustices of the South, its Jim Crow system of servitude, and the constant threat of lynching. The move to northern cities provided access to jobs that were not present in the South, but it also brought additional challenges surrounding access to affordable housing and quality education (Du Bois & Lewis, 1992; Harrison, 1991; Watson-Vandiver, 2018). Since the 1970s, a new trend, reverse migration, has resulted in numerous African Americans returning to the South; however, they are finding that racial and social injustice is still a pervasive problem (Frey, 2004; Rury, 2016; Watson-Vandiver, 2018).

In this reverse exodus, returnees are finding urban schools reeling from economic, social, and political challenges (Davis & Wiggan, 2018; Frey, 2004). Resegregated schools and racialized education disparities are generally the norms in many southern urban cities (Douglas, 2012; Watson-Vandiver, 2018). Hence, within this context, it is necessary to determine how an abolition-democracy model can create a counter space for educational transformation in schools that serve African American students (Du Bois, 1935; Du Bois & Lewis, 1992). Making the connection between curriculum and abolitionist teaching sets the stage for consideration of W. E. B. Du Bois' concept of abolition democracy (Du Bois & Lewis, 1992). Du Bois (1935) noted,

> Two theories of the future of America clashed and blended just after the Civil War: the one was abolition-democracy based on freedom, intelligence, and power for all men; the other was an industry for private profit directed by an autocracy determined at any price to amass wealth and power. The uncomprehending resistance of the South, and the pressure of black folk, made these two thoughts uneasy and temporary allies. (p. 182)

Du Bois (1935) continued, "Abolition-democracy demands for Negroes physical freedom, civil rights, economic opportunity, and education and the right to vote as a matter of sheer human justice and right" (p. 325). As Du Bois rightfully noted, oppressed groups like African Americans must have a curriculum and pedagogy that focuses on their liberation (Du Bois, 1935; Du Bois & Lewis, 1992).

TOWARD AN ABOLITION-DEMOCRACY MODEL

W. E. B. Du Bois argued that a host of democratic institutions (e.g., schools, economic and political institutions) are needed for African Americans to achieve full liberation (Du Bois & Lewis, 1992). An abolition democracy involves reconstructing policies and traditions that mitigate power and privilege, as well as eradicate systems of oppression (Du Bois & Lewis, 1992; Meiners & Winn, 2010). According to Davis (2005), abolition democracy "is not only, or not even primarily, about abolition as a negative process of tearing down, but it is also about building up, creating new institutions" (p. 73). When social institutions and individuals commit spirit murdering, which dehumanizes and creates structural barriers, it fuels the school-to-prison pipeline (Love, 2014; Pane & Rocco, 2014; Tuck, 2012). Stovall (2018) stated that

> imperative to the separation of "school" and education, "school" abolition in this sense seeks to eliminate the order, compliance, and dehumanization that happens in said buildings while allowing for the capacity to imagine and enact a radical imaginary. (p. 51)

Schools and prisons are just two social institutions that must be interrogated to achieve abolition democracy and resolve the problems that set students in the school-to-prison pipeline (Davis, 2005; Morris, 2016; Tuck, 2012). To that end, an Afrocentric curriculum and abolitionist pedagogy is a necessary component of an abolition-democracy model.

AFROCENTRIC CURRICULUM

In schools across the United States, students are exposed to a curriculum that marginalizes or omits the contributions of Africans and African Americans to the development of human civilization (Asante, 1991; Ighodaro & Wiggan, 2011; King & Swartz, 2015; Watson-Vandiver & Wiggan, 2018). This is essentially curriculum violence, when minoritized groups are excluded from the curriculum development process, what often results is a curriculum that focuses on the interests of dominant groups (Ighodaro & Wiggan, 2011; King et al., 2019). In school reform, curriculum development and content-based instructional strategies must be addressed. A curriculum that is inclusive and teaches African and African American history and culture, as well as the contributions of other groups, helps to prepare all students, not just Black students, for success in a multicultural world (Vann & Kunjufu, 1993).

An Afrocentric curriculum helps to support student achievement (Asante, 1991; King, 2005; King & Swartz, 2015; Watson-Vandiver & Wiggan, 2018), while also having a positive effect on students' self-concept (Archer-Banks & Behar-Horenstein, 2012; Aston & Graves, 2016; Baker, 2017; Giddings, 2001). Afrocentricity explains the importance of more accurately teaching about the history of humanity (Asante, 2003; King & Swartz, 2015). It is a human-centered perspective that positions Africa, Africans, and the African Diaspora at the center of analysis (Diop, 1967, 1974; Karenga, 2006). As Asante (1998) noted, Afrocentricity is a social, economic, and political framework that positions Africa and African Diasporic issues at the core of its vision and work (Asante, 1990; King & Swartz, 2015; Wiggan, 2010).

While working for the continued improvement of Africa, the world, and people of African descent and the broader human population/family, Afrocentricity seeks to reclaim and uncover the suppressed contributions of African and African Diaspora (Asante, 1998; King, 2018; Wiggan, 2010). Revealing a more accurate and original historical record from the primary source is transformative for students and teachers (Asante, 2003; Karenga, 1995; King, 2018; King et al., 2013; King & Swartz, 2014). Giddings (2001) advocated for a comprehensive Afrocentric curriculum because it would: (a) assist students in developing the necessary intellectual, moral, and emotional skills for accomplishing a productive, affirming life in society; (b) provide educational instruction that deconstructs established hegemonic pillars of learning; (c) provide instruction that uses techniques in concert with Afrocentric learning styles; (d) assist students of African descent in maintaining a positive self-concept, to achieve a sense of collective accountability; and (e) serve as a model for the Banks (1988) "Transformation" and "Social Action" approach to multicultural education (p. 2). Banks (1988) proposed a transformation approach to curriculum design, wherein the students are taught to view concepts and issues from the perspective of diverse cultural groups.

The U.S. teacher workforce is comprised of 80.1% White teachers who teach diverse student populations. Given this diversity, teachers need the tools to provide instruction to all learners. Thus, this research has implications for teacher preparation programs. Afrocentricity emphasizes the human element by addressing all phenomena from a human-centric lens (Asante, 1991). An Afrocentric curriculum helps to mediate the consequences of curriculum violence (Ighodaro & Wiggan, 2011; Watson-Vandiver & Wiggan, 2018), while abolitionist pedagogy addresses instructional practices (Love, 2019; Meiners, 2011; Meiners & Winn, 2010).

ABOLITIONIST PEDAGOGY

Buttressing an Afrocentric curriculum, abolitionist pedagogy embodies lesson planning and teaching strategies that focus on liberation from racialized and oppressive educational and societal conditions and processes (King, 2018; Love, 2019; Stovall, 2018). Abolitionist teaching is grounded in a critique of injustice. According to Love (2019), this form of teaching "is built on the radical imagination of collective memories of resistance, trauma, survival, love, joy, and cultural modes of expression and practices that push and expand the fundamental ideas of democracy" (p. 100). What does it mean to be an abolitionist teacher? Love (2019) defined it as

> the practice of working in solidarity with communities of color while drawing on the imagination, creativity, refusal, (re)membering, visionary thinking, healing, rebellious spirit, boldness, determination, and subversiveness of abolitionists to eradicate injustice in and outside of schools…you must matter enough to yourself, to your students, and to your students' community to fight. (p. 2)

To further express the urgent need for school reform, Love (2019) contended that abolitionist teaching requires a refusal to take part in practices that contribute to oppression and the school-to-prison pipeline, as well as an insistence on making schools a safe place for students (Morris, 2016; Pane & Rocco, 2014; Yarish, 2019). According to Stovall (2018), school abolition should include a pedagogy that dares to teach by asking the unaskable, positing the necessity of the impossible, and embracing the creative danger inherent in liberationist futures (Ladson-Billings, 2009; Love, 2019; Pane & Rocco, 2014). Acosta et al. (2018) examined how public school desegregation has impacted African American pedagogical excellence within teacher education, and contended that African American pedagogical theory and praxis (including abolitionist teaching) has been under-investigated as a corrective to challenges within U.S. teacher training programs (Meiners, 2011; Meiners & Winn, 2010). Characteristics of effective African American educators include pedagogy that incorporates community solidarity, political clarity, and citizenship (King & Swartz, 2015; Ladson-Billings, 2009; Lee, 2017). Afrocentric curriculum and abolitionist pedagogy require a careful analysis of the judicial system, and the crucial role of litigation in helping to create greater racial equity, inclusion, and liberation through education.

STUDENT ACHIEVEMENT FOR ALL?

Supreme Court Justice and acclaimed civil rights lawyer Thurgood Marshall once noted that as long as there is segregation, equity in education is impossible (Deibel, 2016). His efforts as lead counsel for the National Association for the Advancement of Colored People's (NAACP) legal defense team resulted in the historic 1954 *Brown v. Board of Education* decision, which ruled that *de jure* segregation was inherently harmful to minoritized students, and was a violation of the 14th amendment. Notwithstanding, in the 21st century, the quest for desegregation in schools is still elusive for most African Americans.

Brown v. Board of Education (1954) outlawed separate but equal educational facilities 65 years ago (2019); however, as evidenced by recent litigations (Hansen et al., 2018), segregation is still the norm in the United

States (Mickelson et al., 2017; Reardon et al., 2012). The Civil Rights Act of 1964 "authorized the Department of Justice (DOJ) to enforce anti-discrimination laws and to initiate or intervene in desegregation lawsuits" (United States Commission on Civil Rights [USCCR], 2007, p. 11). *Green v. County School Board of New Kent County* (1968) involved two schools: New Kent, a majority White school, and George Watkins, a majority Black school. After *Brown v. Board*, students had the "choice" of attending whichever school they wanted, yet there was very little change in the nation's school racial demographics. This lack of change was evidence of the ongoing racial violence against Black students who attempted to integrate White schools, and few White students wanted to attend Black schools, which were purposefully underfunded and under-resourced (Hansen et al., 2018). In effect, the freedom of choice plan violated equal protection under the law, which *Green v. County School Board of New Kent County* (1968) set in motion because the New Kent County School District did not stipulate a clear plan to end desegregation.

As a result of continued resistance to desegregation, the Supreme Court in the decision of *Green v. County School Board of New Kent County* (1968) established six specific criteria to judge desegregation efforts, called "Green factors," based on a racial segregation verdict in favor of the Plaintiff Charles C. Green. These Green factors included the following: (a) diversity in student assignment, (b) faculty diversity, (c) diverse staff assignment, and desegregation in (d) transportation, (e) extracurricular activities, and (f) facilities. The Green factors are further described below in a discussion of *Ridley v. State of Georgia (Coweta)* (2006). In the 2007 United States Commission on Civil Rights (USCCR) report, *Becoming Less Separate?*, the USCCR provided information about schools and districts that were under litigation, and their plan to achieve *unitary status*, which meant they had "successfully transitioned from a segregated, racially dual system to an integrated one" (USCCR, 2007, p. xi). USCCR findings indicate that many of the original desegregation orders have been in place for decades. In the Commission's study, 98% of the districts ever under court order were placed under supervision in the 1970s or earlier. A majority of them remain under court order today. The purpose of these orders was to address state-sponsored schemes of segregation and to remedy the effects of intentional discrimination (USCCR, 2007, p. xiii).

Desegregation cases such as *Ridley v. State of Georgia (Coweta)* (2006), *Fisher & United States v. Tucson Unified School District* (2013), and *Cowan & United States v. Bolivar County Board of Education No. 4* (2017) highlight the importance of the judicial system in helping to challenge and change racialized school processes. The litigations helped to mandate desegregation through the attainment of unitary status, meaning districts had to make every effort to eliminate segregation based on race or ethnicity (Hansen et al., 2018), which helps to create inclusive classrooms where, potentially, Afrocentric curriculum and abolitionist pedagogy can be implemented.

In the case *Ridley v. State of Georgia (Coweta)* (1969), the plaintiffs argued that desegregation of schools in Georgia and unitary status has still not been attained. This hard-fought legal battle against the 81 school districts in the state of Georgia has implications for both student success and teacher education (Acosta et al., 2018; Aston &

Graves, 2016; Hansen et al., 2018). In the March 2013 ruling on *Ridley v. State of Georgia (Coweta)* (2016) ruling, the courts mandated specific parameters around how the schools would align with the U.S. Supreme Court (*Green v. County School Board of New Kent County*, 1968) "Green factors." As noted above, the Green factors included the following six criteria for school desegregation: (a) student assignment, including student transfers, classroom assignment, gifted and talented, and discipline; (b) faculty, including faculty assignment and faculty hiring; (c) staff; (d) transportation; (e) extracurricular activities, and (f) facilities. In the 1974 and 2013 Consent of *Ridley v. State of Georgia (Coweta)*, the court ruled that "the school district shall take no action which tends to segregate students or faculty by or within schools based on race, color, or national origin" (*United States v. Ridley*, 1969). Nonetheless, in 2019, the Coweta County School District remains under DOJ jurisdiction and has not attained unitary status.

Similarly, *Fisher & United States v. Tucson Unified School District*, which was originally filed in 1974 and issued a new Consent Order in 2013, addresses school desegregation throughout the 20th and 21st centuries. Representing the concerns of Roy Fisher, an African American, and Maria Mendoza, a Mexican American, the 1974 case alleged intentional segregation and unconstitutional discrimination in Tulsa Unified School District (TUSD). In 1978, the courts ruled that intentional segregation persisted in TUSD, and "the court approved the District's proposed desegregation plan and a settlement agreement was established and directed federal court oversight of the school district" (*Fisher v. Tucson*, 1974). In the following 30 years (from 1978 to 2018), the state of Arizona provided 20 million dollars of funding for desegregation efforts that TUSD promised but did not necessarily deliver (Hansen et al., 2018). Efforts to desegregate TUSD schools relied primarily on magnet school programs as a means to provide opportunities for students from varying racial and ethnic backgrounds to attend (*Fisher v. Tucson*, 1974). Nonetheless, this did not meet the standards for district-wide integration. In the end, unitary status was denied in certain areas—discipline, magnet school assignment—and awarded in others—student assignment, transportation, staffing, quality of education, family and community engagement, extra-curricular activities, and accountability (*Fisher v. Tucson*, 1974). Arizona's unique challenges make the efforts to desegregate schools particularly difficult.

Similarly, *Cowan & United States v. Bolivar County Board of Education* is a 54-year-old school desegregation lawsuit filed on July 24, 1965, wherein 131 minor children, acting through their parents or guardians, filed this action against the Bolivar County Board of Education and numerous of its members, alleging that the defendants:

> Have pursued and are presently pursuing a policy, custom, practice, and usage of operating the public schools of Bolivar County, Mississippi, on a racially segregated basis... In their complaint, Plaintiffs alleged that the action was brought on their behalf and on behalf of all other Negro children and parents... located in Bolivar County, Mississippi, who are similarly situated and affected by the policies, practices, customs, and usages complained of herein. (*Cowan v. Bolivar*, 1965)

Post *Brown* (1954), schools in Mississippi remained largely desegregated with a significant number of private schools serving White students and public schools serving 95% of Black students (*Cowan v. Bolivar*, 1965). Initially, Bolivar School District operated six racially segregated schools for Whites and four segregated schools for Blacks. In a 2017 Consent Order, *Cowan* argued for the consolidation of Cleveland High School and Margaret Green Middle School into desegregated comprehensive schools (*Cowan v. Bolivar*, 1965). Additionally, the modified plan called for students across the district to begin seventh grade in a district-wide middle school and high school serving all students, Black and White. In 2017, over 54 years since the case was ordered, the issue of desegregation of schools is still in question in Cleveland School District, in the Mississippi Delta, and other districts across the country.

As Du Bois noted (1935), abolition democracy is needed for African Americans to gain equal access. In this sense, *Swann v. Charlotte-Mecklenburg Board of Education* (1971) is an example of a school integration model (Douglas, 2012; Holcombe, 1985). In this case, the NAACP sued the Charlotte-Mecklenburg School District in 1968 for its failure to desegregate. Through a court-approved desegregation plan, the district initiated a county-wide bussing initiative that allowed for widespread desegregation of Charlotte-Mecklenburg Schools. Because of its efforts, the *Swann* case became an example for other school desegregation efforts (Douglas, 2012; Holcombe, 1985).

Evidence in the cases above as well as in the history of education points to the need for desegregation and inclusion, and the creation of an abolition democracy for all students (Hansen et al., 2018; Love, 2019). Teachers must be skilled in the ability to prepare students academically, but also to enrich them with citizenship education and prepare them for real-world experiences. Vickery (2016), in a multiple case study, examined the experiences of two African American women social studies teachers for assessing the impact of an inclusive curriculum. Ultimately, the case studies showed that the teachers' background as African American women served as a legitimate source of knowledge and impacted how they enacted a citizenship education curriculum that provided greater exposure (Vickery, 2016).

STUDENT ACHIEVEMENT FOR ALL

After decades of litigations, U.S. public schools still face many barriers to racial equity (Hansen et al., 2018; Reardon et al., 2012). Thus, toward the end of advancing an abolitionist-democracy model, this research utilizes secondary data sources to illustrate student achievement and school inequities. According to the 2018 Brown Center Report (BCR) on American Education, student performance in mathematics and reading are accountability measures used to determine student success and teacher effectiveness (Hansen et al., 2018). A review of the Nation's Report Card published annually by the National Association of Educational Progress (NAEP) makes it appear that academic growth is occurring in schools across the country (Hansen et al., 2018; NAEP, 2018). Over the last 2 decades, increases in reading and mathematics scores suggest that the nation's students are generally achieving below grade level. Looking beyond the data reveals that policies such as No Child Left Behind (2002) and now the Every Student Succeeds Act (2015) have had a significant effect on teaching practices and student outcomes (Hansen et al., 2018; USCCR, 2007). According to the Nation's Report Card, 36% of fourth-grade students are reading at or above proficiency as compared to 34% of eighth-grade students (NAEP, 2018). In mathematics, the proficiency rates are 40% and 33% respectively for fourth and eighth grade (NAEP, 2018). Table 1.1 illustrates these trends.

Racially stigmatizing contexts and instructional practices within schools result in general underperformance (Archer-Banks & Behar-Horenstein, 2012). Systems in place in American schools are modeled after the larger society and thereby complicated by biases, prejudices, and socioeconomic inequities that are woven into the fabric of American society (Artiles et al.,

TABLE 1.1   2017 National Student Achievement by Public School Type (percent at or above proficiency)

	City (Urban)	Suburban	Town	Rural
Grade 4 reading	32%	42%	31%	35%
Grade 8 reading	32%	42%	30%	34%
Grade 4 mathematics	35%	45%	36%	40%
Grade 8 mathematics	31%	39%	29%	33%

Note: From National Assessment of Education Progress (2018a, 2018b)

2016). School suspensions and expulsions plagued by discipline disproportionality are strong predictors of future incarceration (Meiners & Winn, 2010; OCR, n.d.). Additionally, prisons use third-grade performance on standardized reading tests as predictors of the prison population (Davis, 2016). Minoritized students are "steered into detention centers, jails, and prisons from the hallways of school buildings" (Love, 2014, p. 12).

Several research studies highlight the benefits of an Afrocentric curriculum and sound pedagogical practices (Archer-Banks & Behar-Horenstein, 2012; Watson-Vandiver & Wiggan, 2018). Wiggan (2008) addressed high achieving African American students within the school context and the processes that high achieving African American students identify as contributing to their academic success. Wiggan found three main contributors to high school success: teacher practices through engaging pedagogy, participation in extracurricular activities, and performance incentives such as state scholarships. Of these three, teacher practices were the most instrumental in impacting school success.

In "The Genius of Imhotep," Watson-Vandiver and Wiggan (2018) found that while the U.S. school curriculum often overlooks or downplays multicultural history, teachers and students find empowerment through diverse curriculum and pedagogy. Using research conducted at Barbara Sizemore Academy (BSA), a high performing African-centered school, this qualitative case study aimed to determine the perspectives and experiences of students and teachers given the approach to curriculum and teaching. BSA used an Afrocentric curriculum rooted in historical and chronological fact focusing on the primacy of Africa to deconstruct systems of hierarchy in school curriculum while decentering European hegemony (Watson-Vandiver & Wiggan, 2018). Findings indicated that students and teachers at BSA found their African-centered curriculum focused on historical accuracy and was inclusive of all cultures.

DISCUSSION

In light of the above treaties, an Afrocentric curriculum and abolitionist pedagogy can play a role in mediating racialization and marginalization of African Americans in U.S. public schools and establishing an abolition-democracy model of education (Du Bois & Lewis, 1992). After decades of litigation, equity and inclusion still belie the nation's public schools (Hansen et al., 2018; Mickelson et al., 2017). Given the research regarding the quest for unitary status to stop federally mandated DOJ jurisdiction in school districts such as Cleveland, McDuffie, and New Kent County, the effects of segregation are apparent (Reardon et al., 2012; Tatum, 2007). Additionally, the resegregation of schools is an evolving problem. Students are suffering from the same dynamics that framed *Brown* (1954). They are trying to persist in schools that are separate and unequal. More research is needed to develop models for instruction that support the learning needs of African American students and adequately prepare teachers to support their learning (Acosta et al., 2018; Giddings, 2001; King & Swartz, 2015).

Development of an abolition democracy model includes strategies, such as Afrocentric course materials and culturally relevant practices, that educators can use to promote education for freedom (Love, 2016, 2019; Davis, 2005). Ultimately, this work has implications for teacher preparation such that training contributes to the creation of an Afrocentric curriculum and abolitionist pedagogy to promote the development of an abolition-democracy model for education (Love, 2016, 2019; Stovall, 2018). As expressed in the cases above, litigation can be used to promote social justice. The legal cases presented are clear examples of how citizens can use the power of law to disrupt discriminatory practices. While this study focused on a few key cases to illustrate the impact of racialization and marginalization of students, it is limited in its scope. There are other examples of legal cases that address the desegregation of schools; however, for this work, these specific cases were selected because they illustrate the national problem (Hansen et al., 2018; Morris, 2016; Pane & Rocco, 2014).

CONCLUSION

In conclusion, with the U.S. student population exceeding 50.7 million students and becoming increasingly diverse, there is a crucial need to address issues of equity and inclusion (NCES, 2018). With the minority on the cusp of becoming the majority of the nation's public schools, there is a great need for curricular and pedagogical reform (Asante, 1998; Baker, 2017; King, 2018; Watson-Vandiver & Wiggan, 2018). Given that schools are currently sites where students experience injurious practices such as curriculum violence (Ighodaro & Wiggan, 2011),

Afrocentric curriculum and abolitionist pedagogy are necessary for effective educational reform, and to mediate the effects of spirit murdering (Love, 2019; Meiners, 2011; Meiners & Winn, 2010; Stovall 2018).

In this sense, Du Bois addressed the possibilities of an abolitionist future that reconstructs the "structures and traditions that safeguard power and privilege, just as much as taking down those that visibly punish and oppress" (Meiners & Winn, 2010, p. 273). In 2019, at a time when the significance of *Brown v. Board of Education* (1954) is overshadowed by the resegregation of America's schools, the relevance of the Kenneth and Mamie Clark Doll Study (1947) has been lost. In their often replicated and highly acclaimed psychological experiment, the Clarks aimed to determine if Black students who were denied the opportunity to attend integrated schools developed negative identity and self-efficacy (Clark & Clark, 1947). What the Clarks found was as disturbing then as it is now. Young Black grade school children who were asked to identify the "good" doll, the "smart" doll, and the doll they would most want to play with, were far more likely to choose the White doll who looked nothing like them. The Clarks' conclusions regarding the impact of segregation on racial identity had far-reaching consequences that have been replicated several times (Clark & Clark, 1947). Thurgood Marshall used this research to argue in *Brown v. Board of Education* (1954) because he believed segregated schools had a significantly detrimental psychological effect on Black children who were denied the opportunity to attend schools like that of their White peers, and who subsequently believed that they were "less" than their peers. Afrocentric curriculum and abolitionist pedagogy are necessary for effective educational reform. The overall goal of this work was to provide a framework for abolition democracy through Afrocentric curriculum and abolitionist pedagogy. An Afrocentric curriculum can be used to avert spirit murdering and to create a counter space for educational transformation in schools. Major findings support the positive effects of a curriculum that is rooted in an African-centered epistemology. In light of the 2018 BCR, "The United States should place greater emphasis on schools' role in supporting and strengthening American democracy through how it educates its students" (Hansen et al., 2018, p. 2). In that context, our recommendations are as follows:

1. Teacher preparation programs should provide tools for the establishment of abolitionist pedagogy. Train co-conspirators who work together with those who are committed to establishing an abolition democracy (Love, 2019; Meiners, 2011; Meiners & Winn, 2010).
2. Develop Afrocentric curriculum and other inclusive curriculum models (e.g., multicultural curriculum development, anti-racism curriculum, etc.).
3. Catalyze national school reform that addresses the nation's general underperformance and low proficiency levels across all school types (NAEP, 2018).
4. Continue to support the Office of Civil Rights legal initiatives to create and promote greater school equity and desegregation and also the support of the NAACP Legal Defense Team's efforts to create racial parity in schools.
5. Per W. E. B. Du Bois' notion of abolition democracy, teachers should teach with an emphasis on social justice issues and the liberation of marginalized and oppressed student groups.

In sum, while the above discussion and treatment on the topic of this chapter are not exhaustive, it can begin a meaningful discussion on the role of Afrocentric curriculum and abolitionist pedagogy in making schools more humane and democratic for all learners.

REFERENCES

Acosta, M. M., Foster, M., & Houchen, D. F. (2018). "Why seek the living among the dead?" African American pedagogical excellence: Exemplar practice for teacher education. *Journal of Teacher Education, 69*(4), 341–353. https://doi.org/10.1177/0022487118761881

Archer-Banks, D., & Behar-Horenstein, L. (2012). Ogbu revisited: Unpacking high achieving African American girls' high school experiences. *Urban Education, 47*(1), 198–223. https://doi.org/10.1177/0042085911427739

Asante, M. K. (1990). *Kemet, Afrocentricity and knowledge.* African World Press.

Asante, M. K. (1991). The Afrocentric idea in education. *The Journal of Negro Education, 60*(2), 170–180. https://doi.org/10.2307/2295608

Asante, M. K. (1998). *The Afrocentric idea.* Temple University Press.

Asante, M. K. (2003). *Afrocentricity: The theory of social change.* African American Images.

Aston, C., & Graves, S. (2016). Challenges and barriers to implementing a school-based Afrocentric intervention in urban schools: A pilot study of the Sisters of Nia cultural program. *School Psychology Forum, 10*(2), 165–176.

Baker, T. J. (2017). *The effects of an Afrocentric curriculum on reading scores of African American third, fourth, and fifth graders* [Doctoral dissertation, Nova Southeastern University]. Proquest Dissertations Publishing.

Banks, J. A. (1988). Approaches to multicultural curriculum reform. *Multicultural Leader, 1*(2), 1–3.

Brown v. Board of Education of Topeka. (1954). *Oyez.* https://www.oyez.org/cases/1940-1955/347us483

Clark, K. B., & Clark, M. P. (1996). *Racial identification and preference in Negro children.* Bobbs-Merrill.

Clark, K. W. (1947). The gentile bias in Matthew. *Journal of Biblical Literature,* 165–172.

Cowan & United States v. Bolivar County Board of Education No. 4 (Cleveland School District)–Modification Order 2017. https://www.justice.gov/crt/case-document/cowan-united-states-v-bolivar-county-board-education-no-4-cleveland-school-0

Davis, A., & Wiggan, G. (2018). Black education and the Great Migration. *Black History Bulletin 81*(2), 12–16. https://doi.org/10.5323/blachistbull.81.2.0012

Davis, A. Y. (2005). *Abolition democracy: Beyond prisons, torture, and empire; interviews with Angela Davis.* Seven Stories Press.

Davis, A. Y. (2016). *Freedom is a constant struggle: Ferguson, Palestine, and the foundations of a movement.* Haymarket Books.

Deibel, Z. (2016). *Thurgood Marshall and Brown v. Board of Education of Topeka.* Cavendish Square Publishing, LLC.

Douglas, D. M. (2012). *Reading, writing, and race: The desegregation of the Charlotte schools*. UNC Press Books.

Diop, C. A. (1967). *Anteriority of Negro civilizations*. Presence Africaine.

Diop, C. A. (1974). *The African origin of civilization myth or reality*. Lawrence Hill Books.

Du Bois, W. E. B. (1935). *Black reconstruction in America; an essay toward a history of the part which Black folk played in the attempt to reconstruct democracy in America, 1860–1880*. World Pub. Co.

Du Bois, W. E. B., & Lewis, D. (1992). *Black reconstruction in America*. Atheneum.

Fisher v. Tucson Unified School District, 329 F. Supp. 3d 883 | Casetext Search + Citator. (n.d.). https://casetext.com/case/fisher-v-tucson-unified-sch-dist-5

Frey, W. H. (2004). *The new great migration: Black Americans' return to the South, 1965–2000*. Brookings Institute. https://www.brookings.edu/research/the-new-great-migration-black-americans-return-to-the-south-1965-2000/

Giddings, G. J. (2001). Infusion of Afrocentric content into the school curriculum: Toward an effective movement. *Journal of Black Studies, 31*(4), 462–482. https://doi.org/10.1177/002193470103100405

Green v. County School Board of New Kent County. (1968). https://www.oyez.org/cases/1967/695.

Hansen, M., Levesque, E., Valant, J., & Quintero, D. (2018). *The 2018 Brown Center report on American education: How well are American students learning*. The Brookings Institution.

Harrison, A. (1991). *Black exodus: The great migration from the American South*. University of Mississippi Press.

Holcombe, R. E. (1985). *A desegregation study of public schools in North Carolina*. East Tennessee State University.

Ighodaro, E., & Wiggan, G. (2011). *Curriculum violence: America's new civil rights issue*. Nova Science Publishers.

Karenga, M. (1995). Afrocentricity and multicultural education: Concept, challenge and contribution. In B. P. Bowser, T. Jones, & G. A. Young (Eds.), *Towards the multicultural university* (pp. 41–61). Praeger.

Karenga, M. (2006). Philosophy in the African tradition of resistance: Issues of human freedom and human flourishing. In L. R. Gordon & J. A. Gordon (Eds.), *Not only the master's tools: African American studies in theory and practice* (pp. 243–271). Paradigm.

King, J. E. (2005). *Black education: A transformative research and action agenda for the new century*. Routledge.

King, J. E. (2018). *Heritage knowledge in the curriculum: Retrieving an African episteme*. Routledge.

King, J. E., Akua, C., & Russell, L. (2013). Liberating urban education for human freedom. In H. R. Milner & K. Lomotey (Eds.), *Handbook of Urban Education* (pp. 62–87). Routledge.

King, J. E., & Swartz, E. E. (2014). *"Re-membering" history in student and teacher learning: An Afrocentric culturally informed praxis*. Routledge.

King, J. E., & Swartz, E. E. (2015). *The Afrocentric praxis of teaching for freedom: Connecting culture to learning*. Routledge.

Ladson-Billings, G. (2009). *The dreamkeepers: Successful teachers of African American children.* Wiley & Sons.

Lee, C. D. (2017). An ecological framework for enacting culturally sustaining pedagogy. In H. S. Alim & D. Paris (Eds.), *Culturally sustaining pedagogies: Teaching and learning for justice in a changing world* (pp. 261–273). Teachers College Press.

Love, B. L. (2014). "I see Trayvon Martin": What teachers can learn from the tragic death of a young black male. *The Urban Review, 46*(2), 292–306. https://doi.org/10.1007/s11256-013-0260-7

Love, B. L. (2016). Anti-Black state violence, classroom edition: The spirit murdering of Black children. *Journal of Curriculum and Pedagogy, 13*(1), 22–25. https://doi.org/10.1080/15505170.2016.1138258

Love, B. L. (2019). *We want to do more than survive: Abolitionist teaching and the pursuit of educational freedom.* Beacon Press.

Meiners, E. R., & Winn, M. T. (2010). Resisting the school to prison pipeline: the practice to build abolition democracies. *Race, Ethnicity and Education, 13*(3), 271–276. https://doi.org/10.1080/13613324.2010.500832

Mickelson, R. A., Smith, S. S., & Nelson, A. H. (Eds.). (2017). *Yesterday, today, and tomorrow: School desegregation and resegregation in Charlotte.* Harvard Education Press.

Morris, M. (2016). *Pushout: The criminalization of Black girls in schools.* The New Press.

National Center for Education Statistics. (2018). *Fast facts: Back to school statistics.* https://nces.ed.gov/fastfacts/display.asp?id=372

Office of Civil Rights. (n.d.). *Civil rights data collection.* www.ed.gov.

Pane, D. M., & Rocco, T. S. (2014). *Transforming the school-to-prison pipeline: Lessons from the classroom* (Vol. 60). Sense Publishers.

Plessy v. Ferguson, 163 U.S. 537 (1896).

Reardon, S. F., Grewal, E. T., Kalogrides, D., & Greenberg, E. (2012). *Brown* fades: The end of court-ordered school desegregation and the resegregation of American public schools. *Journal of Policy Analysis and Management, 31*(4), 876–904. https://doi.org/10.1002/pam.21649

Ridley v. the State of George, 223 S.E.2d 131, 236 Ga. 147 (1976). https://law.justia.com/cases/georgia/supreme-court/1976/30426-1.html

Royce, E. (2015). *Poverty and power: the problem of structural inequality* (2nd ed.). Rowman & Littlefield.

Rury, J. L. (2016). *Education and social change: Contours in the history of American schooling.* (5th ed.). Routledge.

Stovall, D. (2018). Are we ready for 'school' abolition? Thoughts and practices of radical imaginary in education. *Taboo: The Journal of Culture and Education, 17*(1), 6. https://doi.org/10.31390/taboo.17.1.06

Talley-Matthews, S., & Wiggan, G. (2018). Culturally sustaining pedagogy: How teachers can teach the new majority in public schools. *Black History Bulletin, 81*(2), 24–27. https://doi.org/10.5323/blachistbull.81.2.0024

Tatum, B. D. (2007). *Can we talk about race? And other conversations in an era of school resegregation.* Beacon Press.

The Nation's Report Card | NAEP. (2018). National Center for Education Statistics. https://nces.ed.gov/nationsreportcard/

Tuck, E. (2012). *Urban youth and school pushout gateways, get-aways, and the GED.* Routledge.

United States Commission on Civil Rights. (2007). *Becoming less separate? School desegregation, Justice Department enforcement, and the pursuit of unitary status.* U.S. Commission on Civil Rights. https://www2.law.umaryland.edu/marshall/usccr/documents/cr120079.pdf

United States v. Ridley. (1969). https://www.justice.gov/sites/default/files/crt/legacy/2010/12/14/ridley.pdf

Vann, K., & Kunjufu, J. (1993). The importance of an Afrocentric, multicultural curriculum. *Phi Delta Kappan, 74*(6), 490–491.

Vickery, A. E. (2016). 'I know what you are about to enter': lived experiences as the curricular foundation for teaching citizenship. *Gender and Education, 28*(6), 725–741. https://doi.org/10.1080/09540253.2016.1221890

Watson-Vandiver, M. J. (2018). The history of twentieth-and twenty-first-century Black migration: Implications for educators and schools. *Black History Bulletin, 81*(2), 6–9. https://doi.org/10.5323/blachistbull.81.2.0006

Watson-Vandiver, M. J., & Wiggan, G. (2018). The genius of Imhotep: An exploration of African-centered curricula and teaching in a high achieving US urban school. *Teaching and Teacher Education: An International Journal of Research and Studies, 76*(1), 151–164. https://doi.org/10.1016/j.tate.2018.09.001

Wiggan, G. (2008). From opposition to engagement: Lessons from high achieving African American students. *The Urban Review, 40*(4), 317–349. https://doi.org/10.1007/s11256-007-0067-5

Wiggan, G. (2018). Blacks migrations and urban realities. *Black History Bulletin, 81*(2), 32–33. https://doi.org/10.5323/blachistbull.81.2.0030

Wiggan, G., Scott, L., Watson, M., & Reynolds, R. (2014). *Unshackled: Education for freedom, student achievement, and personal emancipation.* Sense Publishers.

Yarish, J. N. (2019). *Reconstructing home: Abolition Democracy, the city, and Black feminist political thought revisited* [Doctoral dissertation]. University of California Santa Barbara. http://www.escholarship.org/uc/item/8430z7x9

CHAPTER 2

EMANCIPATION THROUGH CULTURALLY RESPONSIVE AND TRANSFORMATIVE LITERACY, CURRICULUM, AND PEDAGOGICAL PRACTICES

Charlotte R. Hancock
University of North Carolina at Charlotte

Greg A. Wiggan
University of North Carolina at Charlotte

Emancipate yourselves from mental slavery. None but ourselves can free our minds.
—From Redemption Song by Bob Marley

Until the lion tells his side of the story, the tale of the hunt will always glorify the hunter.
—African Proverb

Economic, Political and Legal Solutions to Critical Issues in Urban Education   pages 19–37
and Implications for Teacher Preparation
Copyright © 2022 by Information Age Publishing
www.infoagepub.com
19

In U.S. schools, students generally experience a hegemonic curriculum that reflects the interests and perspectives of the dominant group (Dyches, 2018; Ighodaro & Wiggan, 2013). This is reflected in omissions and lack of multicultural perspectives, and lack of critical literacy. However, teachers and students can critically deconstruct hegemony transmitted in curricula and literature to increase student agency and performance (Dyches, 2018). Students and teachers must realize and conceptualize their ability to break free from what Chimamanda Ngozi Adichie (2009) described as the *single story*, an overarching narrative arising from multiple texts, that depicts only one perspective on a culture or way of life. For this reason, we explore in this chapter how culturally responsive and transformative literacy can enhance student achievement and personal emancipation of urban and minoritized students. By analyzing a popular children's biographical book series, we found that the books in these series align with a single story (Adichie, 2009) that depicts White/European males as central to history and present-day society. Through the lens of critical race theory, specifically the role of intersectionality, we recognize and explore how these books implicitly convey to students that White/European males carry the most worth in society by the sheer number of publications available for purchase. The findings reveal the importance of teachers being vigilant in the selection of classroom children's literature.

In April 2020, advocates of multicultural curriculum transformation were victorious in a "hard-fought battle" when the Texas State Board of Education approved an African American Studies high school course (Grisby, 2020, para. 1). This African American Studies course was to be the second ethnic studies course to be offered in the state, adding to the preexisting Mexican American Studies course (Grisby, 2020). However, such efforts in progress were not met without resistance, as was the case with the original proposal of Mexican American studies (Grisby, 2020; Sawchuk, 2018). In a similar vein, Mexican American studies were considered extremely controversial as well in Arizona, with the state legislature eventually banning the course in 2010. This decision, however, was later to be overturned in 2017 by a federal judge ruling the original ban was unconstitutional and driven by racist sentiment (Strauss, 2017). Hence, efforts to include the stories of multiple ethnicities that extend beyond the Eurocentric, White narrative appear to have been consistently met with opposition despite research that demonstrates that multicultural curricula are advantageous to student success (Love, 2016; Watson-Vandiver & Wiggan, 2018).

While it currently appears that supporters of ethnic studies are making advances in curriculum reform, it is essential to examine the ethnic studies curricula that are approved—especially in the case of the approved African American Studies course in Texas that still may be limited in what is included in the approved curriculum (Grisby, 2020). This course is not completely free of censorship, as key historical figures that could be envisioned as threatening the White narrative, such as Malcolm X, will not be included in the curriculum (Grisby, 2020). To get the curriculum approved, negotiations took place that involved the removal of important individuals and organizations (Heilig, 2020). Hence, to what extent do curricular decisions attempt to enslave the mind through an educational form of colonization by conditioning students in ways to think, act, and participate in broader society against their liberation (Wiggan et al., 2014). This is the central aim of this chapter, with a specific focus on elementary literacy curriculum and resources. Most notably, this chapter explores a popular literary resource that is utilized in conjunction with biographical studies at the elementary level. The research question that guides the current work is: How can culturally responsive and transformative literacy help increase student achievement and personal emancipation of urban and minoritized students?

This chapter begins with a review of the literature as it relates to curriculum and resources that limit the ability of students to fully develop a liberated mind. Within the literature review, we will also describe the ways that pedagogy and teacher preparation can aid in transforming current educational practices. After reviewing the literature, we provide the theoretical framework employed for the interpretation of the findings. Next, we describe the methods utilized to explore this specific series of books. Then, we present our findings as related to the research question that guides this chapter. After presenting the findings, we discuss their implications through the lens of critical race theory, arguing that children's literature can either be a hegemonic or liberating tool utilized in schools. Lastly, we conclude with recommendations for the future.

LITERATURE REVIEW

Curriculum and Curriculum Violence

The curriculum is "generally understood to be the program of study and experiences that are related to a field or discipline" (Ighodaro & Wiggan, 2013, p. 3). The curriculum is what directs teachers in what they are to teach and in many instances the order in which it should be taught. According to Ighodaro and Wiggan (2013), the curriculum consists of three essential components—content, process, and evaluation. Further, Ighodaro and Wiggan (2013) asserted that a curriculum "forms a discourse of power and culture, where the interests of dominant groups or power elites are stated and then served through a dominant curriculum, and wherein the curriculum development process, less powerful groups are not allowed to enter the dialogue" (p. 3).

Thus, the curriculum is much more than a program of study; it can also implicitly and explicitly reinforce the perspectives of the oppressor in the minds of the oppressed. Ighodaro and Wiggan (2013) explained the concern surrounding the trauma that *curriculum violence* can create in the lives of students. According to Ighodaro and Wiggan (2013), curriculum violence refers to the deliberate manipulation of education and academic programs in a manner that marginalizes students and compromises their learning experiences, as well as the intellectual and social-psychological well-being of omitted groups, signaling to learners that these groups have no contributions or are not worthy of inclusion (p. 24).

Adichie (2009) cautioned against the dangers of the single story, which attempts to define something, someone, or a group. This revelation of the dangers of a single story stemmed from her personal experiences with children's literature as a young child in Nigeria (Adichie, 2009). She began writing at the age of seven; however, her stories resembled all the widely-available books that she had read as a child (i.e., British and American), with her characters being White and blue-eyed (Adichie, 2009). As she grew, she realized that African literature existed too and that she also had a place within the stories of children's books (Adichie, 2009). Adichie uses her personal story to demonstrate how vulnerable children can be when faced with stories that seem to follow one sole narrative. When children only see the world through one lens in the literature they read, they in essence begin to see themselves through this same lens. Indeed, stories in themselves can be quite powerful as "stories are as prevalent in schools and curricula as they are in every other facet of society, and students are socialized through the stories privileged in school to accept particular ideologies," allowing for hegemony to be transmitted from generation to generation in the school buildings across the nation (Thomas & Dyches, 2019, p. 601). Such use and abuse of a single story can be extremely detrimental to young children.

This is the case with the current K–12 curriculum that has as its core a single, Eurocentric focus that additionally tells all historical stories through this Western perspective. Asante (1998) explained that "the inability to 'see' from several angles is perhaps the one common weakness in provincial scholarship" (p. 1). Asante (1998) discussed his work as one that creates a new reality, deconstructs the current reality that attempts to view the world only through the lens of the Western world, and instead proposes to turn this reality upside down with the worldview that acknowledges Africa at the center of humanity. Asante insisted "that there are other ways in which to experience phenomena rather than viewing them from a Eurocentric vantage point" (p. 1). This vantage point, discussed Asante (1998), "masquerades as a universal view in the fields of intercultural communication, rhetoric, philosophy, linguistics, psychology, education, anthropology, and history" (p. 1). The alternative viewpoint, which Asante (1998) coined

Afrocentricity, places Africa at the center and tells African history through the eyes of Africa, where Africa is the subject, not the object. Further, Asante (1998) described Afrocentricity as an inclusive perspective on the world that would, for example, encourage scholars within the fields of art, literature, and social sciences to imagine the possibility that other realities, including shared realities, exist. A key takeaway from Asante's (1998) work as it relates to this chapter is the importance of current and future teachers realizing that the curriculum and resources that they utilize in the classroom may be upholding a narrative told through one lens, the Eurocentric lens, and thus urges teachers to critically reflect on the damage that telling a single story can have on the lives of their students.

Once teachers are trained to see beyond the single story, the Eurocentric lens through which curriculum is told becomes increasingly apparent and can be seen infused through all parts of the curriculum teachers currently follow. A prime example of such a Eurocentric curricular focus would be that, despite data that lead many historians to believe that much of the current knowledge and innovations of today came from Egypt (Kemet), much curriculum still attributes such contributions to the Greeks and Romans, not the African continent (Asante, 1990; Clarke, 1977; Diop, 1974; James, 2020; Watson-Vandiver & Wiggan, 2018). Another prime example of a Eurocentric perspective on history is the narrative surrounding Christopher Columbus. While many historical accounts taught in schools depict Columbus as an adventurous sailor who discovered a new world and accredit him with discovering the Americas, other perspectives include that of Clarke (1998). Clarke, a Black historian and sociologist, was motivated to learn about the history of the African continent and his people (Sumaila, 2017). However, while trying to find information about the early world history of his people to impress his fifth-grade teacher, Clarke was told by a White lawyer that his people had no history (Sumaila, 2017). Unwilling to accept the words of this White lawyer, Clarke continued to search for answers, and he uncovered that his people had a very intricate and intriguing past that preceded slavery and preceded Europe (Sumaila, 2017). After extensive research, scholars (e.g., Clarke, 1998; Williams, 1994) have produced important works that are counter-narratives to typical K–12 curricula regarding Christopher Columbus, illuminating a connection between Columbus and the Transatlantic Slave Trade. In essence, Clarke (1998) broke free from a Eurocentric focus on this period of history and embraced Asante's (1998) proposal of the need for Afrocentricity in the telling of history. Clarke (1998) described Columbus in his work, *Christopher Columbus and the Afrikan Holocaust: Slavery and the Rise of European Capitalism,* as a villain that set in motion a mass holocaust of the killing of Africans, as a person who discovered nothing, and as a navigator that was completely wrong about where his ship had landed in 1492. Hence, historical perspectives can be quite different depending on which narrative is at the core of the curriculum.

Attempting to move beyond the single story (Adichie, 2009) must be an initiative within curriculum reform. Griffin and James (2018) explained that the curricular choices educators make when selecting certain words over others, adding or omitting certain characters, or using a curriculum that tells a story from a certain or single perspective will meaningfully determine which prisms or conceptualizations students cultivate to understand our world (p. 10). In general, the curriculum has been formed by such a master narrative where all knowledge and viewpoints center on and are taught through a lens that is Eurocentric, White, and male (Brown & Au, 2014). This teaches students that the knowledge of and the lives of White males are what is of worth in U.S. society, silencing and erasing the contributions, the struggles, and the importance of the lives of others.

RESOURCES

Beyond the curriculum, the resources chosen to teach the curricular aims are additionally critical. For example, if educators aim to teach students about historical figures that have contributed greatly to society but choose resources that only reflect one perspective, or only include certain groups and not others, this could be detrimental to students. While some educators may attempt to incorporate literature about diverse ethnic groups into their classroom, the material they choose is key. Quigley (2016) found that the inclusion of Indigenous peoples, also referred to as Natives or first Natives, into her daughter's classroom meant that teachers had selected books that reinforced "decades-old, biased portrayals of Indigenous people living in barbarism" (p. 368). Analyzing multiple children's books incorporated into the K–12 setting that depicted Indigenous life, Quigley (2016) further found a "misogynist portrayal" of Indigenous female characters "as mute," not even providing them with spoken words within this chosen literature (p. 373). Quigley (2016) urged that "now is the time to eradicate racially-biased books that continue to strip Indigenous characters (and people) of dignity" (p. 369). In a similar vein, Thomas and Dyches (2019) examined the hidden curriculum in a widely-used reading intervention program and found implicit messages within the resources implemented with students in need of additional literacy support. Among findings, Thomas and Dyches (2019) found that the books depicted Whites in a positive light, with characters and people that were White being shown as figures that were innovative and successful. In contrast, the resources depicted characters and people of color through a negative light, illustrating these individuals as helpless and inferior (Thomas & Dyches, 2019). Thomas and Dyches (2019) concluded that educators must remain vigilant and uncover hidden curriculum that may exist within the resources that are utilized within the classroom with students.

TEACHER PREPARATION AND
CULTURALLY RESPONSIVE TEACHING

For educators to remain vigilant, they must first be able to analyze materials with a critical eye. It cannot be assumed that educators are equipped to do this without the proper training. Universities and district leaders must train teachers to be culturally responsive to their students and to be able to transform their literacy practices within their classrooms, regardless of the curriculum. Curriculum and standards may direct teachers, for example, to teach with the utilization of multiple perspectives, but are teachers truly equipped to maximize this direction without proper training?

According to Banks (Gay, 2018), the compilation of works and research by a variety of scholars (e.g., Au, 1993; Delpit, 1995; Gay, 2000; Irvine, 2003; Ladson-Billings, 1994; Moll & Gonzalez, 2004; Nieto, 2010) has "constructed a theory of culturally responsive teaching (also called culturally relevant pedagogy) that gives hope and guidance to educators [who wish] to improve the academic achievement of students from diverse, racial, ethnic, cultural, linguistic, and social-class groups" (p. xii). In essence, when teachers build on the strengths that students bring with them to the classroom, recognizing the wealth of knowledge, wisdom, experience, culture, and language with which they arrive, students will achieve more success. Ladson-Billings (1995) found that successful teachers of African American students demonstrated certain characteristics including (a) the belief that all of their students were capable of success, (b) envisioned themselves as part of their students' community—whether they lived in the community or not, (c) took part within the community to show their investment in the people, (d) their fearless nature of being risk-takers when needed to motivate and encourage their students, (e) their ability to take on the role of student or learner and allow the students to take on the role of leader or teacher, (f) their encouragement of students to work together, not against one another in competition, and (g) their dedication to encouraging students to think critically about knowledge. Further, these teachers themselves reflected critically on the school curriculum (Ladson-Billings, 1995).

In line with the findings of Ladson-Billings (1995) that demonstrated the importance of students being supported as a community within the classroom, opposed to being taught to compete with one another, is *Ubuntu pedagogy* (Dillard & Neal, 2020). Ubuntu pedagogy centers around African American female educators exploring their African past to be more grounded in the richness of the African continent as future teachers, and stems from the concept that we are stronger together (Dillard & Neal, 2020). According to Dillard and Neal (2020), "Ubuntu suggests that an individual's personhood is ideally expressed in relationship with others, and through such expression, individuality itself is expressed" (p. 4). Furthermore, Dillard and Neal (2020) suggested three central components in preparing African American teacher development "in the spirit of Ubuntu": (a) There must be "opportunities for Black women teachers to (re)member themselves and their culture and histories from Africa to the U.S. and back again"; (b) for skills to develop, "Black women teachers need multiple opportunities and an invitation to center global Black women's ways of knowing and being"; and (c) the importance of being able to develop spiritually, as "Black women teachers must have spaces both to practice and to bear witness to their spirits and spiritual practices as a central part of their teaching and professional development as women of African heritage" (pp. 13–15).

While some of the solutions include the critical recruitment of more linguistically and culturally diverse teacher candidates, they also include the support and promotion of helping current teacher candidates "understand the culture (their own and others) and the ways it functions in education" (Ladson-Billings, 1995, p. 483). Considering that the teaching force has remained majority White and female, hovering around the 80% mark for the last 20 years (National Center for Education Statistics, 2020), it is imperative that teacher preparation programs also provide learning environments conducive to helping White future teachers to think critically about the educational system and how this system affects the success of students. Ladson-Billings (1995) explained that instead of adding more multicultural education courses that perpetuate diverse learners as "other," that "culturally relevant pedagogy is designed to problematize teaching and encourage teachers to ask about the nature of the student-teacher relationship, the curriculum, schooling, and society" (p. 483). Thus, the skill and ability to reflect critically upon a curriculum is a necessary step in preparing future teachers in a culturally relevant, culturally responsive pedagogical mindset. Further, teacher preparation programs provide the foundation for the development of teacher identity (Carrier et al., 2017; Hong, 2010) making it essential that these programs begin early in laying the groundwork for future teachers to think critically about their belief systems.

THEORETICAL FRAMEWORK

Derrick Bell (2018) contended that "racism is an integral, permanent, and indestructible component of this society" (p. xxi). As such, for those seeking to create real, sustainable change, it is necessary to theorize and analyze the ways that racism is at work in society and in schools. Critical race theory

(CRT) is derived from critical theory, with many recognizing that the origin of CRT extends back to the beginning of the 20th century with Du Bois's (1903) work *The Souls of Black Folk* (Solorzano & Yosso, 2001). Critical theories and CRT focus on the liberation of individuals from societal constraints placed upon them due to race, gender, and social class (Creswell & Poth, 2018). Although CRT had its beginnings in legal studies, including with Crenshaw's (1989) charge to recognize the intersectionality of race and gender as it pertains to discrimination, it has extended over time to the field of education as a way to analyze and theorize the ways schools work (Solorzano & Yosso, 2001). The implementation of CRT in the realm of education dates back to Tate's initial work in 1994 entitled, "From Inner City to Ivory Tower: Does My Voice Matter in the Academy," and the work from Ladson-Billings and Tate (1995) entitled, "Toward a Critical Race Theory of Education." Ladson-Billings and Tate (1995) described their perspective of inequities in schools as based on three central tenets: race remains a persistent factor in inequity in schools, society in the United States has property rights at its foundation, and where race and property rights intersect is the place in which to analyze inequities in the United States.

In addition to Ladson-Billings and Tate (1995), Solorzano and Yosso (2001) built upon this work and posited five tenets as their basis for analysis through a CRT lens in education:

1. The centrality of race and racism and their intersectionality with other forms of subordination
2. The challenge to the dominant ideology
3. The commitment to social justice
4. The centrality of experiential knowledge
5. The transdisciplinary perspective (pp. 472–473)

More than 20 years after CRT's first appearance in the educational realm, it is a theory still often utilized in the field of education as a way to explain the inequities that remain in schools. It is within the intersection of race with class and gender among other forms of subordination—Solórzano and Yosso's (2001) first tenet—that provides for an extension of the interpretation of society and inequality into multiple realms. This chapter recognizes and explores the intersectionality of different forms of discrimination by analyzing how children's books can send implicit messages regarding ethnicity and gender. We argue that children's books can either reinforce the oppressive and discriminatory nature of a society, or, in contrast, can be a form of counter story-telling that helps transform literacy and further teaches students to think critically about the society around them, realizing they have within themselves the power to create change. As Paolo Freire (2017) explained, "A deepened consciousness of their situation leads people to apprehend that situation as a historical reality susceptible of transformation" (p. 85).

Counter-storytelling (Solórzano & Yosso, 2002) is one concrete way to help break the institution of racism. Counter-storytelling provides a space for people who are often neglected and discouraged from telling their stories to share their experiences from their perspectives (Solórzano & Yosso, 2002). This act of storytelling allows the oppressed to break free from the single-story (Adichie, 2009) or the *master narrative* (Montecinos, 1995) to make their voices be heard through their use of counter-storytelling (Solórzano & Yosso, 2002). Solórzano and Yosso (2002) described the master narrative as also the majoritarian story, explaining that "a majoritarian story is one that privileges Whites, men, the middle and/or upper class, and heterosexuals by naming these social locations as natural or normative points of reference" (p. 28). Thus, it is important to analyze master narratives through the perspective of intersectionality, exploring specifically the intersection of race and gender as Crenshaw (1988) has charged.

Hughes-Hassell (2013) asserted that multicultural literature can be one way that counter-storytelling can take place in the classroom. Hughes-Hassell (2013) explained that multicultural literature can "challenge the single story" and further "encourage and empower teens of color and indigenous peoples to take action in their own lives and the world around them" (p. 217). Multicultural literature can accomplish this, according to Hughes-Hassell (2013), by openly discussing the challenges and discrimination that students may face and further demonstrating to students that "they can overcome the constraints placed on them by the dominant culture as represented by the single story" (p. 217). Conversations regarding the importance of multicultural literature are not new, however, stemming back to Nancy Larrick's work in 1965 (Hughes-Hassell, 2013). Thus, it becomes imperative to explore the condition of literacy today in relation to the books children are exposed to in schools almost 60 years since the introduction of this topic in the field. Further, this exploration into whether big publishing companies have worked to overcome the master narrative or permitted the situation to remain unchallenged.

METHOD

For this current exploratory study, we searched the internet for the popular and well-acclaimed children's book series that we will call "Series A" in this chapter. As we were aware that these books were utilized in conjunction with biographical units in elementary settings, we specifically wanted to explore what messages this series may be implicitly or explicitly implying to early elementary students during critical literacy developmental stages.

Series A is an extensive series that focuses on a multitude of key individuals, presenting their stories in a biographical format. While exploring the books available for purchase in Series A, we also encountered additional series the publisher markets on the same website as Series A.

In addition to Series A, we found that there were three additional, accompanying series that were available for purchase. We call these "Series B," "Series C," and "Series D" in this chapter. These additional series varied from the biographical focus that were the focus of Series A. Series B was a compilation of books that focused on specific historical events, rather than individuals, and Series C focused on specific geographical locations from around the world. Series D included only four books, all based on fictional cartoon characters from movies. Thus, we chose to analyze Series A, Series B, and Series C for this chapter and excluded Series D.

Series A produced 166 books for analysis. In Series A, 161 of the 166 books focused on one key individual, with some individuals being from the past ($n = 129$) and some from the present time ($n = 32$). Five of the 166 total books focused on groups of individuals rather than one person in particular, with two books focusing on groups of people from the present and three books focusing on groups from the past. Thus, we chose to analyze these books separately, dividing Series A into Series A1 (present individuals), Series A2 (historical individuals), Series A3 (present groups of important people), and Series A4 (past groups of important people). To further analyze the books in Series A, we separated within each section (Series A1, A2, A3, and A4) by gender and ethnicity. We wanted to analyze if the resources aligned with a Eurocentric focus, so we separated the ethnicities as such: African American/African, Asian, Indigenous, Latinx, and White/European. Within each ethnicity, we separated the books by gender as well. We then analyzed how many books were available for purchase within each category.

The books from Series B depicted historical events that have occurred around the world. Therefore, we analyzed the books' front cover images, and further analyzed the key figure depicted on the front covers by ethnicity and gender in the same way that we analyzed the books from Series A. There were 42 books for purchase within this series. Series C focused on locations around the globe, with a total of 32 books. For this series, we analyzed the books by location since people were not commonly depicted on the front cover, specifically sorting the books by continent to explore which continent was the most prevalently portrayed.

FINDINGS

Table 2.1 demonstrates the findings for Series A1 (present figures) while Table 2.2 depicts the findings for Series A2 (historical figures). The largest

TABLE 2.1 Series A1 Texts	
Ethnicity and Gender	**Number of Books**
African American/African Male	3
African American/African Female	2
Asian Male	2
Asian Female	1
Indigenous Male	0
Indigenous Female	0
Latinx Male	1
Latinx Female	1
White/European Male	15
White/European Female	7

TABLE 2.2 Series A2 Texts	
Ethnicity and Gender	**Number of Books**
African American/African Male	11
African American/African Female	5
Asian Male	3
Asian Female	0
Indigenous Male	1
Indigenous Female	2
Latinx Male	4
Latinx Female	2
White/European Male	76
White/European Female	25

number of books available for purchase was White/European males, followed by White/European females. A few books were available for other ethnicities, with no books being available that focused on Indigenous persons. Regarding gender, there were more books available for males than females for the ethnicities of African American/African, Asian, and White/European.

As was the case with Series A1, White/European males were the largest number of books available for purchase in Series A2, followed by White/European females. African American/African males were the third-largest number of books available, followed by Latinx males. There were zero books available that centered upon Asian women from the past. For each ethnic subdivision, more books focused on males from that ethnicity than females, except for Indigenous historical figures, which had more books available that focused on females ($n = 2$) than males ($n = 1$).

In addition to the books in Series A1 and Series A2, two books focused on groups of people, rather than individuals, from the present (Series A3) and three books from the past (Series A4). For Series A3, one book centered upon two African American females and one book focused on White males. For Series A4, all three of the books focused on White males.

For Series B, we analyzed the books by the figures portrayed on their front covers by image alone to see which people are portrayed most predominantly. Table 2.3 demonstrates our findings.

As was the case with Series A2, Table 2.3 indicates that the majority of images from Series B focused on White/European males ($n = 22$) through display front and center on the cover. The second-largest number of images displayed on the cover of the books was African American/African males ($n = 6$). The diverse males, diverse females, and diversity with both genders' findings indicated in Table 2.3 included covers that portrayed a combination of ethnicities. However, the White/European ethnicity was the most consistently displayed in the combination images. Zero books displayed on their covers Asian males, Indigenous males, Indigenous females, Latinx males, or Latinx females. This is in sharp contrast to the total of 26 books that focused on White/European males ($n = 22$), females ($n = 2$), and both genders ($n = 2$). There was only one book for purchase that displayed African American/African females ($n = 1$) and Asian females ($n = 1$) as the focal point of the cover out of the 42 total books available for purchase. Not included in Table 2.3 are four additional books that either had no people depicted on the cover or the people were too small in size to indicate

TABLE 2.3 Series B Texts by Cover Image	
Ethnicity and Gender	**Number of Books**
African American/African Male	6
African American/African Female	1
Asian Male	0
Asian Female	1
Diverse Male	1
Diverse Females	1
Diversity With Both Genders	2
Indigenous Male	0
Indigenous Female	0
Latinx Male	0
Latinx Female	0
White/European Male	22
White/European Female	2
White/European With Both Genders	2

TABLE 2.4 Series C Texts by Continent	
Continent	**Number of Books**
Africa	2
Antarctica	1
Asia	3
Australia/Oceania	1
Europe	7
North America	12
South America	3

gender and ethnicity. For the texts in Series C, we categorized the locations of the books by continent. Table 2.4 displays these findings.

In this series, the majority of books focused on locations in North America ($n = 12$), with the second-largest number of books focusing on Europe ($n = 7$). The least number of locations mentioned in the books were located in Antarctica ($n = 1$) and Australia/Oceania ($n = 1$). In sharp contrast to North America, Asia, and South America each only had three books that focused on locations in these continents, followed by Africa, which had two books that focused on locations in this continent. Additionally, two books from this series did not fit into the continental categories and therefore were not included in Table 2.4.

DISCUSSION

The findings highlight that the series of books under investigation may very well provide a message to students that counters current efforts to remove systemic racism and oppression within U.S. society. The purpose of this chapter was to critically explore this series to analyze and uncover if these books could potentially be sending implicit messages that tell a single story (Adichie, 2009). The findings indicate that this series of books, by the total number of books published, implies to students that a certain ethnicity and gender carries more worth in society over others.

A DOMINANT NARRATIVE

Findings from this study resemble the findings from the study conducted by Thomas and Dyches (2019), which found Whites at the central focus of the resources. Additionally, the findings from this study reveal that the books create a narrative that White/European males have contributed more to society both historically and in the present than any other ethnicity/gender, which is similar to the points made by Brown and Au (2014) that describe a U.S. curriculum that historically provides a master narrative where White males are dominant. The fact of such a large number of books this subtype further paints a picture that the stories of White males matter more than others and are more worthy of being studied. Although Indigenous people were the first to inhabit the land now called the United States of America, zero books focus on the contributions of this group of people from the present and very few from the past ($n = 3$), resembling the findings from Thomas and Dyches (2019) which found that stories about "Indigenous people were nonexistent" in the literacy intervention resources they investigated (p. 607), and the findings of Quigley (2016) which found that Indigenous voices were silenced. Further, while the human race began in Africa, there are only 16 books about African Americans/Africans from the past in contrast to the number of White/European males ($n = 76$), depicted as central to the past. Further, out of the 16 total books in the African American/African category, only two of these books focus on Africans, centering on the historical figures of King Tut and Nelson Mandela. This series of books appears, by the sheer number of books available per ethnicity and gender, to implicitly teach students that White males are superior, with every other ethnicity and females being portrayed as inferior as it pertains to their importance within and their contributions to society. Similarly, the books in Series B depicted more White males as the main focal point on the cover than any other gender or ethnicity. Additionally, there were more books in Series C that focused on Europe and North America than any of the other continents from around the world.

IMPLICATION ON TEACHER PREPARATION

Of utmost importance is that educators in the field and in training recognize the forms of curriculum violence (Ighodaro & Wiggan, 2013) that surround students daily. Teacher training should yield educators that will make a concerted effort to overcome this form of oppression by providing spaces for counter-story telling (Solórzano & Yosso, 2002) through children's literature (Hughes-Hassell, 2013) that emancipates students from the single story (Adichie, 2009). For teachers to be in a place to analyze the literature in their classrooms, teacher preparation programs must guide future educators in developing the ability to think critically about the curriculum and resources (Ladson-Billings, 1995).

RECOMMENDATIONS

With the findings in mind, we recommend that educators carefully analyze the curriculum and resources being utilized in the classroom, in order to uncover hidden messages of which they may have been unaware. Educators must provide a classroom library to students that includes a balance of key historical figures by ethnicity and gender. Also, being aware that a male, Eurocentric focus drives the production of much curriculum and resources, we highly recommend that educators read the texts they are considering including in their classroom to ensure there are not further detrimental messages within the books that could cause trauma to students by way of curriculum violence (Ighodaro & Wiggan, 2013). It is our duty as educators to demonstrate to students how to liberate their minds so that they continue in this practice for the duration of their lives in all social contexts. Economically, educators can make an impact by choosing to purchase literature that unshackles students from the same, single perspective.

CONCLUSION

By critically examining resources and choosing wisely the materials to be utilized in the classroom, educators can send the message that, regardless of ethnicity or gender, each student is valuable and positively contributes to society. Until the oppressed also are given their due space in the classroom to tell their story, history will always glorify the oppressor. Systemic racism will only be refortified in schools as long as only one side of history is told through one sole perspective. We call for others to seek ways to encourage educators to be vigilant and to make sustainable change in their classrooms and ultimately in the lives of their students.

REFERENCES

Adichie, C. (2009). *The danger of a single story.* TEDGlobal.

Asante, M. K. (1990). *Kemet, afrocentricity, and knowledge.* Africa World Press.

Asante, M. K. (1998). *The Afrocentric idea.* Temple University Press.

Au, K. (1993). *Literacy instruction in multicultural settings.* Harcourt Brace Jovanovich.

Bell, D. (2018). *Faces at the bottom of the well: The permanence of racism.* Basic Books.

Brown, A., & Au, W. (2014). Race, memory, and master narratives: A critical essay on U.S. curriculum history. *Curriculum Inquiry, 44*(3), 358–389. https://doi.org/10.1111/curi.12049

Carrier, S. J., Whitehead, A. N., Walkowiak, T. A., Luginbuhl, S. C., & Thomson, M. M. (2017). The development of elementary teacher identities as teachers of science. *International Journal of Science Education, 39*(13), 1733–1754. https://doi.org/10.1080/09500693.2017.1351648

Clarke, J. H. (1977). The University of Sankore at Timbuctoo: A neglected achievement in Black intellectual history. *The Western Journal of Black Studies, 1*(2), 142–147.

Clarke, J. H. (1998). *Christopher Columbus and the Afrikan holocaust: Slavery and the rise of European capitalism.* Eworld Inc.

Crenshaw, K.W. (1989). Demarginalizing the intersection of race and sex: A Black feminist critique of antidiscrimination doctrine, feminist theory and antiracist politics. *University of Chicago Legal Forum, 1989,* 139–167.

Creswell, J. W., & Poth, C. N. (2018). *Qualitative inquiry & research design: Choosing among* five approaches (4th ed.). SAGE.

Delpit, L. (1995). *Other people's children: Cultural conflict in the classroom.* New College Press.

Dillard, C. B., & Neal, A. (2020). I am because we are: (Re)membering Ubuntu in the pedagogy of Black women teachers from Africa to America and back again. *Theory into Practice, 59*(4), 370–378. https://doi.org/10.1080/00405841.2020.1773183

Diop, C. A. (1974). *The African origin of civilization myth or reality.* Lawrence Hill Books.

Du Bois, W. E. B. (1903). *The souls of Black folk.* Bantam.

Dyches, J. (2018). Investigating curricular injustices to uncover the injustices of curricula: Curriculum evaluation as critical disciplinary literacy practice. *The High School Journal, 101*(4), 236–250. https://doi.org/10.1353/hsj.2018.0013

Freire, P. (2017). *Pedagogy of the oppressed* . Bloomsbury Academic.

Gay, G. (2000). *Culturally responsive teaching: Theory, research, and practice* (1st ed.). Teachers College Press.

Gay, G. (2018). *Culturally responsive teaching: Theory, research, and practice* (3rd ed.). Teachers College Press.

Griffin, A., & James, A. (2018). Humanities curricula as White property: Toward a reclamation of Black creative thought in social studies & literary curricula. *Multicultural Education, 25*(3/4), 10–17.

Grisby, C. (2020, April 29). State board approves African American studies high school course despite controversy. *Spectrum News.* https://spectrumlocalnews.com/tx/san-antonio/news/2020/04/29/state-board-approves-african-american-studies-high-school-course-despite-controversy-

Heilig, J. V. (2020, April 17). Breaking news: Texas has first statewide African American studies course. *Cloaking Inequity.* https://cloakinginequity.com/2020/04/17/breaking-news-texas-has-first-statewide-african-american-studies-course/

Hong, J. Y. (2010). Pre-service and beginning teachers' professional identity and its relation to dropping out of the profession. *Teaching and Teacher Education, 26*(8), 1530–1543. https://doi.org/10.1016/j.tate.2010.06.003

Hughes-Hassell, S. (2013). Multicultural young adult literature as a form of counter-storytelling. *The Library Quarterly: Information, Community, Policy, 83*(3), 212–228. https://doi.org/10.1086/670696

Ighodaro, E., & Wiggan, G. (2010). *Curriculum violence: America's new civil rights issue* (Vol. 27). Nova Science Publishers.

Irvine, J. J. (2003). *Educating teachers for diversity: Seeing with a cultural eye.* Teachers College Press.

James, G. G. M. (2020). *Stolen legacy.* CreateSpace Independent Publishing Platform.

Ladson-Billings, G. (1994). *The dreamkeepers: Successful teachers of African American children.* Jossey-Bass.

Ladson-Billings, G. (1995). Toward a theory of culturally relevant pedagogy. *American Educational Research Journal, 32*(3), 465–491. https://doi.org/10.3102/00028312032003465

Ladson-Billings, G., & Tate, W. (1995). Toward a critical race theory of education. *Teachers College Record, 97*(1), 47–68.

Love, D. (2016, January 26). Stanford study: 'Culturally relevant' teaching boosts GPA, attendance for at-risk youth, so why not make it universal? *Atlanta Blackstar.* https://atlantablackstar.com/2016/01/26/stanford-study-culturally-relevant-teaching-boosts-gpa-attendance-for-at-risk-youth-so-why-not-make-it-universal

Moll, L., & Gonzalez, N. (2004). Engaging life: A funds-of-knowledge approach to multicultural education. In J. A. Banks & C. A. M. Banks (Eds.), *Handbook of research on multicultural education* (2nd ed.; pp. 699–715). Jossey-Bass.

Montecinos, C. (1995). Culture as an ongoing dialogue: Implications for multicultural teacher education. In C. Sleeter & P. McLaren (Eds.), *Multicultural education, critical pedagogy, and the politics of difference* (pp. 269–308). State University of New York Press.

National Center for Education Statistics. (2020). *The condition of education: Characteristics of public school teachers.* U.S. Department of Education. https://nces.ed.gov/programs/coe/indicator_clr.asp

Nieto, S. (2010). *The light in their eyes: Creating multicultural learning communities* (10th anniversary ed.). Teachers College Press.

Quigley, D. (2016). Silenced. *American Indian Quarterly, 40*(4), 364–378.

Sawchuk, S. (2018). *By any other name, Mexican-American studies class finally gets Texas approval.* Education Week. http://blogs.edweek.org/edweek/curriculum/2018/04/by_any_other_name_texas_approves_mexican_studies.html

Solorzano, D., & Yosso, T. (2001). Critical race and LatCrit theory and method: Counter-storytelling. *International Journal of Qualitative Studies in Education, 14*(4), 471–495. https://doi.org/10.1080/09518390110063365

Solórzano, D., & Yosso, T. (2002). Critical race methodology: Counter-storytelling as an analytical framework for education research. *Qualitative Inquiry, 8*(1), 23–44. https://doi.org/10.1177/107780040200800103

Sumaila, M. E. (2017, April 2). *John Henrik Clarke: A great and mighty walk* [Video]. YouTube. https://www.youtube.com/watch?v=CZ4jUoHzMP4

Strauss, V. (2017, August 23). Arizona's ban on Mexican American studies was racist, U.S. court rules. *The Washington Post.* https://www.washingtonpost.com/news/answer-sheet/wp/2017/08/23/arizonas-ban-on-mexican-american-studies-was-racist-u-s-court-rules/

Tate, W. (1994). From inner city to ivory tower: does my voice matter in the academy. *Urban Education, 29*(3), 245–269.

Thomas, D., & Dyches, J. (2019). The hidden curriculum of reading intervention: A critical content analysis of Fountas & Pinnell's leveled literacy intervention.

Journal of Curriculum Studies, 51(5), 601–618. https://doi.org/10.1080/0022 0272.2019.1616116

Watson-Vandiver, M., & Wiggan, G. (2018). The genius of Imhotep: An exploration of African-centered curricula and teaching in a high achieving U.S. urban school. *Teaching and Teacher Education, 76*, 151–164. https://doi.org/10.1016/j.tate.2018.09.001

Wiggan, G., Scott, L. M., Watson, M., & Reynolds, R. (2014). *Unshackled: Education for freedom, student achievement and personal emancipation.* Sense-Springer Publishers.

Williams, E. (1994). *Capitalism and Slavery.* University of North Carolina Press.

CHAPTER 3

COMMUNITY-BASED PROFESSIONAL LEARNING COMMUNITIES (CB-PLCS)

Re-Envisioning a Model of PLCs for Urban Education

Sharon Leathers
Ramapo College of New Jersey

> We can feel sad, hurt, demoralized. But we can't give up.
> —Patrisse Cullors

A vision of a community-based professional learning community (CB-PLC) imagines educational spaces shared by those within teacher education, K–12 schools, and neighborhood communities, as well as policymakers invested in improving the school curriculum and the educational experiences and lives of students in urban education. Schools institute professional learning communities (PLCs; Stoll et al., 2006) to develop teacher collaboration and support; however, PLCs rarely extend beyond the single stakeholder of the classroom teacher, and largely do not exist outside the

Economic, Political and Legal Solutions to Critical Issues in Urban Education   pages 39–53
and Implications for Teacher Preparation
Copyright © 2022 by Information Age Publishing
www.infoagepub.com
39

parameters of the school space. In light of research on the lack of teacher diversity in the educator workforce (Villegas & Lucas, 2004), the pressing need to support teachers of color who are engaged in the work of critical reflection and racial justice (Kohli, 2019), and with the hopes of (re) imagining community-educational spaces, a CB-PLC offers a possibility for advancing the imperative of nourishing and improving the lives lived within urban education.

A few years ago, I attended a traditional, grade-level meeting established as a PLC. For a few months, I had been working in three of the city's schools as a teacher educator and university-school liaison. Although I had visited this school site mainly to support teachers in developing literacy and math practices, their work in the PLCs was largely unknown to me. Due to daily meetings, the school's PLCs were an important component of the teaching schedule. When I learned of this practice, I marveled at the complex scheduling that allowed such a venture to take place. I also considered the possibilities of the impacts on the policy and practices of the school site. During the meeting, the teachers quickly got down to business, reviewing curricular and student routines. They shared insights and questioned school-level policies and programs that did not align with their students' academic, cultural, and intellectual needs. Although they may have been somewhat uncomfortable with my presence, my commitment to the school, along with my former role in the district as a classroom teacher seemingly minimized my disruption of their discussions. The teachers, mainly teachers of color, talked freely with one another. At work was decades of teaching and urban school experience that benefitted grade-level workings, but did not move into vertical, administrative, district planning, or policy. My experiences with PLCs was much the same. As a classroom teacher, I taught in urban school settings in which PLCs met regularly, sharing knowledge, expertise, and experience. However, the innovations, creativity, and problem-solving neither left the grade level nor shifted towards leadership at school or district levels. What might happen if, within urban education, PLC's could expand their potential beyond K–12 level meeting?

The critical points of inquiry raised by this scenario explore what PLCs have to offer, how they might be repurposed to support change more effectively in urban education, and how they can offer much-needed support to students of color and their communities. Simultaneously, how might the practice of a CB-PLC support and sustain teachers of color to elevate knowledge and expertise, and engage more deeply with racial, social, and cultural pedagogies? Unroot antiquated, deficient, and/or inefficient district and school-level policies and practices? Develop caring and nurturing schools and classrooms for students of color? These questions guide the research regarding how to re-envision a model of PLCs for urban education.

URBAN SCHOOLS

I am uniquely positioned to write on this particular topic. I acknowledge my intersecting positionalities as a researcher, educator, and family member within urban school contexts. For the first 3 years of my schooling, I attended urban schools. Further, all of my professional life tracks through urban schools. I taught elementary-age children, collaborated as a university–school liaison, and coordinated an urban teacher residency program. Today, I continue to work within urban education through college–school partnerships.

Within everyday discourse, in school policies, and some areas of research, "urban schools" are continuously named, validated, and reified as recognizable and knowable spaces with implied valences of the deficit. As such, the language of "urban schools," when framed as a unitary, common-sense way of thinking, produces collective, normative, and all too predictable depictions of apathy and failure, and contributes powerfully to patterns created around policy and practice. Students who occupy these spaces are often entangled within these namings and their possible effects.

Historically, education research has obscured or entirely omitted definitions of "urban school." Chou and Tozer (2008) remarked that urban thus obviously comes with its own "baggage" (p. 1). The term may also be used in a self-congratulatory manner, as in, "I teach in an urban school," which is a variant of the more obvious statement, "I teach in the inner city" (p. 1). Often, it persists as a coded marker for conditions of cultural conflict grounded in racism and economic oppression. As such, what are seen as features, characteristics, or conditions of urban schools over time have become, in some ways, modifiers to depict people of color (Noguera, 2003). Recently, researchers of urban schools have argued that the naming is not merely geographical, but suggests that any study involving urban schools cannot take for granted "place" as having a determined and natural meaning (Emdin, 2016; Milner, 2012).

Critical race scholars challenge the language of urban schools, making visible the racialized dynamics connoted through seemingly neutral language and offering alternative framings that challenge these representations. Emdin's (2016) "hood" displaces language of disadvantage and despair, moving beyond the term *urban* to include densely populated and rural areas. At the same time, however, this re-naming also encapsulates the norming characteristic of persons. According to Emdin, these persons are specifically and overwhelmingly African American and Latinx youth. Milner (2012) also disagreed with the construction of the meaning of urban being seemingly based on "shortcomings of students and parents in the school" (p. 558). Therefore, race-neutral terms such as *at-risk, disadvantaged, low socio-economic, high-poverty, high needs, diverse, low-achieving,* and *low-performing* often conflate the conditions of the schools with the students who populate them. Simultaneously, researchers have established the pejorative effects of these racial codings. "CRT scholars in education have noted how educators describe themselves as not 'seeing' race, while they use racially coded language to describe their students and justify using ineffective pedagogies" (Dixson, 2015, p. 175). Thus, these codings—often noted as "cultural differences" (Yosso, 2005)—contribute to deficit language, thinking, and practices within education (Moll et al., 1992) and influence the U.S. curriculum (Brown & Brown, 2015).

Researchers theorizing knowledge with race as an intersection (Anzaldúa, 1987/2012; Delgado Bernal, 1998, 2002; Ladson-Billings, 2000) rely on circulations of racism within the United States particularly and how it has influenced the development of urban schools since the late 1940s and 1950s. As critical race theorists suggest, the tools needed to challenge racism in urban schools are the very tools constructed by racism's institutional ideologies; thus, attempting to challenge common sense thinking, which is seen as wholly rational and true, continues to be problematic. Through a re-interpretation of professional development, and thus teacher development, I hope to disrupt essentialized images of urban teachers, their knowledges around urban schools, and deficit-oriented knowledges around students in urban schools.

Teacher knowledges within educational research capture one example of how power produces various circulations of knowledges. Critical race theory (Ladson-Billings & Tate, 1995) questions normalized epistemological stances in which only particular knowledges are accepted as legitimate. Central to this argument is the supposition that all ontologies and epistemologies are grounded within the cultural, social and historical soil from which they grew. It has been argued by CRT scholars that this soil is indeed fraught with overlapping layers of race. Thus *epistemological racism* exists and warrants ongoing, continued resistance (Scheurich & Young, 1997). Scheurich and Young (1997) detailed institutional, societal, and civilizational worldviews that are predicated and predicted by race. Ladson-Billings (2000) informed that an epistemology is not just a way of knowing, it is a system of knowing. This situating of race shifts it from the beliefs of individuals to a social system through which individual and collective beliefs and behaviors occur.

As one example, there exists a range of characterizations of the relationship between teacher knowledge and practice. "Teacher knowledges" have proliferated in teacher education research (Darling-Hammond, 2010a, 2010b) focusing largely on what urban, early career teachers should know and be able to do. Teacher knowledges can be found in the form of standards (Shulman, 1986), preparing student teachers to teach in high needs settings (Anderson & Stillman, 2010; Weiner et al., 2000) and within urban school–university partnerships (Helfeldt et al., 2009). Specifically, in teacher education research, the question, "Whose knowledge?" has generated significant scholarship. By problematizing the role of the teacher in discussions of teacher effectiveness, researchers in the tradition of teacher/practitioner research have questioned "what it means to generate knowledge, who generates it, what counts as knowledge, and to whom, and how knowledge is used and evaluated in particular contexts" (Cochran-Smith & Lytle, 1999, p. 272). In particular, Zeichner et al. (2013) recognized that knowledge questions about what teachers know and should be able to do (Darling-Hammond, 2006; Darling-Hammond & Bransford, 2005) have been important for considering critical knowledges and skills of teachers, but the authors also offered the question of "whose knowledges" as an oft ignored realm of teacher education. Therefore, the intentions with CB-PLCs lies with re-conceptualizing who has produced and can produce knowledge in professional development.

Reconsidering how teachers engage with professional development and learning is increasingly important given efforts to diversify the teacher workforce and to support teachers of color as they seek to enact social and racial justice, racial literacy, and culturally sustaining teaching within urban school sites. In the face of ever-increasing enrollments of non-White students in U.S. public schools and intensive efforts to recruit teachers of color, the majority of the teacher workforce continues to be overwhelmingly White and female (Carver-Thomas, 2018). Over the course of their public school experiences, White female teachers will instruct the majority of students of color. Over time, this disparity significantly and overtime, this disparity significantly impacts students of color, and public and urban education in multiple ways.

Researchers have situated one impact of this continuing disparity as a democratic imperative. More than 60 years after the *Brown v. Board of Education* (1954) ruling, its promise to provide democratic and equal access to quality education remains largely unfulfilled (Ladson-Billings, 2004). This condition in which many public schools in the United States remain "separate and unequal," coincides with the disparity between the cultures of students of color and those of their teachers, and simultaneously impedes a democratic agenda. As early as the 1980s, researchers recognized possible implications of this inequality in American democracy (Carnegie Forum on Education and the Economy, 1986). These studies asserted that a society devoted to pluralistic ideals could not maintain adequate progress towards those values if students in schools lacked consistent exposure to people of color in authoritative, powerful positions like teaching. Yet, the reality for many teachers of color is that they lack teacher voice (Simon & Johnson, 2015), face racial battle fatigue (Pizarro & Kohli, 2018), and hostile teaching climates (Kohli, 2018). The current accountability culture of high-stakes testing and assessment in public schools (Kumashiro, 2015; Taubman, 2009) becomes dramatically disproportionate in urban school settings, often leaving little room for substantive reform based on teacher input.

Under the subheading, "What Can Teachers Do?" in her text, *Multiplication is for White People*, Delpit (2012) shared a conversation with Asa Hilliard III about the idea of having teachers collaborate to find the "magic bullet" for effecting change. In turn, Hilliard responded that the solution *is* teacher collaboration itself. Specifically, Delpit explored Schmoker's (2006) workaround PLCs as a possible implication to her research on urban school teaching. Schmoker's study focused on persuasive notions of a change via collectivity and agency. Along with the central design of collective planning and assessment with students' cultural knowledge and background, Delpit's main charge for PLCs is an opportunity to engage in problem-solving. At their foundation, PLCs are built on the idea of teacher collaboration within schools as a way to improve them from within. This particular innovation challenged the traditional methods of hiring external professionals to come into school sites with little localized knowledge of the schools or communities, and offered a solution to the isolation that most teachers experience within their daily professional practice. Although the professional expertise was often there, the deliberate and careful attention to the cultural assets of these communities was often missing.

HISTORICAL AND CULTURAL CONTEXT OF PLCS: TEACHER COLLABORATION

When teacher collaboration as a form of school reform emerged, its proponents suggested that interactions within the school site could have a profound impact on various aspects of the school environment (Barth, 1990; Goodlad, 1975; Shaplin, 1964). Examining the ways teachers collaborated within the school setting, researchers studied the impact of promoting school change, implementing new teaching strategies, and redefining school culture. At this time, schools considered various types of teacher collaboration, seen as a way to ease the burden and pressure of schooling. Different approaches to professional development followed. Team teaching presented an alternative to the traditional, one-teacher classroom models (Shaplin, 1964). The Rand group in the late 1970s urged school districts to create teacher centers where peers interacted with each other (McLaughlin & Berman, 1977). Showers and Joyce (1996) discussed peer coaching as having the ability to highly impact teacher behavior in the classroom. Peer coaching included goal-oriented teacher talk, peer observations, curriculum development, and peer review. School administration programs focused on collective leadership that gave teachers a voice in decision-making (Barth, 1990; Fullan & Hargreaves, 1991; Goodlad, 1994; Little, 1981). School-based researchers argued that little or no progress in student achievement and school reform would be made without teachers having a stake. These education reforms offered teachers extensive professional development, but the reforms lacked the structure for the teachers to make clear, consistent changes in classroom practice (DuFour & Eaker, 1998). Others, such as Goodlad (1975), recognized this glaring discrepancy, and helped establish the League of Cooperating Schools. The League constructed teams of teachers in support of collaboration, teacher empowerment, and reform. It was comprised of 18 schools in 18 districts. In time, the teachers affected change within their classrooms and at the school level, as well.

In 1995, the National School Reform Faculty (NSRF) set about changing the ways schools thought about teacher collaboration and school reform (Dunne & Honts, 1998). They proffered PLCs as capable of creating sustainable change from within the school site. Under the Coalition of Essential Schools paradigm, the NSRF trained teachers as coaches and invited other teachers to volunteer to meet monthly, set goals, talk and reflect on teaching practices, examine student work, and identify school issues impacting student achievement (Dunne & Honts, 1999).

Critical Friends Groups (CFGs) produced information about building teacher collaboration helping to alleviate feelings of failure in an isolated profession when teachers do not share their experiences and knowledge (Fullan & Hargreaves, 1991; Lima, 2003; Little, 2003). However, much work was needed. Schools with issues of isolation, habits of autonomy, privacy, and trust adapted slowly to collaboration, but given the appropriate environment, teacher collaboration in professional groups improved student learning. Thus, the number of PLCs grew, but often as they did in my school site, they stayed at the teacher level and neglected to address school reform.

Common today, PLCs traditionally are comprised of teachers within a school site who gather under a school administrator's direction to inquire about teacher and student learning. Over time, the practice and research of PLCs have become more accepted in schools. Nelson et al. (2012) constructed a framework intended for teachers and administrators who navigate professional learning communities. Specifically, the authors' research focused on elements related to the group, rather than the individual, as the unit of analysis. They argue that a PLC's levels of nuanced epistemology and negotiated dialogue shape teacher perspectives and uses of student data and determine the group's capability of transforming pedagogical practice. A nuanced stance is grounded in concept-building with a special emphasis on student data that questions and reflects formatively rather than summatively. Their continuum of dialogue, ranging from disconnected talk to negotiated dialogue, reflects the type of language within the collaborative inquiry. However, it is only through negotiated dialogue, characterized by perspectives that are made explicit, challenged, and transformed, that a PLC can arrive at these transformations.

Many researchers agree that PLCs can be a driving force in improving student achievement, where run-of-the-mill teacher development programs fail (Schmoker, 2006). Wood (2007) described two PLCs, "for teachers and with teachers." In the first, middle school teachers in learning, the community played a limited role in the group's activities, even when acting as facilitators, and relied on external support following what was expected of them. In the second vignette, teachers shared facilitation and leadership, took responsibility for their learning, solved problems, and collaborated with a focus on student achievement, displaying all of Hord's (1997) attributes of authentic PLCs. Most important to note is the differences between these two vignettes. In the first vignette, there was a failed attempt at a PLC. However, teachers were in charge of the group and they attempted authentic PLC work. Why did it fail? Constructing an understanding of professional development *with teachers* requires a culture shift. In part, the teachers in the first vignette were following traditional norms of professional development. In the second vignette, "teachers took ownership of their time and space," thus demonstrating the agency needed for change.

Hord (1997) described approaches to PLCs outside of the school building, where stakeholders across the district can become part of a community. She identified five attributes of PLCs: supportive and shared leadership, collective creativity, shared values and vision, supportive conditions, and shared personal practice. Each of these elements focuses on *with-teachers.* Although Hord referred to varying definitions and purposes of education, she neglected a teacher's perception of professional learning communities whereby teachers see it as yet another initiative with little benefit and many challenges (Wood, 2007). Wood's vignettes of two schools illustrate the dichotomy between teacher engagement (with teachers) and teacher tolerance of new initiatives (for teachers). Bullough's "Eight-Year Study," conducted between 1930 and 1942 by the Progressive Education Association, emphasized the importance of teachers working in collaboration with university faculty and social scientists on the development of inquiry in areas such as curriculum, instruction, and evaluation (Bullough, 2007).

RE-ENVISIONING PROFESSIONAL LEARNING COMMUNITIES

In a CB-PLC, teachers, district and school administrators, preservice teachers and teacher educators, students, parents, community members, and policymakers collaborate to stimulate dialogue and problem-solve to effect sustainable improvement for schools. This expansion of PLCs is promising because of its capacity to have all stakeholders share in agency and leadership. Situating teachers in official leadership positions to lead professional development, revise curricula, and advise policymakers suggests an expansion of the role of the classroom teacher for teachers of color committed to staying within the classroom (Darling-Hammond et al., 2017). While such roles are not new to teacher leaders, CB-PLCs, given status in school, district administration, and city or state legislation, elevate and further legitimize this work. Yet possible and important, is the ability of the CB-PLC to engage in the "Freirian-type" (1970) praxis suggested by Hord (1997). Opening up lines of communication with stakeholders whose opinions and cultural knowledges are valued might be the first step to changing how urban educational policy and practice occur.

I focus on CB-PLCs as an approach to (a) creating and sustaining teacher collaboration for urban educators, and specifically for teachers of color; (b) elevating teacher knowledge and leadership to levels of policymaking; and (c) caring for and nurturing schools and classrooms for students of color. Significantly, while this chapter offers CB-PLCs for urban education settings, teachers collaborating with a diverse body of stakeholders hold an impact on all school communities.

Informed by two PLCs that emerged, one more than 80 years ago, and the other very recently, a CB-PLC revitalizes the work of PLCs by aligning it with a critical stance in which multiple stakeholders participate and engage in advancing the work in urban education. This work cannot and should not rest solely on the shoulders of the classroom teacher. Both of these PLCs embrace the idea that a "learning community classroom functions in partnership with the entire school community, and also with stakeholders outside the school building" (Doolittle et al., 2008, p. 304; Hord, 1997).

Within a CB-PLC, the power of voice and transformation becomes possible. Collins (2009) agreed with the pressing need to center race within educational settings and suggested a domains-of-power framework as a counterargument to color-blind racism. She proposed this framework to support the interrogation of race in education spheres, within and through which color-blindness might be claimed. In Collins' (2009) domains-of-power framework, power is expressed within and through four contexts or domains: structural, disciplinary, cultural, and interpersonal. First, Collins argued how the first three domains are largely invisible. Most racial discourse is realized in the interpersonal domain in which people look to change others' minds about racism and its effects. Additionally, while each domain is named separately, one overlaps with another. Within each domain, power is neither lateral nor all encompassing. Instead, resistances occur within each domain. Collins iterated how all four domains must be in place for racism to persist. The *structural domain* describes the systemic level of racism; the *disciplinary domain* looks at processes and practices mechanized by racism;

the *cultural domain* encompasses the ideologies and beliefs filtered through social institutions and practices and the *interpersonal domain* focuses on the individual level.

Collins' (2009) domains-of-power framework, through which she examined race and racism as systems of power, aligns with the tenets of critical race theory as a way to examine the structures, policies, and procedures embedded within and through urban education. The interplay, interpretations, and assumptions in the literature on PLCs and in alignment with a critical studies lens are complex. For a community to have equity and shared power, all participants need to share in decision-making, but also in the authority needed to decide about PLCs. Currently, principals decide on the creation of PLCs, even when the intent is to give teachers authority within the PLC. Teachers should be able to tell prospective participants about a PLC they wish to create based on an identified problem, just as a principal or other administrative stakeholder would.

Restructuring a PLC as a *community-based* PLC places primary importance on *community* and shifts the community component to include the critical stakeholders that not only work beyond the district and school but also play significant roles in school communities. Therefore, while the naming sounds redundant, it is important for re-thinking and re-learning how communities function within urban school environments. To create lasting and successful change in urban schools, a professional learning community must include more than teachers. CB-PLCs recognize the cultural capital wealth (Yosso, 2005) of school community members and embed critical professional development (CPD) in them (Kohli, 2019; Kohli et al., 2015). CPD is "designed to provoke cooperative dialogue, build unity, provide shared leadership, and meet the critical needs of teachers" (p. 11). Central to CPD is the construction of teachers as intellectuals and agents of social change within schools and communities.

A Community-Based PLC (CB-PLC) in Practice

CB-PLCs operate in opposition to today's climate of urban school reform and accountability. Having teachers, administrators, students, preservice teachers, community members, and policyholders in conversation with one another creates access for developing systemic change. Who might be a member of a CB-PLC?

In K–12:

- Students
- Teachers of color; in-service teachers
- Paraprofessionals/aides

- Principals
- Superintendents

In higher education:

- Preservice teachers
- Teacher education faculty and/or staff

In the community:

- Parents
- Community educational activists
- Locally owned small businesses

In policy:

- Policymakers

Over time, each of these stakeholders contributes to and hears from their CB-PLC members. As policies and practices fall under debate, the CB-PLC provides a forum for discussion and feedback. CB-PLC members can include persons of color seeking to contribute to the dialogue on further development within schools: culturally relevant/sustaining pedagogies, racial literacy, social justice, and other forms of social and cultural change.

LIMITATIONS AND POSSIBILITIES

Although CB-PLCs offer opportunities to restructure professional development and community engagement within urban school settings, it is important to also recognize possible limitations and opportunities. One limitation is that a CB-PLC requires, at its inception, external professional development, which may feel like being positioned between the proverbial rock and a hard place. Thus, professional development is both the solution and the problem. Developing CB-PLCs would require teachers to buy into a system of "professional development" that may have already failed them. Additionally, without proper school organization of time and space, schools will not reap the benefit of CB-PLCs. A teacher's time is already inundated with grading, lesson planning, and preparation, so additional time within the school day is imperative for teachers to meet and work within CB-PLCs.

Possible consequences to this approach include greater teacher agency. Teachers with an increased agency will have greater leadership, skill, and motivation that accompany the capacity to accomplish tasks. Teachers who work directly with policymakers and researchers will better understand both sides of an issue instead of continuing on separate paths. Policymakers will attain greater insight into classroom realities and this realistic view of teaching might assist in the development of policy that benefits students, teachers, and communities.

In summary, CB-PLCs in urban education open up new avenues for research, policy, and practice. Possibilities for research include (a) the structures and impacts of CB-PLCs on school culture, policy, and practices, (b) representations of agency for teachers of color, (c) power relations within CB-PLCs, and (d) shifting the discourse from local to global contexts as we advance in technology for remote communications. Teachers cannot carry the burden of changing urban education on their own. All of us who educate, in teacher education and urban schools, must determine that such change is the charge of all who value urban education.

REFERENCES

Anderson, L., & Stillman, J. (2013). Student teaching's contribution to preservice teacher development: A review of research focused on the preparation of teachers for urban and high-needs contexts. *Review of Educational Research, 83*(1), 3–69.

Anzaldúa, G. (2012). *Borderlands/La frontera: The new mestizo.* Aunt Lute Books. (Original work published in 1987)

Barth, R. (1990). *Improving schools from within.* Jossey-Bass Inc.

Brown, A. L., & Brown, K. D. (2015). The more things change, the more they stay the same: Excavating race and the enduring racisms in US curriculum. *Teachers College Record, 117*(14), 103–130.

Bullough, R. (1985). Professional learning communities and the eight-year study. *Educational Horizons, 85*(3), 168–180.

Carnegie Forum on Education and the Economy, Task Force on Teaching as a Profession (1986). *A nation prepared: Teachers for the 21st century.*

Carver-Thomas, D. (2018). *Diversifying the teaching profession: How to recruit and retain teachers of color.* Learning Policy Institute.

Chou, V., & Tozer, S. (2008). What's urban got to do with it? Meanings of "urban" in urban teacher preparation and development. In F. P. Peterman (Ed.), *Partnering to prepare urban teachers: A call to activism* (pp. 1–20). Oxford University Press.

Cochran–Smith, M., & Lytle, S. (1999). Relationships of knowledge and practice: Teacher learning in communities. *Review of Research in Education, 24,* 249–305.

Collins, P. H. (2009). *Another kind of public education: Race, schools, the media, and democratic possibilities.* Beacon Press.

Darling–Hammond, L. (2006). Constructing 21st–century teacher education. *Journal of Teacher Education, 57*(3), 1–15.

Darling–Hammond, L. (2010a). *Evaluating teacher effectiveness: How teacher performance assessments can measure and improve teaching.* Center for American Progress.

Darling–Hammond, L. (2010b). *Recognizing and developing effective teaching: What policymakers should know and do* [Policy brief]. National Education Association.

Darling–Hammond, L., & Bransford, J. (Eds.). (2005). *Preparing teachers for a changing world.* Jossey–Bass.

Darling-Hammond, L., Burns, D., Campbell, C., Goodwin, A. L., Hammerness, K., Low, E. L., McIntyre, A., Sato, M., & Zeichner, K. (2017). *Empowered educators: How high-performing systems shape teaching quality around the world.* John Wiley & Sons.

Delgado Bernal, D. (1998). Using a Chicana feminist epistemology in educational research. *Harvard Educational Review, 68*(4), 555–582.

Delgado Bernal, D. (2002). Critical race theory, Latino critical theory, and critical race-gendered epistemologies: Recognizing students of color as holders and creators of knowledge, *Qualitative Inquiry, 8*(1), 105–126.

Delpit, L. D. (2012). *"Multiplication is for white people": Raising expectations for other people's children.* The New Press.

Dixson, A. (2015). Yes, we did? Educational equity in a new "post-racial" society. *Teachers College Record, 117*(4), 171–184.

Doolittle, G., Sudeck, M., & Rattigan, P. (2008). Creating professional learning communities: The work of professional development schools. *Theory Into Practice, 47*(4), 303–310.

DuFour, R., & Eaker, R. (1998). *Professional learning communities: Best practices for enhancing student achievement.* Solution Tree Press.

Dunne, F., & Honts, F. (1998). *"That group really makes me think!": Critical friends groups and the development of reflective practitioners.* Paper presented at the American Educational Research Association annual meeting, San Diego, CA.

Emdin, C. (2016). *For white folks who teach in the hood . . . and the rest of y'all too: Reality pedagogy and urban education.* Beacon Press.

Freire, P. (1970). *Pedagogy of the oppressed* (20th anniversary ed.) Continuum.

Fullan, M. G., & Hargreaves, A. (1991). *What's worth fighting for? Working together for your school.* The Regional Laboratory for Educational Improvement of the Northeast & Islands.

Goodlad, J. I. (1975). Schools can make a difference. *Educational Leadership, 33*(2), 108–117.

Goodlad, J. (1994). *What schools are for* (2nd ed.). Phi Delta Kappa Educational Foundation.

Helfeldt, J. P., Capraro, R. M., Capraro, M. M., Foster, E., & Carter, N. (2009). An urban schools–university that prepares and retains quality teachers for "high-need" schools. *The Teacher Educator, 44*(1), 1–20.

Hord, S. M. (1997). *Professional learning communities: Communities of continuous inquiry and improvement* (pp. 127–165). Southwest Educational Development Lab.

Kohli, R. (2018). Behind school doors: The impact of hostile racial climates on urban teachers of color. *Urban Education, 53*(3), 307–333.

Kohli, R. (2019). Lessons for teacher education: The role of critical professional development in teacher of color retention. *Journal of Teacher Education, 70*(1), 39–50.

Kohli, R., Picower, B., Martinez, A., & Ortiz, N. (2015). Critical professional development: Centering the social justice needs of teachers. *International Journal of Critical Pedagogy, 6*(2), 7–24.

Kumashiro, K. K. (2015). *Bad teacher! How blaming teachers distorts the bigger picture.* Teachers College Press.

Ladson-Billings, G. (2000). Racialized discourses and ethnic epistemologies. In N. K. Denzin & Y. S. Lincoln (Eds.), *Handbook of Qualitative Research* (2nd ed.; pp. 257–278). SAGE.

Ladson-Billings, G. (2004). Landing on the wrong note: The price we paid for Brown. *Educational Researcher, 33*(7), 3–13.

Ladson-Billings, G., & Tate, W. (1995). Toward a critical race theory in education. *Teachers College Record, 97*(1), 47–68.

Lima, J. A. (2003). Trained for isolation: The impact of departmental cultures on student teachers' views and practices of collaboration. *Journal of Education for Teaching, 29*(3), 197–218.

Little, J. W. (1981). *School success and staff development: The role of staff development in urban desegregated schools.* National Institute of Education.

Little, J. W. (2003). Inside teacher community: Representations of classroom practice. *Teachers College Record, 105*(6), 913–945.

McLaughlin, M., & Berman, P. (1977). Retooling staff development in a period of retrenchment. *Educational Leadership, 35*(3), 191–194.

Milner, H. R. (2012). But what is urban education? *Urban Education, 47*(3), 556–561.

Moll, L. C., Amanti, C., Neff, D., & Gonzalez, N. (1992). Funds of knowledge for teaching: Using a qualitative approach to connect homes and classrooms. *Theory Into Practice, 31*(2), 132–141.

Nelson, T., Slavit, D., & Deuel, A. (2012). Two dimensions of an inquiry stance toward student-learning data. *Teachers College Record, 114*(8), 1–42.

Pizarro, M., & Kohli, R. (2018). "I stopped sleeping": Teachers of color and the impact of racial battle fatigue. *Urban Education, 55*(7), 1–25.

Scheurich, J., & Young, M. (1997). Coloring epistemologies: Are our research epistemologies racially biased? *Educational Researcher, 26*(4), 4–16.

Schmoker M. (2006). Professional learning communities. In M. Schmoker (Ed.), *Results now: How we can achieve unprecedented improvements in teaching and learning* (pp. 105–123). ASCD.

Shaplin, J. T. (1964). Description and definition of team teaching. In J. T. Shaplin & H. F. Olds Jr. (Eds.), *Team teaching* (pp. 1–23) Harper & Row.

Showers, B., & Joyce, B. (1996). The evolution of peer coaching. *Educational Leadership, 53*(6), 12–16.

Shulman, L. (1986). Those who understand: Knowledge growth in teaching. *Educational Researcher, 15*(2), 4–14.

Simon, S., & Johnson, S. M. (2015). Teacher turnover in high-poverty schools: What we know and can do. *Teachers College Record, 117*(3), 1–36.

Stoll, L., Bolam, R., & McMahon, A. (2006). Professional learning communities: A review of the literature. *Journal of Educational Change, 7,* 221–258.

Taubman, P. (2009). *Teaching by numbers: Deconstructing the discourse of standards and accountability in education.* Routledge.

Villegas, A. M., & Lucas, T. F. (2004). Diversifying the teacher workforce: A retrospective and prospective analysis. *Yearbook of the National Society for the Study of Education, 103*(1), 70–104.

Weiner, L. (2000). Research in the 90s: Implications for urban teacher preparation. *Review of Educational Research, 70*(3), 369–406.

Wood, D. R. (2007). Professional learning communities: Teachers, knowledge, and knowing. *Theory into Practice, 46*(4), 281–290.

Yosso, T. (2005). Whose culture has capital? A critical race theory discussion of community cultural wealth. *Race, Ethnicity and Education, 8*(1), 69–91.

Zeichner, K., Payne, A., & Brayko, K. (2015). Democratizing teacher education. *Journal of Teacher Education, 66*(2), 122–135.

CHAPTER 4

RE-EXAMINING NONCOGNITIVE FACTORS

Promoting the Academic Achievement of African American Males at Urban Universities

Harriet Hobbs
University of North Carolina at Charlotte

Greg Wiggan
University of North Carolina at Charlotte

The function of education is to teach one to think intensively and to think critically.
Intelligence plus character—that is the goal of true education.
—Dr. Martin Luther King Jr.

White supremacist ideology has always judged African Americans by the color of their skin and denied them equal educational opportunities (Watson & Wiggan, 2016; Wiggan, 2007). Allen et al. (2007) posited that the educational gap between African Americans and Whites is the reason for African Americans' subjugated status in society. Negative assumptions

Economic, Political and Legal Solutions to Critical Issues in Urban Education   pages 55–75
and Implications for Teacher Preparation
Copyright © 2022 by Information Age Publishing
www.infoagepub.com
55

about African Americans are deeply interconnected with the utilization of a single test to determine the academic success of African American males, without accounting for school inequalities and structural barriers to achievement (Sedlacek, 2004; Watson & Wiggan, 2016; Wiggan, 2011). To elucidate this issue, Wiggan (2007) highlighted two research studies that assert African American students are intellectually deficient. The first was Stetson's (1897) study that tested 500 African American and White American students who read aloud four stanzas of poetry. The results indicated that African American students outpaced their White counterparts; however, even with these findings, Stetson asserted that African American students were intellectually deficient.

The second study reviewed by Wiggan (2007) was on mental testing by Robert Guthrie (2004), a psychologist who in his book entitled *Even the Rat Was White,* exposed the long history of racist pseudo research on the mental testing of African Americans. In Guthrie's study, the Binet scales for mental measurement were created with a focus on the use of standard English. On the Binet test, White students outperformed their African American counterparts, and unlike the results of Stetson's test, the outcome of this test was greatly publicized (Guthrie, 1998). The Binet test supported the claim of the biological supremacy of White Americans and was used to exacerbate genetic and racial superiority (Guthrie,1998). However, African Americans continue to pursue higher education with faith, perseverance, and desperation, convinced that the deliverance from racial oppression is hidden in the pages of books that African Americans were once forbidden to read (Allen et al., 2007; Anderson, 1988; Wiggan et al., 2014).

Although many state laws during the Civil War prohibited the education of African Americans, their educational pursuits have been traditionally linked to a sense of liberation and a desire to improve the plight of their people (Perry, 2003; Wiggan et al., 2014). However, James (2017) and King and Swartz (2014) found that common core standards still reproduce a hegemonic narrative of Eurocentric history year after year, and continue to omit, misrepresent, and "Whitewash" the history of African Americans and Indigenous groups, sending the message to African American students have little to no value in the context of American history. As a result, scholars have argued the importance for all students, not just African Americans, to learn and understand multicultural contributions and ensure that they are an integral part of multicultural education (James, 2017; Orfield et al., 2005; Watson & Wiggan, 2018; Wiggan et al., 2014).

Public education (K–12) plays a critical role for students of color whose trajectory is higher education. There is a need to explore noncognitive factors in teacher education programs and how they impact African American males' academic achievement in urban universities. Noncognitive factors have been defined as strategies, attitudes, feelings, and behaviors that consider the way students interact within an educational context (Borghans et al., 2008; Garcia, 2014; Wanzer et al., 2019). To better understand African American males' journey in higher education, it is important to highlight their high school completion and bachelor's degree attainment rates. Table 4.1 details the most recent data from the Department of Commerce, United States Census population.

To obtain the data in Table 4.1, 5-year high school completion and bachelor's degree attainment for males by race and ethnicity was compiled. As seen, the high school completion rates for African American males are four times higher than that of their bachelor's degree attainment rate. It is also important to note that African American males' bachelor's degree attainment is less than that of their White, Asian, Pacific Islander, and multiracial counterparts.

Current predictors such as grade point average, retention, and graduation rates should not be the only indicators for predicting academic success for African American males. To better understand these indicators, it is also important to review the fall enrollment data of all males enrolled at postsecondary institutions. Table 4.2 outlines the most recent enrollment and 4-year graduation data collected by the United States Department of Education, National Center for Educational Statistics.

Table 4.2 details the fall enrollment and percentage of male students by race. It can be seen that in 2018, there were fewer African American males (11.6%) enrolled at postsecondary institutions than White males (55.9%) and Hispanic males (20.3%). Overall, the enrollment and percentage points of distribution for African American males at post-secondary institutions declined between 2014 and 2018. Scott et al. (2013) posited that low expectations, miscommunication, under-preparedness, and racist encounters with White professors in classrooms are factors that negatively impact the academic achievement of African American males (Harper et al., 2018; Ladson-Billings & Tate, 1995; Patton et al., 2014).

The 4-year graduation rates of male cohorts between the years 1996 through 2012 are compiled by race in Table 4.3. As seen, among the 2012 cohort that graduated in 2016, African American males were the lowest group to graduate, at 14.9%. Even so, it is important to note that between 1996 and 2012 the graduation rates for African American males have increased by 2–5% (Table 4.3).

Brooms (2016) and Brooms and Davis (2017) indicated that successful mentoring programs have increased the retention and degree attainment of African American males and are one example of how noncognitive factors support their academic success. Hence, examining noncognitive factors is particularly important when considering the academic success of African American male students (Sedlacek, 2004). Some examples of noncognitive factors are maintenance of an academic mindset, fostering

TABLE 4.1 Rates of High School Males' Completion and Bachelor's Degree Attainment

Year	White	Black	Hispanic	Total	Asian	Pacific Islander	American Indian/ Alaska Native	Two or More Races
High School Completion								
2015	93.0	87.2	65.5	90.9	91.3	84.9	81.9	92.5
2016	93.4	87.0	67.2	92.3	92.2	94.9	84.1	92.8
2017	93.7	87.4	69.5	92.5	92.7	89.1	83.0	93.2
2018	93.9	88.3	70.7	92.8	92.9	92.2	79.3	92.5
2019	94.2	88.1	70.8	92.8	92.8	93.3	84.1	91.0
Bachelor's Degree								
2015	36.3	21.1	14.3	55.6	57.3	24.4	18.1	27.2
2016	37.2	21.8	15.4	57.7	59.4	22.2	16.5	25.6
2017	37.8	22.6	15.8	55.7	57.2	26.2	17.7	30.3
2018	38.9	23.7	16.6	58.5	60.1	23.6	15.4	30.0
2019	39.9	24.4	16.9	59.4	60.9	24.8	12.9	31.1

Note: U.S. Department of Commerce, Census Bureau, U.S. Census of Population

TABLE 4.2 Fall Enrollment and Percentage of Males at Degree-Granting Postsecondary Institution From 2014–2018

Undergraduate Male Enrollment by Race/Ethnicity	Fall Enrollment					Percentage Distribution of U.S. Resident Students (Excluded Nonresident Aliens)				
	2014	2015	2016	2017	2018	2014	2015	2016	2017	2018
White	4,299.0	4,188.1	4,087.0	3,990.0	3,867.3	58.9	58.2	57.5	56.7	55.9
Black	924.9	888.4	849.4	831.7	800.5	12.7	12.3	12.0	11.8	11.6
Hispanic	1,261.8	1,298.3	1,343.5	1,378.5	1,402.7	17.3	18.0	18.9	19.6	20.3
Asian/Pacific Islander	511.7	515.0	520.6	525.3	531.5	7.0	7.2	7.3	7.5	7.7
Asian	488.1	492.3	499.2	504.2	511.5	6.7	6.8	7.0	7.2	7.4
Pacific Islander	23.5	22.7	21.4	21.1	20.0	0.3	0.3	0.3	0.3	0.3
Native American/Alaska	56.1	53.2	51.5	49.1	47.1	0.8	0.7	0.7	0.7	0.7
Two or more races	245.9	252.1	255.2	267.2	274.6	3.4	3.5	3.6	3.8	4.0
Nonresident alien	286.8	307.2	309.6	309.4	302.5	†	†	†	†	†

Note: U.S. Department of Education, National Center for Educational Statistics.

† = Not Applicable.

TABLE 4.3 Graduating Rate by Percenttage of First-Time, Full-Time Bachelor's Degree Seeking Males at 4-Year Postsecondary Institutions

Starting Cohort	Total	White	Black	Hispanic	Total	Asian	Pacific Islander	American Indian/ Alaska Native	Two or More Races	Non-Resident Alien
1996	20.8	22.6	9.9	12.5	23.4	—	—	10.9	—	28.6
2000	23.6	25.5	11.7	14.5	27.8	—	—	11.9	—	30.3
2002	24.6	26.6	11.0	15.8	30.4	—	—	12.8	—	30.4
2003	25.7	27.9	10.9	16.4	32.5	—	—	14.1	—	30.8
2004	26.2	28.5	11.2	16.9	32.9	—	—	14.5	—	30.1
2005	27.1	29.6	11.7	18.3	33.5	33.8	14.1	15.0	26.4	29.8
2006	27.9	30.4	12.1	18.8	34.9	35.2	15.4	13.8	29.2	29.7
2007	28.3	31.1	12.1	19.5	34.8	35.0	19.2	14.7	34.0	29.4
2008	29.3	32.1	13.3	20.0	36.1	36.5	18.7	15.4	30.7	33.1
2009	29.5	32.4	13.2	20.3	37.9	38.4	21.0	16.0	27.6	35.2
2010	30.5	33.7	13.4	21.4	38.7	39.1	23.6	13.8	27.2	37.0
2011	31.6	35.2	13.6	22.1	39.3	39.6	25.6	15.1	28.1	38.1
2012	33.2	36.9	14.9	23.1	41.3	41.7	27.8	16.3	28.6	39.6

Note: U.S. Dept. of Education, National Center for Education Statistics graduation rates (— indicates data not available).

a sense of belonging, and having the ability to understand and deal with racism. According to Sedlacek (2011), noncognitive factors are useful for all students because they have been proven as viable alternatives in fairly assessing the abilities of people of color, women, international students, older students, students with disabilities, and others who have experiences that are different from those of young, White, heterosexual, able-bodied, Eurocentric males in the United States.

This chapter re-examines the use of noncognitive factors as indicators in promoting the academic achievement of African American males enrolled at urban universities. Using existing literature, this chapter seeks to answer the research question: To what extent do academic self-efficacy (mindset), a sense of belonging, and the ability to understand and deal with racism, impact the academic achievement of African American male students in urban universities? Using critical race theory (CRT) as the theoretical framework and focusing on the use of noncognitive factors to mitigate racism, the chapter introduces a comprehensive explanation, as well as implications for teacher preparation programs. Finally, the chapter concludes with a call to action and recommendations for university admissions offices, university faculty, and teacher preparation programs.

LITERATURE REVIEW

Many have argued that success, especially for college students, has less to do with grade point averages (GPA) and standardized test scores, and more to do with less tangible and quantifiable qualities such as determination, academic mindset, a sense of belonging, and the ability to understand and deal with racism (Duckworth et al., 2007; Johnson et al., 2007; Moore, 2001; Palmer & Strayhorn, 2008; Sedlacek, 2004; Shorette & Palmer, 2015; Solberg et al., 1993). The CRT framework in education reflects on the larger social, cultural, and economic conditions of students of color and how these factors influence students in their educational journeys. With the need to understand ways to increase the enrollment and academic success of African American males in higher education, noncognitive factors must be explored.

Recently, there has been an increased emphasis on noncognitive factors in education policy and student success (Farruggia et al., 2016; Garcia, 2004; Khine & Areepattamannil, 2016; Palmer & Strayhorn, 2008; Sedlacek, 2011). While there has been a surge of interest and debate about the effects of noncognitive factors in the academic achievement of African American students, they are often understudied at the postsecondary level (Farruggia et al., 2016; Garcia, 2014; Shorette & Palmer, 2015; Tracey & Sedlacek, 1987). The debates focus on the similarities and differences in the process of educational attainment between African American and White students (Sedlacek, 2008, 2011; Tracey & Sedlacek, 1987).

At Historically Black Colleges and Universities (HBCUs), African American students report a strong sense of belonging and experience feelings of engagement, connection, acceptance, support, and encouragement (Allen, 1992). Conversely, Bentley-Edwards and Chapman-Hilliard (2015) and Cokley (1999) found that African American students who attend HBCUs hold more Afrocentric insights relating to their history and culture and experienced a more positive adjustment to their school environment when compared to their African American counterparts at predominately white institutions (PWIs). Contrarily, African American students that demonstrated more African-centered attitudes at PWIs struggled with finding social acceptance and a sense of belonging on their campuses (Anglin & Wade, 2007; Chavous, 2000). This difference in experiences may be related to Kaiser and Pratt-Hyatt's (2009) finding that Whites express increased negative attitudes toward other ethnic minorities who strongly identify with their racial group.

CRT scholars connect the disadvantages of students of color at PWI campuses to a society in which people of color are treated unequally, have higher rates of sickness and death, receive lower quality education and health services, live in poorer social and economic environments, and are more subject to criminal victimization and incarceration (Savas, 2014; Solorzano et al., 2000). Also, Ingram (2013), Palmer et al. (2014), and Savas (2014) asserted that African American students at PWIs experience racial microaggressions in subtle, stunning, and non-verbal ways that offend African American students. Thus, it can be contended that racism still exists on college campuses and therefore we should be discussing with African American males how to understand and deal with racism (Solorzano et al., 2000).

INCLUSIVENESS

Since the educational experiences for students of color have been molded by indoctrination related to miseducation and European theology, the inclusiveness of the curriculum should begin in elementary education and continue throughout the college experience (Wiggan et al., 2014). This means that African American students should not be pressured to learn through conventional teaching philosophies that provide one-size-fits-all approaches (Manning et al., 2014; Savas, 2014). Instead, African American students need a unique pedagogy that encompasses their cultures and traditions and supports them for long-term academic success (Orfield et al. 2005; Wiggan et al., 2014). Within this context, culturally responsive teaching and noncognitive factors should be a part of American schools and higher education (Garcia, 2014; Ladson-Billings, 1995; Savas, 2014; Wiggan et al., 2014).

Accordingly, this chapter addresses the gap in the literature concerning noncognitive factors such as academic mindset, which is defined as the psychological and social attitudes and beliefs that an individual holds toward their academic work (Farruggia et al., 2016; Shen et al., 2016). Academic self-efficacy describes students' beliefs about their ability to execute a course of action to complete an academic task (Bandura, 1997). Understanding individual academic mindsets leads to specific behaviors that can encourage or discourage academic performance (Han et al., 2017). When students lack a sense of academic self-efficacy, they are less likely to persist to overcome academic challenges (Chemers et al., 2001; Han et al., 2017; Shen et al., 2016).

Two additional noncognitive factors that are necessary among African American males at urban universities are the ability to understand and deal with racism, and having a sense of belonging (Harper et al., 2018; Ingram, 2013; Johnson et al., 2007; Palmer et al., 2014; Sedlacek, 1999). Sedlacek (2004) referred to noncognitive factors as variables relating to adjustment, motivation, and student perceptions rather than the traditional verbal and quantitative areas that are measured by standardized tests (Sedlacek, 1998, 2004).

Noncognitive factors can play a central role in the academic success of African American males. Given the entrenched disparities in college graduation rates associated with income, ethnicity, race, and first-generation college status, understanding noncognitive factors among low-income and underserved students has never been more important (Farruggia et al., 2016; Garcia, 2004; Khine et al., 2016; Palmer & Strayhorn, 2008; Sedlacek, 2011). This review of the present literature examines noncognitive factors concerning the academic achievement of African American males. However, there remains a pressing need to re-examine noncognitive factors and their influence on the academic achievement of African American males at urban universities.

THEORETICAL FRAMEWORK

This chapter is framed in CRT, highlighting the works of intellectual scholars, Dr. Derrick Bell and Dr. Kimberlé Crenshaw. The late Dr. Bell is the renowned intellectual architect who drafted the blueprints that guided the initial development of CRT and asserted that despite undeniable progress, no African Americans are insulated from incidents of racial discrimination (Bell, 1992; Hughes et al., 2013). Bell (1992) and Crenshaw (2002) stated that CRT has set the context for contesting the exclusionary practices of elite law schools, and has established a scholarly agenda that places race at the center of intellectual inquiry rather than at the margins of constitutional theory. Additionally, Ladson-Billings (1998) and Ladson-Billings and Tate (1995) asserted that race continues to be a significant factor in determining inequity in the United States.

The perpetuation of racism continued well into the 1990s. An example of a racist theory is in the 1994 best-selling book, *The Bell Curve* by White nationalist, Charles Murray, and Dr. Richard Herrnstein, a psychologist who claimed that race and class differences are largely caused by genetic factors. Murray and Herrnstein (1994) purposefully implied that because of genetic differences, African Americans are intellectually inferior when compared to Whites, by indicating that African Americans scored 15 points below Whites on the IQ Test (Bell, 1995). This theory was rejected because there is no basis for the findings that intelligence is inherited solely based on race (Bell, 1995). For more than four centuries, race and racism have been rooted in the U.S. social, economic, and political systems. It is embedded in the fabric of American society, including the legal and educational systems (Crenshaw, 1995, 2002; Delgado & Stefancic, 2001; Ladson-Billings & Tate, 1995).

The critiques of neutrality, objectivity, color-blindness, meritocracy, and equality are the most common themes linked to the work of CRT (Bell, 1992; Crenshaw, 2002; Delgado & Stefancic, 2001). First, racism is considered ordinary, the usual way that society operates. Second, interest convergence advances the interests of White elites and working-class people within large segments of society. Third, color-blindness is the concept of equality expressed in rules that insist only on treatment that is the same across the board. Finally, social construction holds that races are products of social thought and relations, and they are not objective, inherent, or fixed. Race does not correspond to any biological or genetic reality, but instead is a set of categories that society invents, manipulates, or retires when it is convenient (Delgado & Stefancic, 2001). Race and racism have been central to shaping African American males' experiences, and halts their upward mobility (DeCuir & Dixson, 2004; Palmer et al. 2014). Critical writers in law, as well as in social science, have drawn attention to the ways dominant society racializes different minority groups at different times in response to the shifting needs of society (Delgado & Stefancic, 2001).

Recently, other researchers have applied CRT in higher education (Chaisson, 2004; Harper et al., 2018; Patton et al., 2016; Solórzano et al., 2000). Harper et al. (2018) and Patton et al. (2016) discuss three propositions within the CRT framework in the context of higher education. First, the U.S. higher education system has a white supremacist history that continually affects contemporary postsecondary institutions. Second, imperialism and capitalism reproduce racial oppression and inequities at U.S. colleges and universities. Last, postsecondary institutions are places where racist and white supremacist conceptions of knowledge are produced and rewarded.

Therefore, it is important to examine four tenets of CRT (racism, interest convergence, color-blindness, and social construction) to better understand how race impacts African American males' academic achievement at urban universities (Chaisson, 2004; Ladson-Billings,1998; Solórzano et al., 2000).

A CALL TO ACTION

The literature discussed in this chapter represents a broad examination of the use of noncognitive factors in the fields of education, economics, and neurological science. Garcia (2014) suggests that education policy needs to take action around noncognitive factors by nurturing students' noncognitive skills in educational settings. The integration of noncognitive skills in the education policy agenda could substantially improve how education policy is conceptualized and implemented (Garcia, 2014).

To promote the use of noncognitive factors, scholars have suggested examining students' academic mindset, academic self-efficacy, motivation, and the ability to understand and deal with racism, to improve African American males academic success (Farruggia et al., 2016; Johnson et al., 2007; Khine & Areepattamannil, 2016; Shen et al., 2016; Solberg et al., 1993).

The use of noncognitive factors can be employed on college campuses in academic programs and support services for students. The evaluation of noncognitive factors has been linked to students' academic success and applied across subgroups of students (Sedlacek, 1993, 1998, 1999, 2004, 2008, 2011; Tracey & Sedlacek, 1987). The work from these scholars provides important analyses in the use of noncognitive factors for improving academic success for African American students. Moreover, secondary data provided in the introduction reveals the need to examine noncognitive factors to improve African American males' academic achievement. Since there are gaps in the literature relating to the use of noncognitive factors such as academic mindset, a sense of belonging, and the ability to understand and deal with racism among African American males at urban universities, this chapter argues for the examination of noncognitive factors.

CRT is used as the framework to better understand how race impacts the academic achievement of students of color in college. Furthermore, this chapter discusses African American males who are enrolled at HBCUs, minority serving institutions, and PWIs that are considered "urban" based on their published vision and mission statements. Milner (2012) asserted that researchers, theoreticians, policymakers, and practitioners in higher education do not necessarily possess a shared definition of what is meant by urban education. However, for the context of this chapter, we are addressing urban universities that are in one of the following typologies described by Milner: urban intensive, urban emergent, or urban characteristic.

NONCOGNITIVE FACTORS AND CRITICAL RACE THEORY

Academic mindset, a sense of belonging, and the ability to understand and deal with racism, are noncognitive factors that are independent of cognitive ability (the ability to think, reason, and solve problems), and cannot be captured through tests of intelligence or academic achievement (Camfield, 2015). Tracey and Sedlacek's (1987) seminal work found that African American students' academic ability was determined by their first-semester grade point average (GPA). However, neither GPA nor academic ability was related to their persistence; only noncognitive dimensions were predictive of African American students' persistence. For White students, their academic ability was the best predictor of first-semester grades, and these grades were the major predictor of their subsequent persistence. Noncognitive dimensions were not important in White students' academic success but were crucial in African American students' academic success (Sedlacek, 2004, 2008, 2011; Tracey & Sedlacek, 1987).

Recently, education scholars found that students with more positive academic mindsets had better academic performance, which is associated with a better chance of returning to college for the second year (Farruggia et al., 2016; Shen et al., 2016). Related, Johnson et al. (2007) found that the campus racial climate had strong, significant relationships with students' sense of belonging. Khine and Areepattamannil (2016) found that surveys measuring non-cognitive constructs such as self-efficacy, motivation, the utility for the subject area, and academic self-beliefs influenced academic achievement (Research Collaboration, n.d.; Solberg et al., 1993). Palmer and Strayhorn (2008) affirmed that the HBCU environment contributed to African American males' noncognitive skill development by encouraging and motivating them to learn and to take personal responsibility for their success. It is important to note that Shorette and Palmer (2015) found that African American males felt that the institutional climate at HBCUs was critical in helping them to facilitate noncognitive skills that contributed to their success.

Scholars argue that if the use of noncognitive factors were used early in African American students' academic development it would be reflected in higher standardized test scores, had their educational opportunities been equal to White students (Sedlacek 2004, 2008, 2011; Westbrook & Sedlacek, 1998). The CRT framework for education simultaneously attempts to center race and racism in the research, and challenge the traditional paradigms, methods, narratives, and separate discourse on race, gender, and class by showing how these social constructs intersect and impact communities of color (Solorzano et al., 2000). Researchers firmly believe that noncognitive factors are equally important as cognitive aspects in the educative process and determining employment potential (Farruggia et al., 2016; Khine & Areepattamannil, 2016; Sedlacek, 2008, 2011).

Tracey and Sedlacek (1993) extended their research and demonstrated for 6 years the validity of eight variables using the Noncognitive Questionnaire (NCQ) in predicting grades, retention, and graduation for African American students. The eight noncognitive factors are (a) positive self-concept (possessing strong self-feeling, strength of character, determination, and independence); (b) realistic self-appraisal (accepting and appreciating rewards as well as consequences of poor performance); (c) understanding and dealing with racism (understanding the role of the system in his or her life and how it treats minority people); (d) setting long-range goals (setting goals and proceeding with those goals without reinforcement); (e) availability of strong support person (identifying and receiving help, support, and encouragement from one or more individuals); (f) successful leadership experience (being comfortable in providing advice and direction to others in academic and non-academic areas); (g) demonstrating community service (identifying with their cultural or racial group and becoming involved through community activities); and (h) knowledge acquired in a field (developing creative and culturally relevant views of a field or profession). These eight noncognitive constructs were developed with educational settings in mind, and attempt to account for racial, ethnic, and cultural differences. Therefore, this is the most appropriate model to adopt when examining noncognitive factors (Sedlacek, 2004; Shorette & Palmer, 2015).

Sedlacek (2004, 2008) and Tracey and Sedlacek (1993) argue that if success is measured by retention or graduation, then noncognitive variables have more validity for African American students. While noncognitive factors are useful for all students, they are particularly critical for African American students, since standardized tests and prior grades provide only a limited view of one's potential (Sedlacek, 2008; Sparkman et al., 2012). CRT provides a useful account of how race impacts the academic success of African American males in higher education, which is necessary since scholars posit that academic success looks different for African American and White students in higher education (Khine & Areepattamannil, 2016; Palmer & Strayhorn, 2008; Sedlacek, 1999, 2008, 2011; Tracey & Sedlacek, 1987).

IMPLICATIONS AND RECOMMENDATIONS

It is important to note that after the emancipation from slavery, African Americans did not have access to an equal opportunity in education (Anderson, 1988; Johnson-Ahorlu, 2012). In 1865, during the Reconstruction period, the Freedmen's Bureau was founded and for the first time in U.S. history, public education became available for African Americans (Anderson, 1988; Johnson-Ahorlu, 2012). Since then, African Americans have yet to experience equal opportunities in education. They have consistently been burdened with inferior educational resources and facilities, lower educational funding, and barriers to college access (Johnson-Ahorlu, 2012). Consequently, the opportunity gap affects the academic performance of African American males.

When considering the academic success of African American males, this chapter is a call to action for colleges and universities to adopt a noncognitive framework that examines students' academic mindset, sense of belonging, and ability to understand and deal with racism as a model for measuring and predicting their academic success. Historically, the traditional predictors of student success in college such as the ACT and SAT scores and high school grade point averages have shown to account for only a modest amount of variance (25%) of a students' academic performance in college (Sedlacek, 2008; Sparkman et al., 2012). Hence, using noncognitive factors can help advisors and faculty members learn more about the challenges and strengths that African American males face, and provide them with the appropriate resources to help promote their academic success.

SOCIAL MOBILITY

If higher education is moving away from the political and public policy interest, and seeks to be known as an institution that addresses social inequalities and increases social mobility (Bathmaker et al., 2016), it is important to investigate how noncognitive factors impact African Americans' social mobility. CRT explores the ways in which social and economic conditions influence students of color on their educational journeys. Waller (2014) asserted that a college education is a gateway to upward social mobility for individuals from lower socioeconomic backgrounds. Since social mobility is defined as moving from one social position to another (Tepperman, 2019), it is expected that higher education institutions promote social mobility by making it possible for anyone to succeed who has the ability and motivation to do so (Haveman & Smeeding, 2006). Therefore, noncognitive factors should be part of the discourse when discussing social mobility. This chapter illustrates how important it is to re-examine the role of noncognitive factors and how they may correlate with the academic success of African American males. The next sections provide recommendations for university administrators, admissions offices, university faculty, and teacher preparation programs to support African American males in their pursuit of academic achievement.

RECOMMENDATIONS FOR ADMINISTRATORS

Campus administrators must reimagine how student achievement is measured on college campuses. Accordingly, we propose implementing a modified version of Westbrook and Sedlacek's (1988) model to investigate noncognitive constructs that measure African American males' academic mindset, sense of belonging, and ability to understand and deal with racism, and how these factors contribute to their academic success. These existing subscales have been proven to have strong reliability and validity from previous research (Johnson et al., 2007; Research Collaboration, n.d.; Sedlacek, 1999, 2011; Solberg et al., 1993; Westbrook & Sedlacek, 1998). As the demographics of the student body continue to evolve, campus administrators must be strategic and innovative in accurately assessing and documenting African American males' academic achievement.

RECOMMENDATIONS FOR ADMISSIONS OFFICES

We recommend that colleges and university admissions offices identify and operationalize a set of noncognitive factors that best meets the selection process for the African American male student population. Sedlacek (2011) argues that standardized tests in admissions do not predict grades beyond the first year for any student, nor do they predict retention and graduation for any student in any year. Implementing alternative admissions measures can help level the playing field in the selection process for African American males who show their abilities in ways other than traditional standardized tests and prior grades (Sedlacek, 2011). Considering the use of noncognitive factors is not meant to decrease or minimize the traditional selection process of examining African American males' SAT scores, ACT scores, and GPA for admission, but to offer an equitable approach to college admission and academic success.

RECOMMENDATIONS FOR UNIVERSITY FACULTY

University faculty members must seek alternative methods for assessing African American males' academic mindset, sense of belonging, and ability to understand and deal with racism in the context of the college classroom. University faculty should be trained to diagnose noncognitive factors that are problematic for African American males who are having personal or academic difficulty (Sedlacek, 1998, 1999, 2004, 2008, 2011). Faculty should participate in workshops that are designed to help better understand (a) noncognitive factors, (b) how the factors work with African American males, and (c) how they can identify key noncognitive factors in written materials and interviews so that they can make appropriate referrals. To continually rely on a narrow set of variables perpetuates the inaccurate understandings of African American males' experiences and outcomes

(Harper et al., 2018). Addressing racism encountered on college campuses must be explored in concert with other factors concerning the academic achievement of African American males (Harper et al., 2018). Therefore, noncognitive factors should be part of the faculty discourse.

RECOMMENDATIONS FOR TEACHER PREPARATION

We recommend redesigning teacher preparation programs to introduce and practice the use of noncognitive factors with preservice teachers, to help them nurture noncognitive skills in students who are enrolled in PK–12 urban schools (Garcia, 2014). Darling-Hammond (2017) asserted in her book, *Empowered Educators: How High Performing Systems Shape Teaching Quality Around the World,* that there is a strong emphasis on teacher preparation programs to help students develop inquiry skills and metacognitive skills that contribute to students' academic success. Additionally, Wiggan and Watson-Vandiver (2019) stated that providing students with positive images and lessons about themselves allows students to develop a positive self-concept that enhances their academic achievement on state-mandated assessment. Furthermore, Ball and Foranzi (2009) argued that the tasks of teaching should be congruent with how teachers learn to carry out and organize their work in the classroom. Therefore, teacher educators should provide opportunities for candidates to learn about ways to assess noncognitive factors with diverse students (Ball & Foranzi, 2009; Hollins, 2011).

CONCLUSION

The current cognitive measures of success and academic achievements such as standardized college admissions exams (SAT and ACT) and graduation and retention rates do not appropriately serve people from diverse racial and cultural groups (Sedlacek, 2004). Casting light on noncognitive factors can help students navigate the multiple demands of the college environment and help them persist to graduation (Sommerfeld, 2011). Moreover, African American males' academic performance is affected by the quality and level of academic competition, university policies and practices, race relations on campus, and their relationships with faculty and friends on campus (Allen, 1992). Even though noncognitive factors have received a great deal of attention and debate, the literature is scant on the voices of African American males and their perceptions about noncognitive factors. Therefore, more studies are needed on the use of noncognitive factors through the storytelling of African American males at urban universities.

REFERENCES

Allen, W. R. (1992). The color of success: African American college students' outcomes at predominantly white and historically black public colleges and universities. *Harvard Educational Review, 62*(1), 26–44.

Allen, W. R., Jewell, J. O., Griffin, K. A., & Wolf, D. S. (2007). 75 years of facilitating excellence in black education. *The Journal of Negro Education, 76*(3), 263–280.

Anderson, J. D. (1988). *The education of Blacks in the south, 1860–1935.* The University of North Carolina Press.

Anglin, D. M., & Wade, J. C. (2007). Racial socialization, racial identity, and Black students' adjustment to college. *Cultural Diversity and Ethnic Minority Psychology, 13*(3), 207–215. https://doi.org/10.1037/1099-9809.13.3.207

Ball, D. L., & Forzani. F. M. (2009). The work of teaching and the challenge for teacher. *Journal of Teacher Education, 60*(5), 497–511. https://doi.org/10.1177/0022487109

Bandura, A. (1997). *Self-efficacy: The exercise of control.* Freeman.

Bathmaker, A., Ingram, N., Abrahams, J., Hoare, A., Waller, R., & Bradley, H. (2016). *Higher education, social class and social mobility: The degree generation.* Palgrave Macmillan.

Bell, D. (1992). *Faces at the bottom of the well: The permanence of racism.* Harper Collins.

Bell, D. (1995).Who's afraid of critical race theory? *University of Illinois Law Review, 1995*(4), 893–910.

Bentley-Edwards, K. L., & Chapman-Hilliard, C. (2015). Doing race in different places: Black racial cohesion on Black and White college campuses. *Journal of Diversity in Higher Education, 8*(1), 43–60.

Borghans, L., Duckworth, A. L., Heckman, J. J., & Weel, B. T. (2008). The economics and psychology of personality traits. *Journal of Human Resources, 43*(4), 972–1059.

Brooms, D. R. (2016). Building us up: Supporting Black male college students in a Black male initiative program. *Critical Sociology, 44*(1), 141–155. https://doi.org/10.1177/0896920516658940

Brooms, D. R., & Davis, A. R. (2017). Staying focused on the goal: Peer bonding and faculty mentors supporting Black males' persistence in college. *Journal of Black Studies, 48*(3), 305–326. https://doi.org/10.1177/0021934717692520

Camfield, L. (2015). Character matters: How do measures of non-cognitive skills shape understandings of social mobility in the global North and South? *Social Anthropology, 23*(1), 68–79.

Chaisson, R. L. (2004). A crack in the door: Critical race theory in practice at a predominantly White institution. *Teaching Sociology, 32*(4), 345–357.

Chavous, T. M. (2000). The relationships among racial identity, perceived ethnic fit, and organizational involvement for African American students at a predominantly White university. *Journal of Black Psychology, 26*(1), 79–100. https://doi.org/10.1177/0095798400026001005

Chemers, M., Hu, L., & Garcia, B. (2001). Academic self-efficacy and first year college student performance and adjustment. *Journal of Educational Psychology, 93*(1), 55–64. https://doi.org/10.1037//0022-0663.93.1.55

Cokley, K. (1999). Reconceptualizing the impact of college racial composition on African American students' racial identity. *Journal of college student development, 40*(3), 235–245.

Crenshaw, K. (1995). *Critical race theory.* New Press.

Crenshaw, K. (2002). The first decade: Critical reflections, or a foot in the closing door. *UCLA Law Review, 49*(5), 1343–1372.

Darling-Hammond, L. (2017). *Empowered educators: How high-performing systems shape teaching quality around the world.* Jossey-Bass.

Decuir, J., & Dixson, A. D. (2004). So when it comes out, they aren't that surprised that it is there: Using critical race theory as a tool of analysis of race and racism in education. *Educational Researcher, 33*(5), 26–31. https://doi.org/10.3102/0013189X033005026

Delgado, R., & Stefancic, J. (2001). *Critical race theory: An introduction.* University Press.

Duckworth, A. L., Peterson, C., Matthews, M. D., & Kelly, D. R. (2007). Grit: Perseverance and passion for long-term goals. *Journal of Personality and Social Psychology, 92*(6), 1087–1101. https://doi.org/10.1037/0022-3514.92.6.1087

Farruggia, S. P., Han. C., Watson, L., Moss, T. M., & Bottoms, B. L. (2016). Noncognitive factors and college student success. *Journal of College Student Retention: Research, Theory & Practice, 20*(3), 308–327. https://doi.org/10.1177/1521025116666539

Garcia, E. (2014). *The need to address noncognitive skills in education policy* (Issue Brief No. 386). Economic Policy Institute.

Guthrie, R. V. (2004). *Even the rat was white: A historical view of psychology.* Allyn and Bacon.

Han, C., Farruggia, S. P., & Moss, T. P. (2017). Effects of academic mindsets on college students' achievement and retention. *Journal of College Student Development 58*(8), 1119–1134. https://doi.org/10.1353/csd.2017.0089

Harper, S. R., Smith, E. J., & Davis, C. H. F. (2018). A critical race case analysis of Black undergraduate student success at an urban university, *Urban Education, 53*(1), 3–25

Haveman, R., & Smeeding, T. (2006).The role of higher education in social mobility. *The Future of Children, 16*(2), 125–150.

Hollins, E. R. (2011). Teacher preparation for quality teaching. *Journal of Teacher Education, 62*(4), 395–407.

Hughes, S. Noblit, G., & Cleveland, D. (2013). Derrick Bell's post-*Brown* moves toward critical race theory. *Race Ethnicity and Education, 16*(4), 442–469. https://doi.org/10.1080/13613324.2013.817765

Ingram, T. N. (2013). Fighting F.A.I.R. (Feelings of Alienation, Isolation, and Racism): Using critical race theory to deconstruct the experiences of African American male doctoral students. *Journal of Progressive Policy and Practice, 1*(1), 1–18.

James, G. M. (2017). *Stolen legacy: The Egyptian origins of western philosophy.* Allegro Editions.

Johnson-Ahorlu, R. N. (2012). The academic opportunity gap: How racism and stereotypes disrupt the education of African American undergraduates. *Race Ethnicity and Education, 15*(5), 633–652. https://doi.org/10.1080/13613324.2011.645566

Johnson, D. R., Soldner, M., Leonard, J. B., Alvarez, P., Inkelas, K. K., Rowan-Kenyon, H. T., & Longerbeam, S. D. (2007). Examining sense of belonging among first-year undergraduates from different racial/ethnic groups. *Journal of College Student Development, 48*(5), 525–542.

Kaiser, C. R., & Pratt-Hyatt, J. S. (2009). Distributing prejudice unequally: Do Whites direct their prejudice toward strongly identified minorities? *Journal of Personality and Social Psychology, 96*(2), 432–445. https://doi.org/10.1037/a0012877

Khine, M. S., & Areepattamannil, S. (2016). *Contemporary approaches to research in learning innovations: Noncognitive skills and factors in educational attainment.* Sense Publishers.

King, J. E., & Swartz, E. E. (2014). *Re-membering history in student and teacher learning: An Afrocentric culturally informed praxis.* Taylor & Francis.

Ladson-Billings, G. (1995). But that's just good teaching! The case for culturally relevant pedagogy. *Theory Into Practice, 34*(3), 159–165. https://doi.org/10.1080/00405849509543675

Ladson-Billings, G. (1998). Just what is critical race theory and what's it doing in a nice field like education? *International Journal of Qualitative Studies in Education, 11*(1), 7–24. https://doi.org/10.1080/095183998236863

Ladson-Billings, G., & Tate, W. F., IV. (1995). Toward a critical race theory of education. *Teachers College Record, 97*(1), 47–68.

Manning, K., Kinzie, J., & Schuh, H. J. (2014). *One size does not fit all: Traditional and innovative models of student affairs practice.* Routledge.

Milner, R. (2012).What is urban education? *Urban Education, 47*(3), 556–561. https://doi.org/10.1177/0042085912447516

Moore, J. L., III. (2001). Developing academic warriors: Things that parents, administrators, and faculty should know. In L. Jones (Ed.), *In retaining African Americans in higher education: Challenging paradigms for retaining students, faculty, and administrators* (pp. 77–90). Stylus.

Murray, C., & Herrnstein, R. J. (1994). Race, genes, and IQ—An apologia. *The New Republic, 211*(18), 27–37.

Orfield, G., Marin, P., & Horn, C. (2005). *Higher education and the color line.* Harvard Education Press.

Palmer, R. T., & Strayhorn, T. (2008). Mastering one's own fate: Noncognitive factors associated with the success of African American males at an HBCU. *National Association of Student Affairs Professional Journal, 11*(1), 126–143.

Palmer, R. T., Wood, J. L., Dancy, T. E., & Strayhorn, T. L. (2014). Black male collegians: Increasing access, retention, and persistence in higher education. *ASHE Higher Education Report, 40*(3), 1–147. https://doi.org/10.1002/aehe.20015

Perry, T. (2003). *Up from the parched earth toward a theory of African American achievement: Young, gifted and Black: Promoting high achievement among African American students.* Beacon.

Patton, L. D., Haynes, C. M., Harris, J. C., & Ivery, S. M. (2014). Perhaps the field of education isn't so nice after all: An examination of critical race research in higher education. *NASAP Journal, 15*(2), 135–148.

Research Collaboration (n.d.). *Self-efficacy formative questionnaire technical report.* http://www.researchcollaboration.org/uploads/Self-EfficacyQuestionnaireInfo.pdf

Savas, G. (2014). Understanding critical race theory as a framework in higher educational research. *British Journal of Sociology of Education, 35*(4), 506–522. https://doi.org/10.1080/01425692.2013.777211

Scott, J. A., Taylor, K. J., & Palmer, R. T. (2013). Challenges to success in higher education: An examination of educational challenges from the voices of college-bound Black males. *The Journal of Negro Education, 82*(3), 288–299. https://doi.org/10.7709/jnegroeducation.82.3.0288

Sedlacek, W. E. (1993). Employing noncognitive variables in admissions and retention in higher education. In C. Lee (Ed.), *Achieving diversity: Issues in the recruitment and retention of underrepresented racial/ethnic students in higher education* (pp. 33–39). National Association of College Admission Counselors.

Sedlacek. E. (1998). Admissions in higher education: Measuring cognitive and noncognitive variables. In D. J. Wilds & R. Wilson (Eds.), *Minorities in higher education 1997–98: Sixteenth annual status report* (pp. 47–71). American Council on Education.

Sedlacek, W. E. (1999). Black students on White campuses: 20 Years of research. *Journal of College Student Development, 40*(5), 538–550.

Sedlacek, W. E. (2004). *Beyond the big test: Noncognitive assessment in higher education.* Jossey-Bass.

Sedlacek, W. E. (2008, August). Using noncognitive variables in K–12 and higher education. In *University of Michigan summit on college outreach and academic success: Summary report from meetings at the School of Education* (pp. 35–42).

Sedlacek, W. E. (2011). Using noncognitive variables in assessing readiness for higher education. *Readings on Equal Education, 25,* 187–205.

Shen, C., Miele, D. B., & Vasilyeva, M. (2016).The relation between college students' academic mindsets and their persistence during math problem solving. *Psychology in Russia: State of the Art, 9*(3), 38–56. https://doi.org/10.11621/pir.2016.0303

Shorette, C. R., & Palmer, R. T. (2015). Historically Black colleges and universities (HBCUs): Critical facilitators of noncognitive skills for Black males. *The Western Journal of Black Studies, 39*(1), 18–29.

Solberg, V. S., O'Brien, K., Villareal, P., Kennel, R., & Davis, B. (1993). Self-efficacy and Hispanic college students: Validation of the college self-efficacy instrument. *Hispanic Journal of Behavioral Sciences, 15*(1), 80–95. https://doi.org/10.1177/07399863930151004

Solorzano, D., Ceja, M., & Yosso, T. (2000). Critical race theory, racial microaggressions, and campus racial climate: The experiences of African American college students. *The Journal of Negro Education, 69*(1/2), 60–73.

Sommerfeld, A. (2011). Recasting non-cognitive factors in college readiness as what they truly are: Non-academic factors. *Journal of College Admission, 213,* 18–22.

Sparkman, A. L., Maulding, S. W., & Roberts, G. J. (2012). Noncognitive predictors of student success in college. *College Student Journal, 46*(3), 642–652.

Stetson, G. R. (1897). Some memory tests of Whites and Blacks. *Psychological Review, 4*(3), 285–289.

Tepperman, L. (Ed). (2019). Social mobility. In *The Canadian encyclopedia of historica Canada.* https://www.thecanadianencyclopedia.ca/en/article/social-mobility

Tracey, T. J., & Sedlacek, W. E. (1987). A comparison of White and Black student academic success using noncognitive variables: A lisrel analysis. *Research in Higher Education, 27*(4), 333–348.

Waller, R., Holford, J., Jarvis, P., Milama, M., & Webb, S. (2014).Widening participation, social mobility and the role of universities in a globalized world. *International Journal of Lifelong Education, 33*(6), 701–704.

Wanzer, D., Postlewaite, E., & Zargarpour, N. (2019). Relationships among noncognitive factors and academic performance: Testing the university of Chicago consortium on school research model. *AERA Open, 5*(4), 1–20. https://doi .org/10.1177/2332858419897275

Watson, M. J., & Wiggan, G. (2016). Sankofa healing and restoration: A case study of African American excellence and achievement in an urban school. *The Journal of Pan African Studies (Online), 9*(1), 113–140.

Watson, M., & Wiggan, G. (2018). The genius of Imhotep: Lessons from a high achieving urban minority school. *Teaching and Teacher Education, 76,* 151–164. https://doi.org/10.1016/j.tate.2018.09.001

Westbrook, F. D., & Sedlacek, E. W. (1998). A workshop on using noncognitive variables with minority students in higher education. *The Journal for Specialists in Group Work, 13*(2), 82–89. https://doi.org/10.1080/01933928808411780

Wiggan, G. (2007). Race, school achievement and educational inequality: Towards a student-based inquiry perspective. *Review of Educational Research, 77*(3), 310–333.

Wiggan, G. (2011). *Education for the new frontier: Race, education and triumph in Jim Crow America.* Nova Science Publishers, Inc.

Wiggan, G., Scott, K., Watson, M., & Reynolds, R. (2014). *Unshackled: Education for freedom, student achievement, and personal emancipation.* Sense Publishers.

Wiggan, G., & Watson-Vandiver, M. J. (2019). Urban school success: Lessons from a high-achieving urban school, and students' reactions to Ferguson, Missouri. *Education and Urban Society, 51*(8), 1074–1105. https://doi.org/10 .1177/0013124517751721

CHAPTER 5

CULTURAL CAPITAL, URBAN EDUCATION, AND SCHOOL PRIVATIZATION

A Critical Race Social Reproduction Analysis

Jordan Boyd
University of North Carolina at Charlotte

Greg Wiggan
University of North Carolina at Charlotte

> *Education is the passport to the future, for tomorrow belongs
> to those who prepare for it today.*
> —Malcom X

Privatized suffering is not a new phenomenon in the United States. From the prison industrial system to privatized war, the wealthy have simply perpetuated the cycle of social reproduction through modernized stratagem at the expense of working-class people in America ("Trey" Marchbanks et al., 2018). This chapter examines the myriad ways that the privatization

Economic, Political and Legal Solutions to Critical Issues in Urban Education   pages 77–89
and Implications for Teacher Preparation
Copyright © 2022 by Information Age Publishing
www.infoagepub.com
77

of education acts as a means of stratification for marginalized students in America. Additional arguments include those stemming from charter schools, and the various ways that the institution of alternative schooling can be detrimental to the potential success of minority students (Wilson, 2019). From the perspective of critical race social reproduction theory (CRSRT), this chapter argues that social and cultural capital, and lack thereof, within these methods of stratification combine to further expound on the immorality of both the privatization of education and charter schooling. The ultimate aim of this research is to critically examine school privatization through the lens of CRSRT and propose distinct solutions to remedy the issue. Applicable research questions are posed in this way: How has school privatization perpetuated the cycle of social reproduction in the United States? Barring the grave toxicity of such a cycle, how might CRSRT illuminate the detrimental effects of school privatization on marginalized groups in the United States, particularly Black youth?

Accordingly, this paper addresses critical race theory (CRT) and social reproduction theory (SRT) as individual fields of thought as a means of clarifying their synthesis as CRSRT, the key theoretical lens through which this topic is examined. Then, this text discusses the literature that is currently available on the topic of school privatization. Next, this work presents possible solutions and recommendations to reform the policies that have long fueled the critical issues of school privatization and social reproduction.

THEORETICAL FRAMEWORK

CRT refers to a broad social scientific approach to the study of race, racism, and society. CRT is a critical interpretive framework used to advocate for racial and social justice, and to mobilize marginalized groups to create racial equity, and social and political change (Ladson-Billings & Tate, 1995). Originating with Derrick Bell, a constitutional scholar, CRT was developed to examine society and culture as they relate to race, power, and the legal system (Bell, 1980; Ladson-Billings & Tate, 1995). It is also further developed and supported by the work of Kimberlé Crenshaw. Bell's concept of interest convergence is a key tenet of CRT (Bell, 1980), which explains racial progress or justice in relation to the legitimating interest of the dominant group. Kimberlé Crenshaw and Derrick Bell popularized CRT within the subfield of critical legal studies in the 1980s (Bhambra, 2017). Both Crenshaw and Bell referred to the fact that despite the civil rights legislation in the United States, the social and economic conditions of African Americans had not improved. Relatedly, SRT helps to explain cultural capital and transmission in society and in schools.

According to Pierre Bourdieu (2011), the cycle of social reproduction is fueled by four imperative types of capital that can just as easily marginalize an individual as they can assist one. Social capital is one of the four types of capital and it encompasses all of the connections that one can make through membership in a group (Bourdieu, 2011). Respectively, the second type of capital is referred to as cultural capital, or the collection of embodied, objectified, and institutionalized capital as a means of social reproduction (Bourdieu, 2011). Embodied capital entails all aspects of culture that an individual acquires beginning at birth, objectified capital consists of material and symbolic cultural goods, and institutionalized capital is a form of objectification in its manifestation through academic qualifications (Bourdieu, 2011). In this paper, social capital as well as all three forms of cultural capital will be utilized to probe the concept of education privatization and charter schooling for minorities. A deviously popularized method of social reproduction is the privatization of education; much like the prison industrial system and privatized war, this phenomenon is far from underdeveloped. While cultural reproduction theory has less of an emphasis on racial and ethnic relations, CRT helps to sharpen the analysis. Thus, while reproduction theory explains social and cultural transmission, CRT provides a cogent racial analysis centered on issues of race. In sum, the paper frames CRSRT for its analysis and discussion.

LITERATURE REVIEW

Bell (1980) proclaimed that the justification for the original success of civil rights law passage was largely based on the U.S. judicial system's covert support of the interests of America's White elite. Much like the subtle representations of quid pro quo between the lawmakers of old and the White elite who benefited therein, education policymakers have replicated an identical system of wealth production based on the seemingly progressive passage of undeniably oppressive laws for the continuous enrichment of the White elite (Giroux, 2013). For example, McLaren and Farahmandpur (2001) explained the relationships between corporate models of education and global economic policies of "advanced capital societies" (p. 139–140). Their research asserted that decreased government funding has fostered a perturbing relationship between public education and private corporations, who seek to capitalize on a $5.5 trillion industry (Kamentez, 2016). Being that schools are a microcosm of society, one must assume that the global economy acts as a macrocosm of that which is taking place economically within a given society. Decreased government funding in other countries has resulted in the herding of students by the millions into the realm of privatized education, thus initiating a harvest of billions to be reaped by stakeholders of various capacities.

From a CRSRT perspective, it is imperative to note that the figure mentioned earlier in this text reflecting the proximate value of contemporary privatized education, $5.5 trillion, is nearly equivalent to that of the global health care industry (Kamentez, 2016). Most of that money circulates within government bureaucracies, thus perpetuating the cycle of social reproduction for non-possessors of such capital as well as stakeholders who capitalize on such totalitarianism. According to Kamentez (2016), Pearson, the largest education company in the world, would like to become education's first major conglomerate, serving as the largest private provider of standardized tests, software, materials, and now the schools themselves. To this end, the company is testing academic, financial, and technological models for fully privatized education on the world's poor by way of the Pearson Affordable Learning Fund. The author detailed Pearson's preparatory landmarks to accomplish such a task in this way:

> Pearson allocated the fund an initial $15 million in 2012 and another $50 million in January 2015. Students in developing countries vastly outnumber those in wealthy nations, constituting a larger market for the company than students in the West. (Kamentez, 2016)

In the United States, of course, charter schools are funded by taxpayers but operate as for-profit entities, thus leading into discussions on domestic school privatization. Per CRSRT, all acquisitions of wealth are considered objectified capital and, particularly in the realm of education, are instantaneously applied to the cycle of social reproduction, thus perpetuating the wealth of the White elite (Pearson), and further broadening the gaps of opportunity and success for marginalized youth in the contemporary urban school.

METHOD

Secondary data analysis was the method through which data was synthesized for this research. According to Smith (2008), secondary data analysis is best described as the extraction of knowledge on topics other than those which were the focus of the original survey (p. 4). This approach was most suitable based on the application of CRSRT to previously conducted research and the ease of cohesion between data that already exists and social issues that are currently plaguing the contemporary urban school.

To best allot for academic scope and understanding for CRSRT to be applied in this text, secondary data analysis aligns with the exposition of the critical issues found herein in its ability to embrace a whole spectrum of empirical forms; they can include data generated through systematic reviews, documentary analysis as well as the findings from large scale data sets such as the National Census or international surveys (Smith, 2008). The expansive nature of secondary data analysis is called upon in this text's usage of the National Education Association (NEA) and the National Center for Education Statistics (NCES). Each of these data sources will be used to address the detrimental rise of school privatization and statistics on the disproportionate presence of White teachers in majority-minority schools across the nation.

DISCUSSION

Through the lens of CRSRT, the social and cultural capital belonging to an individual will act as an imposing determinant of wealth and positionality. This chapter will examine the capital belonging to Betsy DeVos, former U.S. Secretary of Education. As of February 7, 2017, Betsy DeVos was confirmed as Secretary of Education by way of a 51–50 Senate vote; the original 50–50 tie was broken by Vice President Mike Pence. As secretary of education, DeVos, possessing no experience in public education (as a pupil or otherwise), was charged with the responsibility of advising the president on federal policies, programs, and activities related to education in the United States. Through circumspection, one may find it difficult to conceptualize DeVos as a viable candidate for the position of education secretary, also known as the head of the U.S. Department of Education. However, a CRSRT analysis would deem her appointment as a classic representation of applied cultural capital in action. In order to break down DeVos' cultural makeup in its entirety, one must look to the root of her existence; her genealogy. According to Greg Toppo (2017) of *USA Today*, Betsy DeVos (born Elisabeth Prince) is daughter to an entrepreneur who made millions in the auto parts trade. This fact alone reflects DeVos' social capital. In addition to the tangible wealth DeVos was born into, it is central to acknowledge that her ease of matriculation into power stems from significant social capital through her family name. According to Bourdieu (2011), social capital can manifest itself through social institutions and is thereby guaranteed by the application of a common name.

Betsy DeVos is married to Dick DeVos, son of Richard DeVos Sr., a founder of Amway. Though Prince is DeVos' maiden name, she married into the DeVos lineage with substantial wealth to support her as she transitioned from her family to an equally wealthy bloodline, solidifying the connection of two prominent family names (Toppo, 2017). The couple, who have reported assets totaling $583 million to $1.5 billion, are longtime Michigan Republican Party activists and donors; they have the ultimate group membership. According to Bourdieu (2011) such membership "provides each of its members with the backing of the collectivity-owned capital, a 'credential' which entitles them to credit, in the various senses of the word" (Bourdieu, 2011, p. 88).

From a CRSRT perspective, DeVos reflected no forms of social or cultural capital to justify her appointment to the position of secretary of education, despite the delicacy of such an influential role in the U.S. government and the impact of the secretary's decisions upon urban school stakeholders across the nation. Ultimately, through DeVos' membership in the Michigan Republican Party, and in congruence with the connections inherently made through the relationships pertaining to both her maiden name, Prince, and her married name, DeVos, she acquired the social capital necessary to obtain the position of secretary of education, with no legitimate association with the contemporary urban school. According to *Education Votes*, a primary advocate of the NEA, as of March 2017 DeVos supported the Trump budget proposal to slash funding for the Department of Education by 13.5% (Education Votes, 2020). This proposal called for a collective $9 billion in cuts in education, including after-school programs, career and technical education, and programs to hire and train teachers. From a CRSRT perspective, all of the programs that such a proposal would destroy (after-school, career and technical education, and programs to hire and train teachers) can all be classified as initiatives that have historically been staples in the upholding, progression, and succession of urban schools across the country. Putting an end to such programs would further perpetuate the cycle of social reproduction for children of working-class parents across America.

Due to DeVos' application of social and cultural capital, CRSRT posits that the power and influence that belongs to the secretary of education then belonged with her while she held the position; consequently, such power acted as a polarizing influence as she implemented her ideal projections for the state of public education in America. One of DeVos' immediate goals as secretary of education was to shift from public to private education, an irrefutable method of social stratification in the concept's complete disregard for the well-being of working-class minorities and other marginalized populations in the United States. According to Fred Hobson (2017) of the *News & Observer*, the shift from public to private institutionalization has maintained a growing perception over the past few decades. For example, private colleges and universities, by their very nature, have become more desirable—especially for parents who can afford them—than public universities (Hobson, 2017). Where does that categorize the parents who cannot afford to send their children to private school, or those who cannot afford to buy a home in an upscale neighborhood with a community school that possesses the resources necessary for equipping a child with scholarship-worthy test scores? CRSRT argues that each of these stipulations further perpetuate the cycle of social reproduction: forward for the wealthy, and backward for all others.

The institution of privatized higher education is not far-removed from the current state of K–12 education. In fact, under the governance of Education Secretary DeVos, mass privatization became exactly where America was headed. Only with the power to manipulate national rankings can the conservative agenda influence a nationwide shift from public to private institutionalization. Membership in the Republican Party will allot its members the social capital necessary to further distance American education from the public existence of old, to the desired privatized state as motivated and reaffirmed by Secretary DeVos.

A CRSRT examination of this line of intent and decision-making voices a resounding dissonance between America's educational needs and DeVos' agenda as an educational leader. The United States is not comprised primarily of wealthy individuals who come from wealthy families and marry into other wealthy families; in fact, this nation's circumstance at the macro level is quite the contrary. According to the Federal Reserve (n.d.), White households owned 85.5% of the wealth in 2019, Black households owned 4.2%, and Hispanic households owned 3.1%. While nearly 90% of America's wealth as of 2019 belonged to White Americans, its education system is predominantly occupied by minority students who commonly reside at the opposite end of the wealth spectrum. America's desks are in fact filled with the sons and daughters of day laborers, teachers, preachers, landscapers, estheticians, artists, coal miners, and various other individuals who make up the true fabric of this nation. CRSRT argues that this discrepancy between DeVos, who once represented the U.S. Department of Education, and the students whom she was charged with the responsibility of serving, is a direct reflection of an imbalance of capital throughout America's stratum of wealth. As capital is made readily available for this nation's power elite, a void of the same opportunities is further broadened for America's marginalized youth.

A crippling result of the shift from public to private education presents itself in the form of charter schools. As many schools (urban and otherwise) continue to lose students to charter schools and alternative private educational opportunities due to the inadequacies of contemporary public education, many working-class parents are left with two options: leave their child in the failing community school, or risk sending their child to a charter school in hopes of reaping the benefits of increased resources and an improvement in their academic achievement. According to Merriam-Webster (n.d.), a *charter school* is defined in this way: "a tax-supported school established by a charter between a granting body (such as a school board) and an outside group (as of teachers and parents) which operates the school without most local and state educational regulations so as to achieve set goals." Tax-supported autonomy is the essential theme that one

should deduce from the aforementioned definition. All justifiable reserva-
tions regarding charter schooling can be found in the institution's funding;
tax dollars earned by the inhabitants of a given community are delegated
to charter schools across the nation, even if the taxpayer's child is not enrolled in a charter school. The existence of a network of connections, social
capital, gives only those who actively maintain membership in a group the
privileged flow of information to communicate this knowledge to one another, then govern themselves accordingly.

A national shift from public to private education has led directly to a mass
influx of charter schooling that did not always exist, particularly for Black
students. In an Education Week article, Prothero (2017) argued why such
an influx is detrimental to Black students. It reads: "Black families and communities are losing control of their public schools." Although charter schools
typically garner support from members of the Republican Party, Education
Week conducted a survey in 2016 and deduced that 45% of African-American respondents said they either "completely support" or "somewhat support" charter schools, compared with 29% that either "completely oppose"
or "somewhat oppose" charters (Prothero, 2017). Nationally, Black students
make up 28% of charter school enrollment, compared with 15% of non-charter enrollment; White students make up 35% of total charter school enrollment and 50% of the public, non-charter sector (Prothero, 2017). However,
the racial makeup of charter schools varies greatly from state to state.

Black students make up large majorities of charter school enrollment
in Louisiana, New Jersey, and Tennessee—in areas where states have tak-
en over low-performing districts or schools. According to Miller (2020), a
2017 poll reflects 42% of Black parents believe the education provided to
Black students is not as good as that for Whites, as well as 90% who do not
believe that schools in Black communities receive the same level of funding as schools in White communities. Figure 5.1 represents the 2015–2016
percentage distribution of teachers in public elementary and secondary
schools, by school classification and teacher minority status.

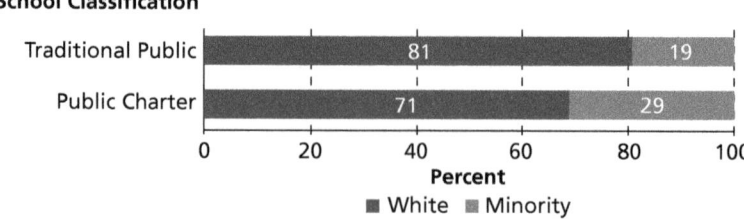

Figure 5.1 School classification. *Source:* National Center for Education Statistics
(n.d.), Figure A.3.

Locale

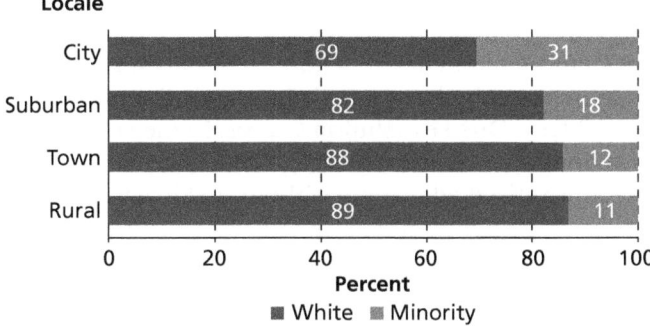

Figure 5.2 School locale. *Source:* National Center for Education Statistics (n.d.), Figure A.4.

Figure 5.2 represents the percentage distribution of teachers in public elementary and secondary schools, by school locale and teacher minority status. As depicted in both graphs, in traditional public schools, public charter schools, and across the spectrum of school locale, White teachers continue to disproportionately occupy classrooms across America (Miller, 2020). The tumultuous relationship between White teachers in predominantly minority classrooms is a seasoned phenomenon, and although it is not to be misinterpreted as a distrust in the capabilities of White teachers, it is a direct input that commonly results in the negative output of disproportionate minority contact. Despite the perceived emancipatory effect of school choice, charters are often created, funded and governed by White people. Therefore, the importance of employing Black teachers is no longer as imperative as the collection, production, and reproduction of capital therein.

CONCLUSION/SOLUTION

Through the scope of CRSRT, the first possible solution to the problem of school privatization as a means of social reproduction is to deprive it of its primary source of capital: students. The ceasing of privatization practices in education that stakeholders long for is rooted in elimination. One should not assume elimination implies "a complete termination of," however, it should be conceptualized as the most efficient ridding of a malignant cancer that has spread throughout the body for many years. The cancer of systemic oppression in the form of school privatization infiltrated America's skeletal structure many years ago, and is as far from benign as the disease can be. The stakeholders of the American urban school and marginalized youth must act as the surgeon under these circumstances, whose tools manifest in the form of information. School boards, parents, and community members must be made aware of the toxicity that is school privatization and its predatory contractors across the nation, particularly in communities of color in which an influx of charter schools have taken root, only to collect their earnings in roughly three years' time and disappear like a sudden flame (Wilson, 2019). One key solution to assist in the eradication of predatory charter schooling is to cease feeding America's marginalized youth to the machine of privatized education; without fuel it will surely perish.

The second possible solution that CRSRT offers toward putting an end to school privatization and social reproduction is a reestablishment of government funding allotments based on the wealth of a school, or lack thereof. For many years, local school districts were primarily responsible for funding K–12 education in the United States, typically through property taxes. However, since the 1970s, state and local governments have held nearly equal responsibility for funding K–12 education, with each providing just under half of all funds (federal support totals less than 10 %; Chingos & Blagg, 2017). According to Chingos and Blagg (2017) state governments have much greater power to influence the distribution of funds across school districts by setting policies that may affect both the state and local contributions to public education. States largely exercise this power by using education funding formulas, which determine the minimum level of per-student funding in each district. Per CRSRT, rather than allocating federal/state money to the more affluent schools. Through the lens of CRSRT privatization undermines logical education policy. Instead of allocating federal and state funds, these funds should be sent to the school losing the student, rather than to the private charter looking to gain attendees. Darling-Hammond (2010) argued that for every dollar spent on an urban student, up to three dollars are spent on a more affluent school. The wealthier schools do not need more federal dollars because they have a surplus of cash via the social capital of a strong PTA along with the objectified capital of the students' parents (Bourdieu, 2011). As classroom sizes shrink, the spending will become more comparable, possibly allowing teacher pay raises, building renovations, and/or the purchasing of stronger curriculum.

To encapsulate the arguments of this text in totality, by way of CRSRT, a quotation is upheld from Justin Stith, the national coordinator for the Alliance for Educational Justice; it reads, "The education of Black children in this country is caught between a policeman and a privatizer" (Prothero, 2017). Though posed as a metaphorical statement, there is truth in Stith's words. The two representations of the oppressor in his statement, both policeman and privatizer, represent the possession of social and cultural capital that entraps black students in the process of education. To earn the membership into any police force, figurative or literal, one must invest time. Not unlike the policeman, to acquire the social and cultural capital necessary to become a privatizer, one must invest time and possess substantial amounts of predated capital (objectified and institutionalized). Stith said of this process that our children are "caught"; implying that the two entities with the power of imposition are blocking each exit, thus leading to educational inequity and institutional bondage.

Those exits are deliberately blocked as a means of stratification through the application of social and cultural capital in education. In traditional schools, students of color are disproportionately represented in suspensions, expulsions, and special needs programs: the policeman. In charter schools, parents are misleadingly convinced that their child will gain opportunities for academic success that one would presumptively not gain at a traditional school, for the administrative acquisition of economic capital: the privatizer. Through the acquisition of social and cultural capital, individuals like Betsy DeVos can perpetuate the conditions highlighted by the CRSRT in the privatization of education, prisons, and even war. The overarching reality of American life is that substantial capital is not needed for socioeconomic law enforcement; when manifested in ways that will benefit other members of America's White elite, substantial capital is the law.

Interest convergence, a central tenet in the late Derrick Bell's cultivation of CRT, should be considered the final and perhaps most impactful implication on the journey toward disrupting privatized education and ill-intentioned charter schooling in America. According to Bell (1980), interest convergence is the proposition that Black people achieve civil rights only when the interests of both Black and White people converge. Within the context of this chapter and dialogue on privatized education, interest convergence can be most notably applied in the form of viable teacher preparation programs. CRSRT engages with all matters of marginalization, particularly within the context of race, with the understanding that a substantial amount of capital is weaponized in the process. Teacher preparation programs are often the birthplace of weaponized capital in the timelines of both effective and ineffective classroom teachers.

When colleges and universities across the nation fail to instill in the hearts of future educators an appreciation for cultures unlike their own, the cycle of mediocre education practices and social reproduction is perpetuated. As addressed in Figures 5.1 and 5.2, White teachers disproportionately occupy classrooms across America, regardless of locale (NCES, n.d.). With this reality in mind, teacher preparation programs offer a crucial opportunity for teacher educators to converge the interests of the marginalized youth they will work with the interests of teachers themselves. Future educators enroll in teacher preparation programs with the general hope to one day become a teacher; this interest is safely assumed. Unbeknownst to these future educators is that a great interest of their future students is to be uplifted, engaged, and educated by teachers who understand and value their cultures. CRSRT, along with the work of professor Bell (1980), aligns its principles with the notion that interest convergence in the form of culturally reimagined teacher preparation programs will surely uproot the foundations of social reproduction in America. In turn, such a revitalization will soon nullify parents' needs to extract their children from local public schools in favor of the privatized charter. With stronger teacher preparation programs that emphasize the cultural wealth of students of color, the marginalized will finally receive the education deserved and promised by the U.S. Constitution.

REFERENCES

Bell, D. (1980). 'Brown v. Board of Education' and the interest-convergence dilemma. *Harvard Law Review, 93*(3), 518–533. https://doi.org/10.2307/1340546

Bhambra, G. (2017). *Critical race theory.* Global Social Theory. https://globalsocial theory.org/topics/critical-race-theory/

Bourdieu, P. (2011). The forms of capital. In A. R. Sadnovik (Ed.), *Sociology of education: A critical reader* (2nd ed.; pp. 83–93). Routledge.

Chingos, M. M., & Blagg, K. (2017). *Making sense of state school funding policy.* Urban Institute.

Darling-Hammond, L. (2010). *The flat world and education: How America's commitment to equity will determine our future.* Teachers College Press.

Education Votes. (2020). *Betsy DeVos and her no good, very bad record on public education.* https://www.nea.org/advocating-for-change/new-from-nea/betsy-devos -six-worst-moves-2019

Federal Reserve. (n.d.). *Board of Governors of the Federal Reserve System: Distribution of Household Wealth in the U.S. since 1989.* https://www.federalreserve.gov/ releases/z1/dataviz/dfa/distribute/chart/#quarter:122;series:Net%20worth; demographic:race;population:all;units:shares;range:1989.3,2020.1

Giroux, H. A. (2013). Neoliberalism's war against teachers in dark times. *Cultural Studies? Critical Methodologies, 13*(6), 458–468.

Hobson, F. (2017). *The privatization of America.* https://www.wbur.org/hereandnow/ 2017/05/10/america-privatized-military

Kamentez, A. (2016). Pearson's quest to cover the planet in company-run schools. *Wired.* https://www.wired.com/2016/04/apec-schools/

Ladson-Billings, G., & Tate, W. (1995). Toward a critical race theory of education. *The Teachers College Record, 97*(1), 47–68.

Mclaren, P., & Farahmandpur, R. (2001). Teaching Against globalization and the new imperialism: Toward a revolutionary pedagogy. *Journal of Teacher Education, 52*(2), 136–150. https://doi.org/10.1177/0022487101052002005

Merriam-Webster. (n.d.). Charter School. In *Merriam-Webster.com dictionary.* https:// www.merriam-webster.com/dictionary/charter%20school

Miller, R. (2020). Why Charter schools are failing Black students. *The Progressive.* https://progressive.org/charter-schools-failed-black-students-miller-200303/

National Center for Education Statistics. (n.d.). *Spotlight A: Characteristics of public school teachers by race/ethnicity.* https://nces.ed.gov/programs/raceindicators/spotlight_a.asp

Prothero, A. (2017). Charter schools aren't good for Blacks, civil rights groups say. *Education Week.* https://www.edweek.org/leadership/charter-schools-arent-good-for-blacks-civil-rights-groups-say/2016/08

Smith, E. (2008). *Using secondary data in educational and social research.* McGraw Hill Open University Press.

Toppo, G. (2017, February 7). What you need to know about Betsy DeVos. *USA Today.* https://www.usatoday.com/story/news/2017/02/07/facts-about-education-secretary-betsy-devos/97605238/

"Trey" Marchbanks, M. P., Peguero, A. A., Varela, K. S., Blake, J. J., & Eason, J. M. (2018). School strictness and disproportionate minority contact: Investigating racial and ethnic disparities with the "school-to-prison pipeline." *Youth Violence and Juvenile Justice, 16*(2), 241–259. https://doi.org/10.1177/1541204016680403

Wilson, E. K. (2019). Charters and choice: The New White flight. *SSRN Electronic Journal, 14*(234). https://doi.org/10.2139/ssrn.3353473

CHAPTER 6

PRIORITIZING TEACHER WAGES ON A NATIONAL SCALE

Jordan T. Register
University of North Carolina at Charlotte

Olanrewaju T. Oriowo
University of North Carolina at Charlotte

Nicole E. Shanley
University of North Carolina at Charlotte

Marquis R. Mason
University of North Carolina at Charlotte

You want to know what I make? I make kids wonder,
I make them question.
I make them criticize.
I make them apologize and mean it.
I make them write.
I make them read, read, read.

Economic, Political and Legal Solutions to Critical Issues in Urban Education
and Implications for Teacher Preparation
Copyright © 2022 by Information Age Publishing
www.infoagepub.com
pages 91–112

I make them spell *definitely beautiful, definitely beautiful, definitely beautiful*
over and over and over again until they will never misspell
either one of those words again.
I make them show all their work in math
and hide it on their final drafts in English.
I make them understand that if you've got *this,*
then you follow *this,*
and if someone ever tries to judge you
by what you make, you give them *this.*
Here, let me break it down for you, so you know what I say is true:
Teachers make a goddamn difference! Now what about you?
—Excerpt from Taylor Mali, "What Teachers Make"

Taylor Mali's (2002) poem begins with a question: "What's a kid going to learn from someone who decided his best option in life was to become a teacher?" What a question! Pregnant with the context that one almost doesn't have to explain, this question broadcasts the paradox of the teaching profession. What is wrong with wanting to become a teacher? The common saying, "Those who can't, teach," often reflects the idea that choosing to teach means one has tried and failed at other respected and lucrative careers, making teaching a last resort; a calling for the incompetent. Aside from the fact that, if this statement were true, then there is lunacy in sending children to be taught by failures, it also causes one to wonder why teaching is held in such low regard. The most common reason for teacher strikes is pay; salaries and compensation are the way the world ascribes value or worth to what a person does, so what does it say about teachers when the most accepted fact is that it is a low paying profession that lacks the respect of society (García & Weiss, 2019)? Furthermore, for the many who view teaching as a calling, is that the same as making a vow of poverty? Many people fail to understand why teachers would demand more money, expecting that teachers should be satisfied with educating future doctors, lawyers, and entrepreneurs, even if they can only dream of the lifestyle they made possible for others.

The purpose of this chapter is to explore school funding and its relationship to teacher wages across the United States. The following review of literature will provide a brief overview of how education became a state responsibility, the role of the federal government in influencing the educational climate, and the effects of both on teacher compensation. Specifically, it explores how a teacher's worth is determined by various states in the United States, a phenomenon that is intimately tied with school funding. School funding will then be discussed both in the context of the United States and in countries that are considered successful in terms of student achievement on international tests, teacher compensation, and teacher satisfaction (Darling-Hammond, 2017). Given the inequitable funding programs that currently exist in the United States (Baker, Farrie, & Sciarra, 2018; Baker, Weber, et. al, 2018), a solution will be offered which attends to the best interests of students and the value of high-quality teachers. The chapter will culminate by offering a weighted, progressive funding model to be implemented uniformly across states, in addition to related implications and recommendations.

EDUCATION: A STATE OR FEDERAL RESPONSIBILITY?

The political domain of education has been murky since the establishment of the U.S. Constitution. Its failure to explicitly include education has influenced many to see it as a state responsibility rather than a national concern (Black, 2019). How significant was this omission? According to Black (2019), by never using the word "education," federal courts have maintained that education was never expected to be managed at the federal level, thereby relegating it to the realm of the state. After more than 20 years in the courts, it became clear that nothing short of an amendment to the U.S. Constitution would persuade the resolute federal courts. There was one sliver of hope: A case brought by the state of Mississippi argued that the rights to citizenship promised by the 14th amendment indicate "an intent to make education a guarantee of citizenship" (Black, 2019, para. 5). Since the admission of southern states into the Union was contingent upon their adoption of the 14th Amendment and the revision of their state's constitution to include a guarantee of education (Black, 2019), one might be persuaded, but, alas, the Supreme Court is unwavering.

Contributing to a contentious situation, the federal government exerts influence over how states carry out their charge using the Elementary and Secondary Education Act (ESEA). First enacted in 1965, this civil rights law, subsequently renamed the No Child Left Behind Act (NCLB, 2001), and recently, the Every Student Succeeds Act (ESSA, 2015), came to govern education. Though each reincarnation of this law has maintained a common purpose of "equal opportunity for all students," the ESSA has aimed to guarantee high-quality instruction from highly qualified teachers as evidenced by progress on statewide assessments (U.S. Department of Education [USDOE], n.d.). This federal law defines what constitutes a highly qualified teacher but offers no guidance as to what such a teacher should be worth, leaving teacher salaries entirely in the domain of the state. The ESEA does not speak to funding but, rather, offers federal grants for the purchase of textbooks, scholarships for college students with low socio-economic status (SES), centers supporting special education, and more. It also provides grants for districts that serve large populations of low-income students. NCLB does not address funding but dictates accountability measures for students, teachers, schools, and the state.

While enabling school systems to make decisions that are regionally appropriate to their students, the delegation of educational responsibility to the states also implies that they assume the bulk of financial responsibility (Baker, Farrie, & Sciarra, 2018; Baker, Weber, et al., 2018). Given the differential earning power of state and local governments across the United States, it follows that school funding, and as a result, teacher compensation, differ substantially across the country (Baker, Farrie, & Sciarra, 2018; Baker, Weber, et al., 2018; Maciag, 2016).

WHAT SCHOOLS ARE SPENDING ACROSS THE UNITED STATES

School funding is a central component affecting teacher pay scales and student learning (Baker, Weber, et al., 2018). In the United States, schools are funded irregularly both across and within states, influencing differential educational opportunities for students depending on where they reside and different earning potential for teachers (Baker, Farrie et al., 2018). In their report, *Is School Funding Fair? A National Report Card*, Baker, Ferrari, et al. (2018) and his colleagues explored the distribution of both state and federal funding across United States' schools with a particular emphasis on supporting students in need. In 2018, there was a $12,400 difference in yearly per-pupil funding between the highest and lowest contributing states (Baker, Farrie, & Sciarra, 2018). Additionally, many of these states demonstrated flat and regressive funding patterns, indicating that high needs schools received equal or less funding than their wealthier counterparts (Baker, Farrie, & Sciarra, 2018, p. iv).

The amount of funds spent per pupil varies greatly across the United States (see Figure 6.1). For instance, on the low end, states like Utah and North Carolina spend less than $7,000 and $9,000 respectively, while New York spends over $22,000 per child (Baker, Farrie, & Sciarra, 2018; Maciag, 2016). Several factors explain these vast spending differences, the first of which is revenue. scholars suggest that the amount of money spent on students depends more on the number of available funds than the cost to educate students (Maciag, 2016). Both Maciag (2016) and Baker, Farrie, et al. (2018) suggested that school spending is directly related to the district's funding sources, including the state's gross domestic product (GDP) and local property taxes. According to Maciag (2016), the districts with the

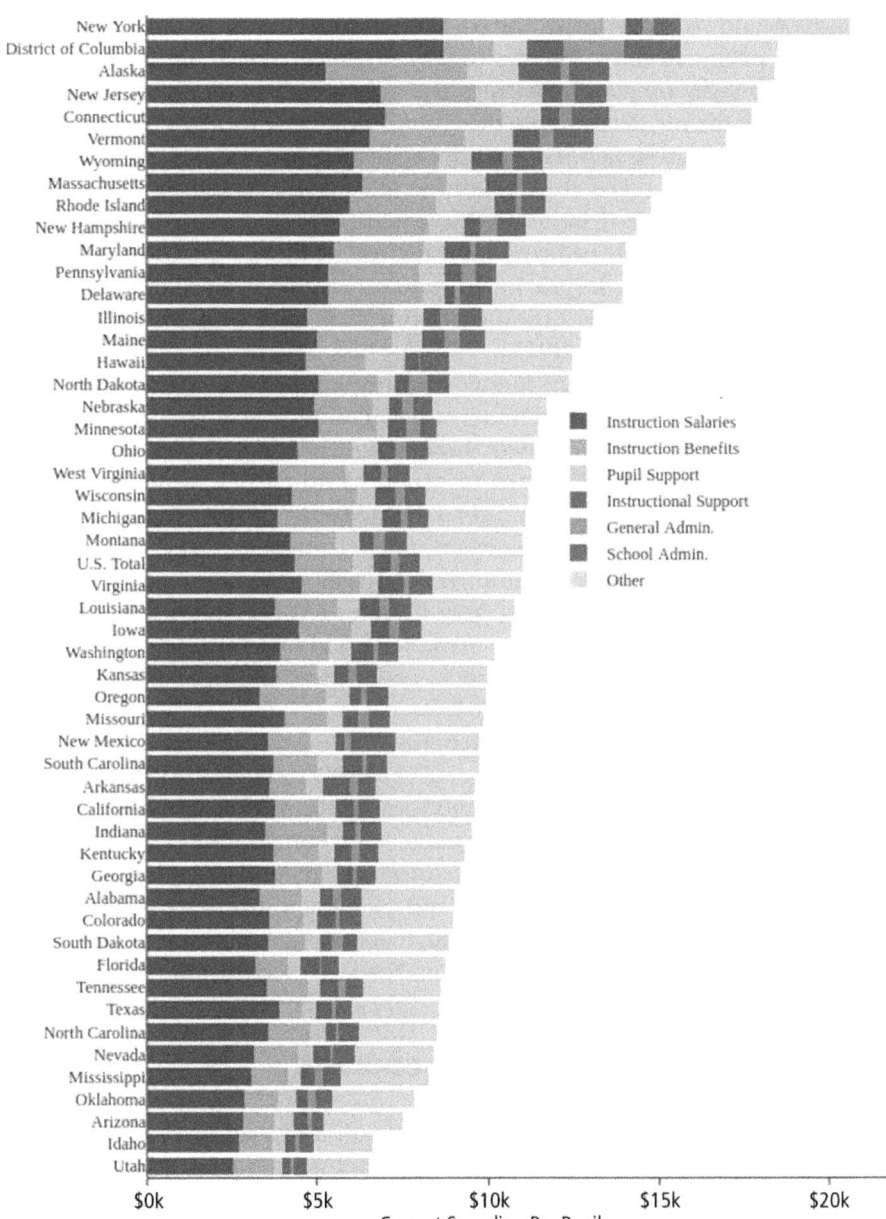

Figure 6.1 Fiscal year 2016 public elementary-secondary school per pupil spending by function. *Source:* U.S. Census Bureau (n.d.).

greatest spending can typically be sourced to local funding sources in areas with high property taxes. Maciag (2016) further posited that districts that rely more heavily on state resources typically have less money in total, yet demonstrate the more equitable distribution of those funds across districts.

Other contributing factors to school spending include the cost of living, state demographics, class sizes, administrative costs, state and local policy, teacher wages, and staff benefits (Cavanagh, 2017). As can be expected, states with a higher cost of living typically spend more on education. That being said, some states, despite having a lower cost of living than the national average, rank in the top quintile of education spending (e.g., Wyoming and Rhode Island; Maciag, 2016).

State demographics also influence differential spending patterns. For instance, some states have a much larger population of school students and/or more rural districts which incur higher transportation costs. Such states simply may not be able to afford to spend as much per student as other states, especially if they have a lower GDP (Maciag, 2016). Class sizes and administrative costs also differ between states (Cavanagh, 2017). While class sizes are closely related to the number of teachers on the payroll, administrative costs depend heavily on how fragmented the states are. Because highly fragmented states, like New York, have a greater number of separate districts, they require more funding to cover the building, administrative, and administrator costs (Maciag, 2016).

Teacher salaries and employee benefits, however, constitute the greatest expense in education (Baker, Weber, et al., 2018; Cavanaugh, 2017). Given the differences in wealth between state and local governments, as well as the different funding policies used across states, teacher compensation varies greatly. Further, the amount of money allocated to teachers depends on the student body and the human, technological, and pedagogical resources needed to educate them (Maciag, 2016). As a result, teacher wages may suffer to provide educational materials for students (Baker, Farrie, & Sciarra, 2018).

THE COST TO EDUCATE

The cost to educate a single child depends on a myriad of factors that include (but are not limited to) their socioeconomic status, language orientation, and whether or not they qualify for accommodations for exceptional needs (Baker, Farrie, & Sciarra, 2018; Baker, Weber, et al., 2018; Freedberg, 2019; Hill, 2012; Maciag, 2016). In the 2017–2018 school year, the amount of money required to educate a child in California (a state just over the halfway mark for state education spending) was approximately $9,000, and it was suggested that the cost to educate a student with an individualized education plan (IEP) or 504 plan was triple that amount (Freedberg, 2019).

Further, this amount varies based upon the type of disability the student has, and has been seen to range from $1,000 to $100,000 per student per year in some cases (Freedberg, 2019). The federal Individuals with Disabilities Act (IDEA, 1990) mandates that students with disabilities are offered the services that they need to receive fair and equal educational opportunities. Unfortunately, the costs required to cover such expenses are vast, and although the federal government set out to cover 40% of special education expenses (average national per-student expenditure multiplied by the total number of students needing services in each state), they have failed to meet these conditions, creating an estimated $3.2 billion gap between what they are paying and what they should be paying (Freedberg, 2019).

Emerging multilingual students also require additional funding for schooling. Emerging multilingual students made up approximately 10% of the U.S. student population (about 5 million students) in 2017 and their population is expected to grow (NCES, 2020a). It seems that the cost to educate emerging multilingual learners is widely undetermined and underaddressed on both the national and state levels (Hill, 2012). This is partially due to the differences in English language programs across states as well as policies that influence the goals, outcomes, and effectiveness of English language programs (Garcia, 2016). That being said, scholars and policy advisors are typically in agreement that to effectively support emerging multilingual students, extra funding is necessary (Hill, 2012). They further argue that such students require support beyond what they are given while receiving services as ELLs. To provide a truly equitable education to emerging multilingual learners, they must be supported beyond becoming proficient in conversational English or passing an English assessment, again requiring additional financial support (Garcia, 2016).

Finally, there is the consideration of students living in poverty. It is widely accepted that students from low-income families require additional educational resources to compensate for the disadvantages of poverty (Barshay, 2018). Unfortunately, the exact amount is difficult to determine due to differences in cost of living, labor costs, and poverty rates across states (Baker, Weber, et al., 2018). However, after declaring the United States was well behind other countries on international tests like the Program for International Student Assessment, a team of researchers from Rutgers University, in collaboration with the Education Law Center, created an algorithm that predicts the cost to support all U.S. students in reaching average test scores (Baker, Weber, et al., 2018). They reported that it would cost a poor district triple the amount of a wealthy district to reach average test scores (measured from 2013–2015), which are still well below proficient (Baker, Weber, et al., 2018; Barshay, 2018).

According to Baker, Farrie, et al. (2018), a progressive funding model is one that distributes funds equitably and according to need. Although the exact amount required to educate students is difficult to determine, it is clear that U.S. schools require additional and more equitable funding (Baker, Weber, et al., 2018). Further, it has been noted that the majority of recommended student–teacher ratios for all students are not being met (especially those with exceptional needs; NCES, 2018, 2019b). The composition of schools and available resources are the major determinants of the amount of funding that districts need to be able to support their unique group of students. Supporting diverse students further requires high-quality teachers who are equipped to teach students with a vast range of needs. This means not only attracting high-quality teachers, but ensuring that they can support themselves and their families, and are afforded the necessary resources for supporting students.

SCHOOL FUNDING

To understand teacher compensation in the United States, we must examine how schools are funded both within and across states. According to the National Center for Education Statistics (NCES, 2020a), there has been, on average, a 24% increase in education expenditure among Organization for Economic Cooperation and Development (OECD) countries between 2005 and 2016. U.S. education spending, in comparison, has only increased by 8%, which roughly coordinates with the increase in public school enrollment in a comparable time frame. Gertler and Gilchrist (2018) claimed that federal funding has been on the decline since the 2008 recession, placing a greater financial burden on the states. In the absence of funding directives to support these edicts, and edicts they are, there is no unified manner among states for assigning resources to schools.

In the United States, individual states maintain the responsibility of funding K–12 schools. Funding models are unique and dependent upon state policy and the capability of local districts to generate revenue. As of 2018, 9% of school revenue came from the federal government while the remainder was split between state and local governments depending on local districts' financial capability (Baker, Farrie, & Sciarra, 2018). According to Baker, Farrie, et al. (2018), state revenues are not always allocated according to need (progressive funding). Instead, states may fail to attend to local districts' ability to generate the revenue necessary for educating their unique group of students. In such cases, flat and regressive funding models, respectively, allocate the same resources to all schools or allocate more resources to wealthy schools (more on this later), and serve to exacerbate educational inequities by failing to support the neediest schools.

The U.S. Department of Education (USDOE, 2017) reported that about 92% of funding for primary and secondary education comes from state, local, and private sources, limiting the federal financial contribution to just 8% . This suggests that how each state directs these financial resources will impact the proportion allotted to teacher compensation. Where state financial resources and management allows greater per-pupil spending, one can logically expect higher teacher wages. According to the National Center for Education Statistics (NCES, 2020a), resourcing patterns by federal, state, and local governments differ substantially. For instance, in the 2016–2017 school year, 22 states received greater than 50% of their revenues from state governments, 16 states received over half of their funds from local sources (primarily from local property taxes), and the remaining 12 received less than half of their funding from both state and local sources (NCES, 2020b).

The Education Commission of States (Dachelet, 2019), maintained that there are at least five different funding mechanisms in play within the 50 states, District of Columbia, and Puerto Rico: foundation formula, resource allocation model, hold-harmless, hybrid, and other. Table 6.1 provides definitions and descriptions for the various terms related to the funding practices mentioned in this section. While it seems that some states have a uniform, yearly base amount per student, other states vary this amount by grade band. These amounts range from $3,561.30 in New Hampshire to $11,525 in Connecticut, though Massachusetts stands apart in that its base amount is determined by grade level and 11 different cost function areas (Dachelet, 2019). Resources for special education are determined using multiple weight systems, census-based systems, a resource allocation model, flat-weight system, reimbursement model, high-cost, or block grants. It is not clear which strategy delivers ideal financial distribution to optimize student success and teacher wages. However, such differential funding mechanisms are directly tied to school districts' ability to allocate resources to teachers, and as a result, are a necessary consideration when seeking to improve teacher compensation.

As previously stated, the variation in funding mechanisms across states is intimately tied to variation in teacher compensation. In a report published by the National Council for Teacher Quality, Kency Nittler (2019) shared the findings from the analysis of teacher funding structures in 100 of the largest districts in the country as well as the largest districts in each state. Nittler highlighted:

1. More than 50% of large districts still use a funding structure that adjusts teacher salaries according to educational attainment and years in service. About 25% use alternative methods including pay-for-performance. The implication is that compensation is less a reflection of quality and effectiveness and more a marker of the passage of time.

TABLE 6.1 State Funding Models and Descriptions

Funding Model	Description
Base Amount	This is the minimum guaranteed dollar amount that each district receives per student, if available in statute. The dollar figures are the most recent year available in statute, as of July 2019.
Block Grant	Under a block grant model, the state requires districts to apply for funding, and districts must make a case for why they should receive additional funding. Block grants can either use zero-base budgeting and start from scratch each year, or the grants can be calculated based on past years' spending on services.
Categorical	Under categorical funding, the state distributes money to districts or schools based on certain conditions. For example, a state may provide a funding supplement for a small or isolated school district, based on that designation alone.
Census Based System	Under a census-based system, the state assumes that each district has the same percentage of a student population, regardless of the actual demographics of the district. For example, a state could assume that 4% of students in each district are gifted/talented, regardless of the individual district composition.
Flat Weight System	Under this funding mechanism, districts receive funding for each student who meets the identification criteria. The weight or dollar amount is the same regardless of the student's individual characteristics. For example, all English language learners in a state would receive the same weight, regardless of their proficiency level.
Foundation Formula	Under a foundation formula, districts receive a base amount of funding per student with additional money or weights added to meet the needs of high-need student populations.
High-Cost Students System	Because of the financial burden some education services can impose on a district, some states provide additional funding for very high-cost students. This is often coupled with another funding mechanism to help offset the cost of some services. For example, while districts are responsible for the cost of special education services up to a certain threshold, if costs exceed that threshold, that state would then provide additional funding to the district.
Multiple Weights System	Under a multiple weights system, more than one weight or dollar amount is assigned based on certain factors. For example, in special education funding, the weights can be assigned based on severity of disability (e.g., mild, moderate, or severe) or a multiple weight formula may be more generalized (e.g., tiered amounts based on grade level).
Reimbursement System	Under this model, districts submit actual expenditures to the state, and the state reimburses districts for all or a portion of their actual spending.
Resource Allocation Model	Under a resource allocation model, states distribute resources rather than assigning weights or dollar values based on certain criteria. For example, the state would provide funding for a prescribed number of teaching positions based on student counts.

2. When adjusted for cost of living, the average teacher salary was $44,236 and the average maximum base salary available was $78,947. Nittler noted that it takes about 24 years of service for teachers to reach this maximum, and in some cases, a doctoral degree is required. The slow realization of wage increases could prompt more teachers to leave the industry.

3. A 5-year trend shows that, when adjusted for inflation, starting and maximum teacher salaries have increased only slightly, decreasing in some districts.

More variation in funding stems from the fact that some states place the onus on local districts to determine compensation structures (Nittler, 2019). These highlights show that teachers who remain in education can expect their pay to reflect tenure rather than quality or effectiveness, attributes that are highly valued (and remunerated) in industries outside of education (Chingos & West, 2012). It also suggests that, unless changes are made, teachers can expect starting and maximum salaries to remain relatively unchanged, making the profession financially unappealing.

Teacher compensation is unquestionably related to the attractiveness of the field. Failure to provide a uniform and competitive wage to teachers may influence the teacher shortages, high rates of teacher turnover, and comparatively low student performance on international tests that have become synonymous with the U.S. education system (Carnoy & Rothstein, 2013; Darling-Hammond, 2017; Garcia et al., 2019). As shown in relevant and international educational literature, competitive teacher compensation has significant positive effects on teachers' professionalism and self-worth (Darling-Hammond, 2017). Countries that prioritize teachers, including their wages, have increasingly positive student outcomes as shown on international tests, graduation rates, and other important measures of academic success (Darling-Hammond, 2017).

TEACHER COMPENSATION

In the United States, teachers currently are paid up to 30% less than their non-teaching counterparts with the same levels of education and accumulated student debt (Baker, Weber, et al., 2018). Though most university students pursue a college degree under the guise of entering a higher income bracket, ironically, novice teachers are granted beginning salaries comparable to, and often lower than, those without a college degree (Allegretto et al., 2019; Fayer et al., 2017; Weir, 2019). According to the National Education Association (NEA), when adjusted for inflation, teacher salaries have decreased in the last 10 years, placing teachers in a worsened economic position (NEA, 2020). The Economic Policy Institute (EPI), in a collaborative effort with the Center on Wage and Employment Dynamics, reported that teacher wages, when compared to that of other college graduates, "has been eroding for over half a century" (Allegretto et al., 2019). Across the country, this wage penalty ranges from 0.2% to 32.6% and the states with the largest penalties are Arizona, North Carolina, Oklahoma, and Colorado (Allegretto et al., 2019). While popular rhetoric would blame this trend on the Great Recession, the EPI report showed that the penalties are a reflection of state policies that began before the recession, and featured tax cuts after the recession (Allegretto et al., 2019).

In contrast, teachers in some of the most successful education systems in the world, in terms of student achievement on international tests and teacher satisfaction, hold comparable, and sometimes higher, salaries than other graduates while also receiving financial and other support (like housing or child-care subsidies) during teacher preparation programs (Darling-Hammond, 2017). Such incentives for teaching in areas like Finland, Canada, Singapore, Shanghai, and Australia, result in a teaching field that is competitive and highly esteemed both in practice and culture. This competition enables teacher preparation programs and school districts to be selective and holds high expectations for practice, resulting in greater and more equitable student outcomes (Darling-Hammond, 2017; NCEE, n.d.). Comparatively, teachers in the United States enter the teaching profession with wages similar or below those without similar levels of schooling, hold considerable student debt, do not receive opportunities for career advancement without entering into administration or leaving the teaching profession, and do not feel respected as professionals despite their training (Darling-Hammond, 2017). This lack of interpersonal, professional, and financial support contributes to greater levels of teacher attrition, many of whom leave the profession completely within the first 3 years of teaching (Triplett et al., 2019). The volatility of the teaching profession in the United States contributes to further instability in U.S. schools, resulting in inequitable outcomes for students, most negatively affecting the country's most vulnerable children (Garcia et al., 2019; Triplett et al., 2019).

Differences in teacher salaries depend directly on schools' ability to allocate resources. Wage variance among U.S. teachers across states is affected by factors such as cost of living differences, politics, and GDP across states (Baker, Farrie, & Sciarra, 2018). Since a uniform teacher salary is neither mandated nor supplemented by the federal government, impoverished states are often forced to choose between providing competitive wages for teachers or tangible resources for their students (Baker, Farrie, & Sciarra, 2018; Baker, Weber, et al., 2018). While some states can allocate close to 70% of their monetary resources to teacher and staff salaries, others allocate just over 50% (National Center for Education Statistics, 2019a). In the most recent data available through the National Center for Education Statistics (NCES), on average, instruction costs (salaries and benefits) account for 61% of state current expenditures. Figure 6.2 offers a disaggregated view at the state level and reveals that more than half of the states are below the national average for salary allocations.

Teacher and teaching quality depend heavily on the compensation and resources afforded to them. Teachers tend to migrate to where they feel most supported, both professionally and financially (Darling-Hammond, 2017). Because teacher compensation varies by state and school district, there is a disparity of both qualified teachers and quality teaching throughout the United States, with a disproportionate number of underqualified teachers holding vital positions in the neediest schools (NEA, 2019b; Triplett et al., 2019). School resources and associated teacher wages within states depend on four key factors: differences in per-pupil funding as determined by public policy, additional provision of funds for poor districts, states' fiscal efforts as compared to their income levels and GDP, and the degree to which wealthier families opt out of public schools, taking with them their social and political clout (coverage; Baker, Farrie, & Sciarra, 2018). In their examination of resource allocation between states, Baker, Farrie, and Sciarra (2018) found that funding levels illuminate discrepancies with the

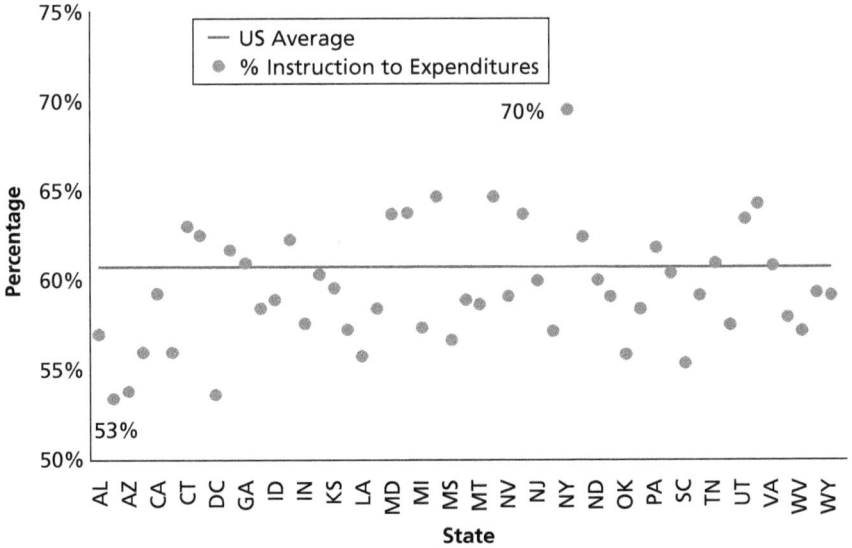

Figure 6.2 Proportion of instruction cost to current expenditures by state. *Note:* The labeled data points represent the lowest and the highest percentages relative to the U.S. average (NCES).

opportunity gap widening in lower funded states. Specifically, Baker, Farrie, and Sciarra, 2018 reported that "the funding differential between the highest (New York) and the lowest (Idaho) funded states is over $12,400 [per pupil] . . . States with higher funding levels can offer more competitive salaries, while in the lowest funded states teacher salaries are the least competitive with other professions (pp. iii–iv).

Of great concern is the reality that impoverished schools often serve larger populations of students who live in poverty and need special education or language supports (Baker, Weber, et al., 2018; NEA, 2019b; Triplett & Ford, 2019). Students in poverty, emerging bilingual students (EL/ELLs), and those with exceptional needs, benefit from smaller teacher-to-student ratios in that they are positively impacted by smaller class sizes, support staff, and social services (Baker, Weber, et al., 2018; NEA, 2019a, 2019b). NCES' (2019b) most recent data showed that the national average pupil/teacher ratio is 16:1, ranging from 10.8:1 in Vermont to 23.3:1 in California and Arizona. It is important to note that the number of teachers includes special education teachers and other specialist teachers. Considering class sizes, the ratio looks slightly different. For self-contained classes, there is a national average of 20.9 students per classroom at the primary level, 16.6 students per classroom in middle schools, and 16.3 students per classroom in high schools (NCES, 2018). In contrast, for departmentalized instruction (instruction to several classes of different students) primary classes have 26.2 students per classroom, middle school has 24.9, and high school has 18.6 students per classroom (NCES, 2019).

Given that the average recommended class size is 15 students, it seems that the United States is missing the mark (NCES, 2019c). Likely, the teacher shortages and turnover, both related to funding and inadequate compensation (Garcia et al., 2019), have influenced schools' ability to staff according to students' needs. When schools are not allocated enough money to cover necessary resources, administrators may be unable to hire necessary staff, while teachers may feel overwhelmed and under-supported, negatively affecting their retention (Garcia et al., 2019; Wang, 2019). As such, new and equitable funding mechanisms must be developed which consider the unique needs of the students, including the physical, intellectual, and human resources required to educate them.

PROGRESSIVE RESOURCE ALLOCATION

Baker, Farrie, et al. (2018) recommended that states adhere to "progressive" funding patterns. Progressive funding implies that more resources are targeted to poorer schools while schools with more resources (likely due to high property taxes, financial assistance from family donors, or Parent

Teacher Organizations) received less financial assistance. Impoverished schools require additional personnel and supplementary funding to attain desired student outcomes. States who employ "flat" or "regressive" funding patterns, characterized by their allocation of the same or fewer funds to high-poverty districts, fail to support students with diverse needs through their inability to employ and retain a sufficient number of high-quality teachers, support staff, and additional resources to provide equitable learning opportunities (Baker, Farrie, & Sciarra, 2018; Baker, Weber et al., 2018). Further, the additional stress associated with teaching vulnerable populations of students, with inadequate resources and compensation, often results in high rates of teacher attrition to more privileged schools or out of the profession altogether, contributing to a disparity of high-quality teachers in the schools that need them most (Baker, Farrie, & Sciarra, 2018; Darling-Hammond, 2017; Triplett et al., 2019).

National data suggests that states that successfully target resources to their highest poverty schools have better student outcomes, and those that provide competitive wages have better quality teachers and less teacher attrition (Baker, Farrie, & Sciarra, 2018). International studies further indicate that the most successful education systems, in terms of student performance on international tests and teacher satisfaction, allocate resources with explicit attention to equity in access and quality of education (Darling-Hammond, 2017). Within these systems, local and national governments work together to dispense monetary and human resources across school districts based on need, meaning that some schools, districts, and regions receive more aid than others. Further, these countries place a high value on teaching as a profession, providing competitive wages, opportunities for advancement, and often financial support during teacher preparation programs. In such areas, teaching is a competitive and highly respected profession, comparable in both compensation and esteem to lawyers and medical professionals (Darling-Hammond, 2017).

To elicit high-quality student outcomes on a national scale, teachers must be uniformly and competitively compensated throughout the United States. Because students and teachers are held to the same national standards under ESSA for high-quality learning and teaching, their compensation should be nationally regulated as well. If we wish to provide an equitable education to all students, we must ensure that they receive appropriate and equitable resources. This means ensuring the employment of the highest-quality teachers and providing them with the tools, encouragement, support, and compensation they need to thrive as human beings and as professionals. While this will require significant national reforms in education policy and funding, changes in how teachers are developed and students are assessed can be made to benefit stakeholders at little cost to taxpayers.

SOLUTION

Federal legislation must be implemented to equalize funding per pupil and teacher compensation across the nation. Such a law would implement a progressive funding model to regulate how much and to whom the states' resources should be distributed. Its goal would be to provide enough funding to cover student education costs and to create desirable teaching jobs through competitive wages in every state (Baker, Farrie, & Sciarra, 2018). The national education cost model (NECM) has been used to identify and compare valuable information regarding states and their respective schools' demographics, expenditures, population characteristics, economic conditions, and student performance measures (Baker, Farrie, & Sciarra, 2018). Using this or a similar model, states with the most equitable teaching outcomes, competitive teacher wages, and quality teachers can be analyzed to determine the optimal funding measures required to fulfill ESSA's mandate. This includes differential funding for students from low-income families, for those with special needs, and emerging bilingual students.

Teacher Compensation

The NECM can be used to determine an optimal proportion of school funding that yields competitive and uniform teacher wages. An ideal percentage measure should be determined and implemented across states to promote a uniform compensation base for funding which should be dispersed according to individual schools' population demographics. Regarding individual teacher wages, it is argued that beginning salaries should become higher and nationally mandated (at the expense of later pay increases) and that subsequent raises are acquired based on education level, certifications and CEUs earned, and extra responsibilities taken. Beginning teacher salaries should be comparable to salaries (upwards of 90%) offered to graduates with similar levels of education, certification, and personal investment (Darling-Hammond, 2017). A salary schedule is also proposed that increases wages yearly (in addition to the cost of living increases) rather than on a fixed schedule. High-quality teachers often enter the profession with student loan payments, living expenses, and young families to care for. Competitive wages at the beginning of their careers may encourage qualified individuals to not only choose a career in teaching but to stay in one. Furthermore, teachers who wish to increase their salary can do so through continued learning and leadership, which has positive implications for teachers, schools, and students, such as an improved sense of professionalism, collaboration, and pedagogical content knowledge (Darling-Hammond, 2017; Darling-Hammond et al., 2017).

Per Pupil Funding

Several measures should be collected based on national data and individual school population characteristics. Together, these values form the proposed nationally regulated, baseline funding algorithm. The NECM can be used to determine annual, nationally agreeable, individual student funding values (ISFVs) on four levels: the cost to educate a single student above the poverty line and without documented special needs (S), the amount of additional money required to educate a student in poverty (P), the amount of additional money required to educate a student with exceptional needs (N), and the amount of additional money required to support emerging bilingual students (B). ISFVs consider optimal student–teacher ratios for impoverished students and those who need additional learning and/or language support. Data collection at the school-level includes the total student population (TS), the total number of students from low-income families (TP), the total number of students in the exceptional children's program (TN), and the total number of students who are considered emerging bilinguals (TB). Population characteristics and ISVFs are combined to produce the following weighted, school funding formula, where F represents a single school's allotment:

$$F = TS(S) + TP(P) + TN(N) + TB(B)$$

Using this formula, each school receives funding that is proportional to its diverse student body (U.S. Census Bureau, 2018). State education budgets are determined by the sum of the F measures (ΣF) of its schools but are allocated to individual schools rather than to the state itself to ensure that funds reach their intended target. Importantly, such funds must be allocated within schools according to appropriate student–teacher and resource ratios (NCES, 2018, 2019c). For instance, schools with larger populations of emerging bilingual students should employ a larger proportion of ESL teachers while schools with greater populations of students with exceptional needs (EC) should have a more substantive EC program. Schools should not allocate additional resources targeted to special education or language programs to fund athletic, extracurricular, or advanced programs that do not directly benefit the intended recipients of those funds. Also, districts and states should be held responsible for students who transfer within and across districts. Each student will have an associated ISFV whose funds will follow them, should they happen to leave their home school. To account for this, funds should be accounted for, prorated, and redistributed on a monthly or quarterly basis.

Accountability

To hold states accountable, schools and states must be required to provide financial statements every quarter and undergo yearly audits. Schools that fail to comply may enter a probationary period where an educational financial advisor will be required to come in and work with the school administration until appropriate allocations are made. Schools will be required to submit mixed methods, holistic reports of student learning, teacher quality, and teacher attrition measures which will be analyzed yearly to determine the effects of the equitable funding policy. Schools that are underperforming in regard to equitable funding allocation will be paired with successful schools to observe their methods and engage in school-to-school mentorship (Darling-Hammond, 2017).

The consequence of fluid education funds is that teachers and staff may be required to transfer schools from time to time. To ensure that both students and teachers do not suffer from this practice, teacher education programs and school districts must take a systems approach to teaching, in which teachers expect to be where they are needed and adapt to their students and environment (Darling-Hammond, 2017).

RECOMMENDATIONS: A SYSTEMS APPROACH TO TEACHING

To offset the cost of increased teacher wages, revenues must be reallocated within the educational sphere as well as outside of it. Since the latter depends on polarized political whims, the first should be prioritized. An exceptional amount of financial resources in education are allocated to students and teacher accountability measures including standardized testing and teacher professional development (Wiggan, 2012). A significant body of research has clarified the detrimental effects of standardized testing on equitable student outcomes, preparation for the 21st century, and participation in the global democracy and economy (Darling-Hammond, 2017; Stromquist et al., 2014; Wiggan, 2012). Further, teacher professional development has been proven ineffective when performed externally and intermittently (Darling-Hammond et al., 2017; Ladson-Billings, 1995). With that in mind, funds traditionally allocated to standardized testing and external professional development should be redistributed to support increased teacher wages, and shift the responsibility of assessment and professional development back to teachers. With this reallocation, teachers would receive the autonomy to assess students at the school level and according to their instruction. Holistic assessment measures (MCEIA, 2020) should be determined and calibrated across the district, with local universities, post-secondary institutions, and employers, through professional learning communities that ensure student outcomes are both relevant to 21st-century skills and equitable across schools. Professional development related to such outcomes should be led by teachers, based on their participation in action research within their classrooms and schools. The increased competition of teacher candidates and expectations for professionalism associated with heightened competition would ensure that high-quality teachers would be prepared, willing, and highly capable of taking on such roles, as evidenced by nations that implement a systems approach to education (Darling-Hammond, 2017).

FINANCIAL IMPLICATIONS

The financial implications of this model are intimately tied to individual states' abilities to dispense the amount of money required to adhere to it, and to the federal government's ability to hold states accountable for compliance. It is argued that federal funding initiatives such as Title I and IDEA must be distributed according to states' fiscal capabilities as well as student populations, poverty levels, and documented student needs. States with higher gross state product and income levels will receive less funding, while the states that struggle to cover educational expenses will receive more aid. Although this may require an increase in the federal education budget, the economic and social benefits of investing in equitable and high-quality education are sizable and worthy. The greatest obstacle is legislative; this solution might require tax reforms since the previous decrease in education budgets were due to tax cuts. Realistically, it could take more than ten years for positive results to be consistent. This means that despite changes in political administrations, education funding programs should remain constant. Teachers need to believe that these changes are real and not subject to political whims. In other words, the country will need to prove that teachers and their students are a priority.

SUMMARY

We began this chapter with an excerpt from Taylor Mali's (2002) poem, "What Teachers Make." It is an uplifting ode to educators who are preparing the next generation to take up the mantle of the last, who realize the importance of embedding themselves in the communities they serve, and who partner with parents to support the developing identities of their students. While the pun in Mali's title reminds us that the teaching profession holds great social significance, it also draws attention to this issue of teacher pay. The data regarding teacher compensation makes the promises of greater earnings due to a college degree ring hollow. The quality of teaching and of teachers can be dramatically improved when compensation is aligned to the perceived worth of the profession. This alignment has been demonstrated to alter the trajectory of education in the countries that are ranked highest on international assessments that drive competition. While we have suggested one way to establish this alignment, it is now the responsibility of the United States to show, once and for all, what it believes is the value of a teacher.

REFERENCES

Allegretto, S., & Mishel, L. (2019). *The teacher weekly wage penalty hit 21.4 percent in 2018, a record high.* Education Policy Institute. https://www.epi.org/publication/the-teacher-weekly-wage-penalty-hit-21-4-percent-in-2018-a-record-high-trends-in-the-teacher-wage-and-compensation-penalties-through-2018/

Baker, B. D., Farrie, D. D., & Sciarra, D. D. (2018). *Is school funding fair? A national report card* (7th ed.). Education Law Center.

Baker, B. D., Weber, M., Srikanth, A., Kim, R., & Atzbi, M. (2018). *The real shame of the nation: The causes and consequences of interstate inequity in public school investments.* Rutgers University & Education Law Center.

Barshay, J. (2018, March 26). *What would it cost to get all students to average? Most low-income schools don't receive enough money to help kids hit average math and reading scores, a new study shows.* U.S. News. https://www.usnews.com/news/national-news/articles/2018-03-26/how-much-would-it-cost-to-get-all-students-up-to-average

Black, D. W. (2017). *The constitutional right to education is long overdue.* The Conversation. http://theconversation.com/the-constitutional-right-to-education-is-long-overdue-88445

Carnoy, M., & Rothstein, R. (2013). *What do international tests really show about U.S. student performance?* Economic Policy Institute. https://www.epi.org/publication/us-student-performance-testing/

Cavanagh, S. (2017). *K–12 spending: Where the money goes.* EdWeek. https://marketbrief.edweek.org/marketplace-k-12/k-12-spending-where-the-money-goes/

Chingos, M. M., & West, M. R. (2012). Do more effective teachers earn more outside the classroom? *Education Finance and Policy, 7*(1), 8–43. https://doi.org/10.1162/EDFP_a_00052

Dachelet. K. (2020). *50-State Comparison: K–12 Funding.* Education Commission of the States. https://www.ecs.org/50-state-comparison-k-12-and-special-education-funding/

Darling-Hammond, L. (2017). *Empowered educators: How high-performing systems shape teaching quality around the world.* Jossey-Bass.

Darling-Hammond, L., Hyler, M. E., Gardner, M., & Espinoza, D. (2017). *Effective teacher professional development.* Learning Policy Institute. https://static1.squarespace.com/static/56b90cb101dbae64ff707585/t/5ade348e70a6ad624d417339/1524511888739/NO_LIF~1.PDF

Fayer, S., Lacey, A., & Watson, A. (2017). *STEM Occupations: Past, present, and future.* U.S. Bureau of Labor Statistics, Spotlight on Statistics. https://www.bls.gov/ spotlight/2017/science-technology-engineering-and-mathematics-stem-oc- cupations-past-present-and-future/pdf/science-technology-engineering-and- mathematics-stem-occupations-past-present-and-future.pdf

Freedberg, L. (2019). *California spending over $13 billion annually on special education.* EdSource. https://edsource.org/2019/california-spending-over-13-billion -annually-on-special-education/619542

García, A. (2016). *New report examines equitable school funding for ELs.* New America. https://www.newamerica.org/education-policy/edcentral/new-report-examines -equitable-school-funding-els/

García, E., & Weiss, E. (2019). *U.S. schools struggle to hire and retain teachers.* Economic Policy Institute. https://www.epi.org/publication/u-s-schools-struggle-to-hire -and-retain-teachers-the-second-report-in-the-perfect-storm-in-the-teacher -labor-market-series/

Gertler, M., & Gilchrist, S. (2018). What happened: Financial factors in the great recession. *Journal of Economic Perspectives, 32*(3), 3–30.

Hill, L. (2012). *California's English learner students.* Public Policy Institute of Califor- nia. https://www.ppic.org/publication/californias-english-learner-students/

Ladson-Billings, G. (1995). Toward a theory of culturally relevant pedagogy. *Ameri- can Educational Research Journal, 32*(3), 465–491. https://doi.org/10.3102/ 00028312032003465

Mali, T. (2002). *What teachers make.* https://taylormali.com/poems/what-teachers -make/

Maciag, M. (2016). *Education spending per student by state.* Governing. https://www .governing.com/gov-data/education-data/state-education-spending-per-pupil -data.html

MCEIA. (2020). *Beyond standardized tests: A new vision for assessing student learning and school quality.* https://www.cce.org/uploads/files/MCIEA-White-Paper_ Beyond-Standardized-Tests.pdf

NCEE. (n.d.). *Top performing countries: Finland.* Center on International Education Benchmarking. http://ncee.org/what-we-do/center-on-international-education -benchmarking/top-performing-countries/finland-overview/finland-system -and-school-organization/

National Center for Education Statistics. (2018). *Public elementary and secondary teach- ers, enrollment, and pupil/teacher ratios, by state or jurisdiction: Selected years, fall 2000 through fall 2016.* https://nces.ed.gov/programs/digest/d18/tables/ dt18_208.40.asp

National Center for Education Statistics. (2019a). *Average class size in public schools, by class type and state: 2017–18.* https://nces.ed.gov/surveys/ntps/tables/ntps 1718_fltable06_t1s.asp

National Center for Education Statistics. (2019b). *Public school expenditures.* https:// nces.ed.gov/programs/coe/indicator_cmb.asp

National Center for Education Statistics. (2019c). *Public school expenditures by state.* https://nces.ed.gov/programs/digest/d19/tables/dt19_236.75.asp

National Center for Education Statistics. (2020a). *Education expenditures by country.* https://nces.ed.gov/programs/coe/indicator_cmd.asp

National Center Education Statistics. (2020b). *English language learners in public schools.* https://nces.ed.gov/programs/coe/indicator_cgf.asp#:~:text=(Last%20 Updated%3A%20May%202020),%2C%20or%203.8%20million%20students

National Education Association. (2017). *School funding: Learn the facts and how to use them.* https://educationvotes.nea.org/2017/07/19/school-funding-learn -facts-use/

National Education Association. (2019a). *Background of special education and the individuals with disabilities education act (IDEA).* http://www.nea.org/home/19029 .htm

National Education Association. (2019b). *Backgrounder: Education students from poverty and trauma.* https://files.eric.ed.gov/fulltext/ED591937.pdf

National Education Association. (2020). *Teacher compensation: Fact vs. fiction.* https:// www.nea.org/resource-library/teacher-compensation-fact-vs-fiction

Nittler, K. (2019, May 30). *The ins and outs of teacher salaries* [Blog post]. National Council on Teacher Quality. https://www.nctq.org/blog/The-ins-and-outs-of -teacher-salaries

Stromquist, N. P., & Monkman, K. (Eds.). (2014). *Globalization and education: Integration and contestation across cultures.* Roman and Littlefield Education.

Triplett, N. P., & Ford., J. E. (2019). *E(Race)ing inequities: The state of racial equity in North Carolina public schools.* CREED.

U.S. Census Bureau. (n.d.). *2016 education spending per student by state.* https://www .governing.com/gov-data/education-data/state-education-spending-per -pupil-data.html

U.S. Census Bureau. (2018). *Classroom diversity on the rise.* https://www.census.gov/ library/visualizations/2018/comm/classroom-diversity.html

U.S. Department of Education. (n.d.). *Every student succeeds act (ESSA).* https:// www.ed.gov/essa?src=rn

U.S. Department of Education. (2017). *Federal role in education.* https://www2 .ed.gov/about/overview/fed/role.html

Wang, K. (2019). *Teacher turnover: Why it's problematic and how administrators can address it.* The Science of Learning Blog. https://www.scilearn.com/teacher -turnover/#:~:text=Teacher%20turnover%20continues%20to%20concern ,annual%20turnover%20rate%20to%2016%25

Weir, M. (2019). *10 alarming facts about teacher pay in the United States.* Business Insider. https://www.businessinsider.com/10-alarming-facts-about-teacher-pay -in-the-united-states-2019-10

Wiggan, G. (2012). *Education in a strange land: Globalization, urbanization and urban schools: The social and educational implications of the geopolitical economy.* Nova Publishers.

CHAPTER 7

ONE SIZE DOES NOT FIT ALL

Understanding Lemovian Techniques and Multi-Tiered Systems of Support to Create a Better Framework for Behavioral Supports

Mike Friedberg
Northeastern Illinois University

> *The secret in education lies in respecting the student.*
> —Ralph Waldo Emerson

I am a White male teacher. I have taught in Chicago Public Schools since 2012, in schools that predominantly served students of color, mostly Latinx. I acknowledge my privilege in doing this work. Influenced by Kendall (2012), I commit to personal work by searching for an understanding of my past behaviors and biases. I acknowledge that there are different perspectives on experiences, both of students and teachers, and I seek to build relationships across racial boundaries. Additionally, I have researched in the field of critical race theory (CRT; Delgado & Stefancic, 2012) and have been influenced by the concepts of "Whiteness as property" (Harris, 1993), the racial contract (Mills, 1997), racial trauma (Carter, 2007),

Economic, Political and Legal Solutions to Critical Issues in Urban Education   pages 113–136
and Implications for Teacher Preparation

the interest-convergence dilemma in education (Bell, 1980), and storytelling and counter storytelling in CRT (Delgado, 1989). I also seek to be as antiracist as possible, from the conceptual framework of Ibram X. Kendi (2019). In doing so, I assert that I am imperfect in this work. I have spoken words and used disciplinary techniques, including those I critique in this research, that have perpetuated assimilationism, regardless of my intentions.

I have worked with Black and Latinx youth since 2007, first in community centers, and then as a public school teacher. It was through my student teaching and clinical experiences in the 2 years before becoming a full-time teacher that I was exposed to Lemovian techniques. Finally, I have published multiple blog posts on the above-mentioned techniques. The first post gained the attention of Doug Lemov (or his staff) and was posted on social media through the official "Teach Like a Champion" Twitter and Facebook accounts. Considering that, I did not seek to promote or repudiate Lemovian techniques in this study.

The initial research for this study started in 2016 and was completed in 2018 and presented at a research symposium at Northeastern Illinois University. The original process was seeking to understand if the techniques could be applied to students who have difficulty conforming to specific behavioral expectations (due to trauma from institutional racism, which is explained more in-depth in this chapter). However, through the process, other themes emerged. Since completing the initial research, I have become influenced by the field of CRT. Therefore, I incorporated new research to explore ideas regarding teacher preparation and CRT. At that time, there was little research on the effectiveness of Lemovian techniques, and more work still needs to be done. To expand my search, I considered topics such as charter schools and classroom management. These topics are not directly about Lemov's texts, but they serve to give context to, and offer a unique perspective on, Lemov's work.

Disagreements exist over the best approach to classroom management, particularly in addressing students with behavioral needs. Through this lens, the term *behavioral needs* is meant to reflect how trauma caused by poverty and institutional racism may lead to students not conforming to a set of behavioral expectations. The intent is to examine these systems, not blame the student. Here I define behavioral needs as challenges to conform to strict, punitive, disciplinary policies rooted in White supremacy that have often marginalized students of color by failing to take systemic racism into account.

The works of Doug Lemov (2010, 2015) have received recognition in conceptualizing classroom management despite failing to adequately address not only students with behavioral needs but institutions of racism. In the videos included with the books, as well as in Lemov's words, it is clear that the techniques are rooted in repetition, speed, efficiency, obedience, and teachers asserting power over students. There are repeated examples of teachers correcting students when they do not replicate the desired synchronized results of their peers, including tasks such as passing out papers and moving around a classroom. The videos cast the instructors as extremely authoritative. The techniques are colorblind at face value, yet analysis shows that it is clear that the construction of racist systems and racist ideas have perpetuated inequities in public schools (Kendi, 2019). Teacher preparation programs must address how schools have disproportionately marginalized students of color, especially regarding disciplinary practice (Wilson et al., 2020). An equitable approach will be paramount, and doing so will require us to challenge contemporary teaching techniques.

However, it is unclear if Lemovian techniques can be successful with students with behavioral needs in non-charter public schools. One of the benefits argued by supporters of charter schools is that these organizations have more autonomy than traditional public schools and thus can avoid the bureaucracies that hinder progress (Anonymous, 2017). However, charter schools may not limit the number of consequences, such as suspensions and expulsions, in comparison with their non-charter public school counterparts. This autonomy could lead to higher rates of suspensions and expulsions, including for not conforming to certain behavioral techniques (DeAngelis & Shakeel, 2017). Expelling these students is known as "cream skimming" (Altonji et al., 2010). (To be fair, it is clear that charters have heard these criticisms of punitive models of discipline and many are working to create more equitable approaches [O'Neill, P., 2019].) The purpose of this study is to investigate the effectiveness of teaching techniques in the controversial and popular book, *Teach Like a Champion* (Lemov, 2010, 2015) when they are applied to students with behavioral needs in non-charter public schools. Specifically, the driving question and focus of this study is how do teachers at charter schools and traditional public schools perceive and compare classroom management techniques for students with varying levels of behavioral needs?

RATIONALE

This research is important because, due to the spread and justification of standardized testing, Lemov's ideas have quickly gained traction in the education world (Iyengar et al., 2017; Munter & Haines, 2019). Lemov focuses intensely on quantitative data in the form of test scores and has influenced other schools and districts to do the same. However, it is unclear whether the techniques are successful in non-charter schools with students with behavioral needs, particularly because charter schools may have higher expulsion rates than non-charter schools (Golann, 2015). Thus, students who do not conform to strict behavioral expectations in a charter school can be expelled easily, whereas doing so in a public school can be difficult.

Additionally, this research seeks to add to the dialogue concerning effective classroom management practices with students who may not conform to behavioral expectations, but would benefit from using restorative practices (Fronius et al., 2016; Guckenburg et al., 2015a). These scholars show us that teachers need to shift their focus away from behavior that may be viewed as problematic and start asking why a student is behaving in a particular manner. Additionally, teachers must acknowledge their roles in creating a culturally relevant environment where students can feel safe, have their culture(s) affirmed and validated, and meet behavioral expectations (Ladson-Billings, 2016). This can be through multicultural perspectives, as opposed to traditional, Eurocentric curriculums. Kim and Connely's (2019) research showed that preservice teachers' attitudes towards diversity and a culturally relevant curriculum can have significantly positive consequences for their multicultural efficacy. Pedagogy that is culturally relevant and responsive can affirm a student's identity and give them a sense of belonging in school (Alexander, 2016). Therefore, the goal of this work is to examine how effective Lemov's techniques can be in different environments and to promote possible suggestions for implementation of alternatives to create safe, restorative classrooms where all students can flourish.

LITERATURE REVIEW

Teach Like a Champion

Doug Lemov is the author of *Teach Like a Champion* (2010, 2015) as well as the director of the charter school network Uncommon Schools. Lemov and *Teach Like a Champion* first gained attention with an article in *The New York Times*. Green (2010) highlighted how Lemov had been a successful teacher and principal, but could not reproduce his success with other teachers and schools. According to Green, part of the conclusion that Lemov reached was that teachers were not being properly trained like professionals in other careers, such as athletics where players are given specific, concrete feedback. Teachers were simply told that they had to "get better," but were not given opportunities to do so, let alone feedback on how to improve their craft. Green further summarized Lemov by explaining that many teacher education programs had students teach broad, or study abstract theoretical perspectives, but did not advise how to properly apply best practices in their classrooms. In sharp contrast, Lemov believes that concrete, replicable techniques can be used to improve teacher practice.

Consequently, for 5 years Lemov arduously observed teachers, looking for what separated the effective from the ineffective. Uncommon Schools would eventually fund his work, and the product became Lemov's (2010) first book, *Teach Like a Champion: 49 Techniques That Put Students on a Path to College.* Classroom management is central to the book, specifically being able to get students to follow instructions as closely as possible, particularly in classroom procedures such as passing papers, using hand signals, and sitting in class. While some of the actions may seem punitive, such as reprimanding kids for not exhibiting synchronistic body movements in a robot-like fashion with the rest of the students, Green (2010) argued that Lemov's goals for teachers are "an exercise in purpose, not power," in addition to evaluating whether Lemovian management skills alone are sufficient for teaching content. This assertion is questionable at best, as the techniques are profoundly rooted in control. They are also not suited for modification for students who may have difficulty conforming to strict, punitive behavioral expectations, because these students are not properly addressed. Finally, as I will discuss in depth in the following chapter, there is profound racism underlying the book, despite a guise of colorblindness.

It is a common misconception that there is something in great teachers that makes them great, asserted Doug Lemov (2010, 2015). Instead, he argued, there are concrete, reproducible techniques that distinguished educators use to produce high standardized test scores. This is the focal point of his work: Use the techniques and students will score well on assessments. The techniques themselves are militaristic. There are themes of repetition, compliance, and obedience, and the entire book is not about classroom management by any means. Yet the discussions around teaching are rooted in the teacher's ability to assert their authority and to control students. There is no mention of creativity, culturally responsive teaching, trauma-informed pedagogy, socioeconomics, or race, except for the disparities in standardized test scores between White children and their peers of color. This colorblind pedagogy is lacking in discussion in many critical components, with the implications that the techniques can boost test scores, and create "champion teachers," a term used repeatedly.

The techniques may be effective with some students, such as those who may conform easily to punitive behavioral expectations, however Lemov's (2010, 2015) techniques were not created to address students with high behavioral needs nor incorporate restorative practices. In the DVD that accompanies the texts, students follow the directions flawlessly for the most part. For students who do not have difficulty with such strict expectations that appear to be rooted in teachers asserting their power, the techniques may be successful. There is no proof that they would work with students who have a history of social-emotional challenges as a result of centuries of systemic racism, denial of wealth through government policy, and failure to repair this damage (Coates, 2014.) In his work, Lemov made no mention of institutional oppression, and in not doing so, perpetuates these power constructs. Lemov emphasized the effectiveness of his techniques, and the implication is that they will be universally successful, yet there is scarce mention of differentiating for students who do not conform to behavioral expectations.

Classroom Management

Identifying best classroom practices has proved controversial since very little research effectively demonstrates correlations between teaching techniques and positive outcomes. There is also ambiguity in defining exactly what problematic behavior is, and its effect in classrooms. Consider how Fallon et al. (2012) described school-wide problem behaviors as noncompliant, combative and destructive. These terms are problematic in their lack of objectivity. They do not question institutional racism or acknowledge how the effects of poverty can lead to such behaviors (Flouri & Midouhas, 2016), only that they are problematic. They also omit the disparity in consequences that are disproportionate to African American students, particularly males, which can lead to feelings of learned helplessness and internalized self-hatred (Fallon et al., 2012). Part of the problem is that teachers may be at various stages of identity development and addressing racism. They may lack cultural context in contemporary pedagogy (Caraballo et al., 2020), and perception of equity (Darling-Hammond, 2010), as some teachers misunderstand different standards of behavior (Verstegen, 2015) within the lens of CRT (Stovall, 2016). The problem is that racism can be perpetuated amongst teachers to students, regardless of the instructor's intentions. This can have devastating consequences, most notably continuing the school-to-prison pipeline (Grace & Nelson, 2019). As Wormeli (2016) noted, if schools do not work to acknowledge racism, they can continue bigoted policies and inequitable outcomes.

Dixson and Ladson-Billings (2017) clarified what it means to be culturally relevant for educators and scholars. Behavioral supports that are universally applied may be ineffective due to cultural conflicts, particularly if the dominant culture of the teacher is imposed on non-dominant groups (Day-Vines & Day-Hairston, 2005). Consequently, students can feel alienated and marginalized as a result of their teacher's methods of discipline (Weinstein et al., 2003). This can perpetuate a cycle of negativity and learned helplessness on the part of the student and thus continue the perceived misbehavior. Lemov (2010, 2015) made no mention of these factors.

Notably, zero-tolerance discipline policies in school have not improved behavior, eliminated expulsions, or reduced suspensions (Skiba, 2014). Instead, they have exacerbated the opportunity gap (Cowan Pitre, 2014) and created an "educational debt," which is the disparity in resources in

White, affluent schools as opposed to traditionally underfunded schools with students of color (Ladson-Billings, 2006), having negative impacts on these students (Bernstein, 2014). The perpetuation of these consequences has furthered the school to prison pipeline, in which classroom exclusion and criminalization of misbehavior have contributed to increased involvement in the justice system (Fowler, 2011). Additionally, students of color and those with disabilities are suspended at far higher rates than their peers (USDOE, 2014). Carmichael et al. (2005) found correlations between students with histories of disciplinary problems and the eventual entry into Texas prisons. It is plausible to conclude that zero-tolerance policies in schools that give students severe consequences for minor infractions are comparable to adults being sent to prison for misdemeanors. Schools can be unintentionally complicit in perpetuating the prison pipeline for students of color. Discipline policies involving law enforcement can also increase the likelihood of students entering the juvenile system (USDOE, 2014). Black students in particular are disproportionately disciplined, even when controlled for variables such as socioeconomic status (Gregory et al., 2010; Skiba et al., 2002). Moreover, Green et al. (2018) analyzed how suspensions, detentions, and traditional punitive models of school discipline have been ineffective in motivating students to conform to behavioral expectations. Belser et al. (2016) instead argued for procedures that do not exclude students from class, but instead, utilize "frameworks of prevention and intervention" (p. 260). Effective teachers create engaging, positive learning environments that place not only focus on academics but social-emotional learning as well (McDonald, 2013). Additionally, successfully working with students with behavioral needs calls on multifaceted theoretical perspectives, including social-emotional learning. Successful classroom management "is not an end in itself" but is "more than just rules, rewards, and consequences" (Egeberg et al., 2016, p. 13).

Lemov's (2010, 2015) work does not mention these but is rooted in B. F. Skinner's work on behaviorism (1957), which suggested that student behavior is rooted in extrinsic consequences. While Skinner's work has some validity, it does not address socioeconomic factors or the realities of trauma and social-emotional challenges. Egeberg et al.'s (2016) work is a more appropriate lens for classroom management. An approach that is increasingly gaining popularity, particularly for Black and Latinx students who have been disproportionately disciplined in contrast to their White peers in schools (Thompson, 2016), is known as the multi-tiered support system (MTSS; Belser, et al., 2016). Schools and counselors that properly utilize MTSS seek to implement restorative practices in schools and decrease suspensions and expulsions. While MTSS interventions can be utilized for academic as well as social-emotional needs, the focus of this research is the latter. Figure 7.1

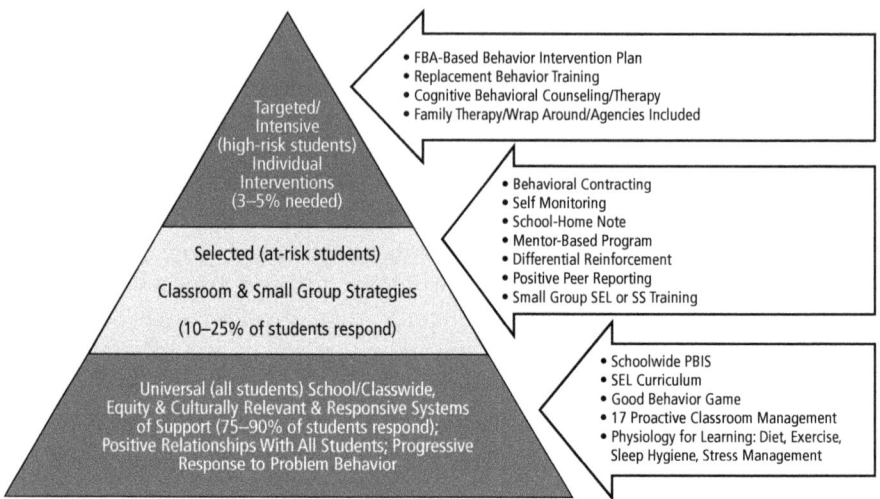

Figure 7.1 Evidence of supports and approximate ratios per classroom. *Source:* California Department of Education, 2018.

is from the California Department of Education (2018) and illustrates how support is given for various tiers of students.

As outlined in Figure 7.1, students with behavioral needs are first identified by the counselor and/or instructor. They are then provided interventions over a given time. The problem is identified, behavioral expectations need to be as objective as possible, and students are grouped into "tiers" based on the severity of the behavior. The data are analyzed and appropriate intervention is provided. Table 7.1 illustrates some examples of behaviors, quantifiable objectives, and appropriate interventions.

Using the MTSS model, if the student cannot meet the objective, they are moved on to the next tier. Generally, Tier 1 students should account for 80% of a classroom, Tier 2 students should make up 15%, and Tier 3 students (who require the most support) should not constitute more than 5% of a classroom. This will vary depending on the school and community, but generally, tiers should be within those ratios. While all classrooms are unique in their needs, and guidelines of ratios may vary between districts, these proposed ratios are meant to give teachers an idea of how to prioritize the needs of students.

Teach Like a Champion Techniques

In *Teach Like a Champion,* Lemov (2010, 2015) did not include any peer-reviewed research or empirical studies to support the validity of his techniques,

TABLE 7.1 Examples of MTSS Interventions		
Behavior	**Objective (quantifiable)**	**Intervention**
A fourth-grade girl has self-control issues and is constantly disrupting class.	In 6 weeks, student disruptions will occur no more frequently than twice per hour.	The teacher will monitor student disruptions with a form and set up an incentive system. The teacher will use progress monitoring.
A high school junior is at least 2 hours late to school 3 days a week.	In 5 weeks, the student will be late by no more than 2 hours once a week.	The social worker will meet with students twice a week for at least 2 minutes. The goal will be to learn about possible circumstances outside of school that might be making the student repeatedly late. The social worker will then create a plan for the student to arrive to school on time.
An eighth-grade boy refuses to follow instructions, especially from female teachers, and frequently either gets kicked out of class or voluntarily leaves.	In 6 weeks, the student will follow instructions with no more than two redirections per class period and will no longer be kicked out of class.	The counselor and teachers meet with parents to discuss observations of the student as well as circumstances occurring outside of school. Staff and parents work together to determine what is causing the behavior. The student will have a system where he checks in and checks out during the school day with a male teacher of his choice. The counselor will create a data collection tool to determine if the child may have symptoms of oppositional defiant disorder. As the weeks progress, the student will complete a reflection sheet about skills that work for coping with anger, and what he can do to stay in class.

only that he gathered them from observing teachers he deemed effective. This is extremely problematic and questions the integrity of the text. Why are schools using the book if it is so subjective? If the techniques are so valid, why is there not any peer-reviewed research to support them? Why is Lemov a household name in education, and scholars publishing peer-reviewed research on similar and adjacent topics not given the same credibility? These are legitimate questions that the text does not answer. Instead of research, Lemov discussed high scores on standardized tests. The implication is that proper utilization of these techniques, with a strong focus on classroom management, will lead to improved growth on achievement tests. Here are some of the techniques that Lemov (2015) defines in his second edition, followed by their intrinsic failures to meet the needs of all students:

1. *Right is right*—"When you respond to answers in class, hold out for answers that are 'all-the-way right' or to your standards of right" (p. 100). What about English language learners (ELLs) and diverse

learners (DLs)? The text does not properly address how to use this technique with those students who might not present perfect answers or behave in ways that do not match strict expectations. Evnitskaya and Berger's (2017) research demonstrated that students' willingness to participate is not absolute but is shaped by a myriad of aspects, such as being a non-native speaker.

2. *Do it again*—"Give students more practice when they're not up to speed—not just doing something again, but doing it better, striving to do their best" (p. 373). This seems intrinsically acceptable but is suggested for rote tasks. There is no peer-reviewed research that demonstrates that having students walk the hallways in silence or repeatedly entering the classroom can help students, including students with individualized education plans (IEPs). Research suggests that students with ADHD should not be repeating negative behaviors (Special Education Programs, 2003). Lemov made no mention of this.

3. *Strong voice*—"Affirm your authority through intentional verbal and nonverbal habits, especially at moments when you need control" (p. 412). Framing "control" in this sense is authoritarian and does not promote democratic classrooms. This technique does not address peace circles or restorative practices which should make the need to control students nonexistent. Ideally, we should strive for true democratic classrooms where teachers do not need to assert control through their words and actions to intimidate students into submission. This authoritarian style could lead to increased tension in a classroom. Holmes (2017) asserted how a preservice teacher development program designed to teach de-escalation, building students' self-confidence, and conflict-resolution skills led to a decrease in disciplinary actions.

4. *Make visible compliance*—"Ensure that students follow through on a request immediately and visibly by setting a standard that's more demanding than marginal compliance. Be judicious in what you ask for, specifically because it will uphold the standard or compliance" (p. 393). This technique does not address social-emotional challenges. What if the student has experienced something traumatic recently and is struggling with this authoritative manner of making compliance visible? This does not adequately address the ways in which many students may struggle with following a demanding, rote task relating to trauma due to their home situation or even something broader such as systemic racism. Research asserts that the stereotype threat, which may cause students to have anxiety when they are associated with a particular group, can be extremely detrimental, and that self-affirmation is effective against it. Activi-

ties of self-affirmation had other long-term benefits (Rozek, 2015). Demanding compliance from students is the opposite of students affirming themselves.

5. *No opt-out*—"Turn 'I don't know' into success by ensuring that students who won't try or can't answer practice getting it right" (p. 90). Like the previous technique, this fails to address how a student's struggle to answer a question correctly may be related to dealing with personal challenges. These students should not receive a consequence for experiencing social-emotional trauma or be embarrassed for being diagnosed with a learning or behavioral disability. Scholars assert how restorative practices can better help students' self-confidence and increase their willingness to participate and be engaged, as opposed to forcing them to speak (Osher et al., 2018).

6. *Least invasive intervention*—"Maximize teaching time and minimize 'drama' by using the subtlest and least invasive tactic possible to correct off-task students" (p. 395). This technique fails to adequately define what "off-task" means. From the videos and descriptions, it appears that this may be as simple as not starting a packet correctly or even holding a pencil at the appropriate time. Lemov did not acknowledge how anti-Blackness has affected how teachers disproportionately "correct" Black students, regardless of how discrete the intervention is (Marcucci, 2020).

7. *Art of the consequence*—"Ensure that consequences, when needed, are more effective by making them quick, incremental, consistent, and depersonalized. It also helps to make a bounce-back statement, showing students that they can quickly get back in the game" (p. 406). Again, there is no mention of restorative justice. Furthermore, the idea of incremental consequences is too ambiguous, in addition to not mentioning how trauma may affect student behavior and how consequences may exacerbate it.

The major failure with Lemovian techniques is that they are too broad and not defined for students with high behavioral needs, such as students who may be experiencing personal or institutional trauma or have difficulty conforming to strict behavioral expectations. They do not address those who may have diagnosed disabilities, either cognitive or behavioral. They do address institutional racism. They do not address how teachers should strive to be culturally relevant. They do not address best practices for Black and Latinx students. These omissions show an obliviousness to the needs of children, viewing them simply as machines without emotions.

Uncommon Schools and Implementation of Lemovian Techniques

Because I do not work for Uncommon Schools, it is challenging to understand exactly how the techniques are implemented. I interviewed a Teach Like a Champion employee and was told that professional development is ongoing. Teachers receive weekly training on specific techniques, which are followed up with an administrator or coach. The instructor is given feedback on what they did well and how they could improve it. The implementation is rolling with simultaneous feedback and development. According to the interviewee, Uncommon seeks to create a culture with the techniques so that classrooms and discipline can be proactive rather than reactive (Anonymous, personal interview, 2017). This creates a shared language for planning and observation. Certain Uncommon campuses also use a token economy with "scholar dollars," which are used for rewards and consequences. Students can use these to buy prizes—ranging from a slice of pizza to visiting a college. Scholar dollars are used from kindergarten through high school, as are Lemov's techniques. Again, the organization seeks to create a culture with continuity where students are clear on their expectations throughout their enrollment at Uncommon Schools (Anonymous, personal interview, 2017).

Accordingly, it is unclear what research, besides Lemov's extensive observations, drives the pedagogical reasoning for scholar dollars, and the systems of rewards and punishments at Uncommon Schools. For this study, MTSS is utilized as the theoretical framework (Belser et al., 2016). Specifically, this research looks at best practices for working with students with high behavioral needs. MTSS is extremely important for any research on classroom management, but is particularly pertinent to Lemov's work, as he did not acknowledge interventions, social-emotional or cognitive. To a lesser extent, B. F. Skinner's (1957) operant conditioning, falling under the general psychology of behaviorism, is referred to. Skinner's work discusses stimuli and responses, specifically through both positive and negative reinforcement. To clarify, the purpose of examining Skinner and Belser's research is to apply these theoretical frameworks to Lemovian techniques.

Charter Schools

Uncommon Schools is a charter school network. While my research is not broadly about charters, the context in which they exist and operate is crucial to understanding Lemov. Charter schools have existed for over 20 years and are concentrated in predominantly urban areas. (For this research, I used Milner's [2012] definition of "urban," which is not based on race but on concentrated populations, often of lower socioeconomic status.) Charter schools have a focus on deregulation (allowing charter schools to operate outside the realms of traditional public schools), accountability (schools must meet certain objectives outlined in their charters), and choice (parents are given opportunities based on the concepts of free-market competition). These changes from traditional public schools are intended to lead to increased staff autonomy and pedagogy, improved equity, parent satisfaction, and an end goal of student achievement (Miron & Nelson, 2002). They are divergent from the traditional public school model. Because Lemov is a director of a network of charters, it is important to understand their uniqueness, differences, and autonomy.

Charter schools are controversial. Much of the complaint about them has stemmed from the fact that the teachers are not unionized and have little to no job protections. Karanxha (2013) cited examples of administrators at a failed charter school who "conducted psychological warfare" on the teachers, such as being brought individually into rooms with the principal, or being confronted and told that their concerns and criticisms of the toxic environment "were a threat to the school" and "endangering everybody's job" (p. 595). Fernandes and Menezes-Filho (2020) argued that evaluating charter schools based on test scores is not a strong criterion due to the free-market equilibrium in their nature. Because charters do not have the same regulations as traditional public schools, they argued, they should not be assessed in the same manner, such as through standardized tests. Golann's (2015) research demonstrated that certain charter models can stunt the higher-level thinking skills of their students by forcing them into a "teach to the test" mindset, where higher-level thinking becomes irrelevant and students are only able to perform on certain types of standardized tests. They can also have unintended consequences for the students, such as decreased motivation, increased stress, and weakened relationships with teachers. This may occur as students are disciplined punitively through minor infractions, are held to unrealistic individual expectations, and are given an overwhelming amount of work that is not properly differentiated based on their needs (Golann, 2015).

As a result, many charters and large corporations have a "no excuses" attitude towards low standardized test scores (Golann, 2015). "No excuses" is often synonymous with the idea of high standards. Lemov's implication appears to be that in many public schools, Black and Latinx students may be held to lower standards and thus have lower test scores. Uncommon Schools proudly proclaimed how their philosophy holds students accountable to the highest standards possible (Lemov, 2010, 2015). Low-income students of color should be held to the same expectations as their White affluent counterparts. The implication of the text is that teacher willpower can raise standardized test scores by extraordinary gains. Lemov's work did not consider the denial of wealth, safety, systemic racism, and lack of basic human services that many low-income children of color face. This does not mean that the students should not be held to high academic standards; it is acknowledging the reality of a myriad of socioeconomic factors. Being cognizant of these realities is essential because not doing so repudiates the research showing how poverty and trauma have dramatic consequences on children. In contrast, multi-tiered approaches will be essential to healing the trauma of students of marginalized groups (Berger, 2019).

There has been increased criticism regarding the techniques that charter schools use to obtain "achievement." Bruhn (2014) highlighted the backlash of the film *Waiting for Superman* as educators in New York City made the following assertions: Charter schools do not exist to fix the "achievement gap" (a problematic term that should be replaced with "access gap," but Bruhn uses this terminology), the privatization/reform movement will not in actuality improve education, and union safeguards (which Uncommon Schools do not have) protect children. These ideals are vastly different in comparison to those presented by Lemov (2010, 2015), whose schools are not unionized and imply that Uncommon can solve all problems within urban education. That said, a 2013 Center for Research on Education Outcomes (CREDO) study asserted that Uncommon Schools had a "significant and positive" effect on Black and Latinx students. However, Black students enrolled in Uncommon Schools did not achieve significantly higher test scores in reading, although they did in math. Still, in comparison to the other charter schools in the study, Uncommon Schools had the greatest positive effects on students and had the strongest growth for 10 out of the 12 subpopulations that the network serves (Woodworth & Raymond, 2013, p. 89). The CREDO study is limited in its analysis, focusing predominantly on standardized test scores. Quantitative surveys from students and parents and qualitative interviews would better provide a more holistic picture of Uncommon Schools, including information on school culture and climate. To clarify, while my study is not focused on test scores, it is important to acknowledge them because Lemov implied that they are evidence that his techniques work. Again, the texts contain no peer-reviewed research to assert their effectiveness, only standardized test scores. While it is important to acknowledge the CREDO study, as little research exists to determine the effectiveness of Lemovian techniques, it is extremely limited in its implications. It is impossible to extrapolate sufficient data on the effectiveness of these techniques by examining test scores alone.

Charter Schools and Discipline

While the research on Lemovian techniques is limited, the research on school discipline is not. This context is essential to understanding Lemov, as he focuses on behavioral norms and strict classroom management. Golann (2015) argued that when charter schools emphasize "working-class behavioral norms, they can develop an environment that promotes achievement" (p. 115). Lemov's (2010 , 2015) text emphasized Golann's assertions as there is a strong emphasis on order. For example, in Golann's (2015) study, one charter high school principal was asked "how to discipline students without deadening their spirits" (p. 115). The principal responded that the kids feel like they are in prison, although she wanted to enact a warm/strict model throughout the school.

> I have a vision for rigor; I have a vision for warmth—I want it to be a warm place. I have a vision for high conduct and I have a vision—and this is what doesn't always mesh well with no excuses—but I have a vision for the gradual release of structure. I want the kids to leave here at the end of 12th grade as young adults, and not as adolescents. And so I'm trying desperately to find the way to maintain our structure, and at the same time enable them to leave as young adults…And that's the problem that I'm having, I don't know how to do that. (Golann, 2013, p. 115)

According to Golann's (2015) research, many students struggle with gaining independence and identity in charter schools as well. One student in the aforementioned principal's school observed that the students would not know what to do if the structure was loosened, because they had never experienced school with fewer constraints than the charter model to which they were accustomed. It is clear that the strict charter model has removed the "warmth," in the words of the principal, and "deadened their spirits." This should not be the consequence of any school, charter or non-charter. This also leads to questions of how student behavior may also be reflective of socioeconomic conditions in a neighborhood faced with challenges such as poverty, violence, police brutality, and other forms of trauma. Behavior reflects systems, not the people in the community. To examine behavior, we must understand institutional racism through policies such as redlining, food deserts, and limited access to healthcare (Ponds, 2013). Golann (2015) suggested that students receive more opportunities for activities to develop assertiveness, reasoning skills, and initiative through student-led activities and advisories. KIPP schools have introduced character-building into their curriculum, and while this is a positive move, Golann asserted that students learn more from social interactions and rules than "lessons on character" (p. 116). Students are more than test scores, and strong schools will need to incorporate a social-emotional curriculum to help students grow holistically, as well as learn to apply the material into their everyday lives.

With this in mind, it is clear that in *Teach Like a Champion* (Lemov, 2010, 2015) obedience is the primary focus, not character. From reading the text, it is difficult to assert how much of a factor student choice is at Uncommon

Schools. Additionally, there do not appear to be any restorative justice practices. Golann (2015) argued that while the intense disciplinary actions of charter schools may produce some results, it is not clear that they are necessary.The schools do not mention behavioral interventions, restorative justice, or other alternative practices.

However, to better analyze Lemov's work, we need to better understand where his schools stand. It is hard to tell from videos, because students may behave differently when being recorded. *Teach Like a Champion* emphasizes "warm/strict," which is when the teacher is "both warm and strict at the same time, to send a message of high expectations, caring, and respect" (Lemov, 2015, p. 438). Being warm and strict simultaneously are not mutually exclusive. Teachers can have extremely high expectations with smooth-running classrooms with the enforcement of consequences while students are still able to feel comfortable, at ease, and that their teacher is approachable.

Indeed, this is a powerful concept: conveying clear expectations, holding students accountable without being an authoritarian, and emphasizing care for others. Lemov (2015) describes the technique with the following components: "Explain to students why you're doing what you're doing...Distinguish between behavior and people...Demonstrate the consequences are temporary...Use warm nonverbal behavior" (pp. 438–439). Golann (2015) used this exact term and suggested that these "no-excuses schools" should train their teachers in being warm/strict. She also suggested analyzing which specific parts of discipline are correlated with achievement as well as student engagement. Warm/strict should be multifaceted, expressing intrinsic motivation, willingness to participate, teacher and student buy-in, student retention, student engagement, and attitudes toward school.

Therefore, it appears that warm/strict is one technique that Lemov may have gotten right, but what forms should it take in a charter school? Golann (2015) suggested alternatives to extreme strictness, and called for schools to use flexible disciplinary methods. Golann (2015) also claimed that giving students more choices might change their perception of what they believe to be unfair school rules. Again, there is no evidence that these practices exist at Uncommon Schools. Despite observations that the warm/strict style may be effective, teachers in many charter schools were often seen as too authoritarian in disciplining their students. This is a common complaint of charter school parents, as highlighted by Bruhn (2014), who interviewed mothers who explained that they had been lured to charter schools based on false promises but were shocked at their children experiencing punitive consequences for minor misbehavior, rigid codes of discipline, and general unhappiness. The latter is not the goal of charter schools but has nevertheless become a consequence of some.

Additionally, Olsen (2019) demonstrated how several factors, including disciplinary incidents, can lead to lower teacher retention rates, particularly in rural "no excuses" charter schools. Other research demonstrated how teacher retention rates lead to stabilizing schools and can be improved in charter schools' unionization (Jabbar et al., 2020). Additionally, a 2016 study of Illinois charter schools asserted that improving teacher retention can lead to better school outcomes (White, 2016). Reform advocates such as Candal (2016) also asserted the importance of teacher retention for successful charter schools. In sum, charter advocates should be concerned with teacher retention rates and how disciplinary systems in their schools may affect those rates.

Finally, while little peer-reviewed research exists on Uncommon Schools, two recent Instagram pages, @_theuncommontruth, and @blackatuncommon have documented severe criticisms of racism and punitive discipline, both from student and staff perspectives. The following are all accounts from the @blackatuncommon page:

> For the first 6 weeks, kids had to be silent during lunch. After 6 weeks, kids could talk IF they earned talking privileges. In what world is lunch, one of the few times kids are allowed to be social, doing something meant to be social, eat lunch, become a privilege to talk. Why did kids have to earn the "right to speak." If kids spoke on the walk from class to lunch, they either got detention or a silent table. A silent table meant you could [not] speak the entire lunch period. Teachers who "let kids slide and speak" were immediately pulled to the side and forced to give a consequence or force kids to go to the silent table. It was racist, disgusting and unacceptable. (September 1, 2020)

> The dollar system reveals the worst parts of capitalism and creates an incredibly toxic classroom culture. Having a financial-based punishment/incentive disciplinary system is problematic in all settings, but especially problematic and downright cruel in spaces where poverty rates are high due to #racism #inequity #whitesupremacy. Try #restorativepractices. (July 2, 2020)

> I remember my sixth-grade year at RPC. The very first day I had to serve detention because I didn't have the sweater vest that we were supposed to wear with our uniform. My mom forgot to buy me one and despite explaining this to the dean and assuring him that I'd have one the next day, he said he didn't care and that it was my job to look "presentable" before I stepped foot into the building. (July 30, 2020)

> I am the mother of a former high schooler . . . my daughter was an exemplary student and always stayed on task . . . I later found out . . . in her 11th-grade year . . . that the pressure placed upon the black children there is tremendous . . . the school over polices the students and makes the actual good kids feel as if they are never good enough . . . this school will sell parents a false dream of higher quality education . . . while making the children feel imprisoned with subtle racism . . . I took my daughter out . . . and regret not doing it earlier. (June 27, 2020)

I have been in the U Schools system since 5th grade. I have come home cry-
ing and hated my school, and my life, at some points. A lot of my issues with
anxiety and fear of authority trace back to 5th grade. When I didn't have a
book during silent breakfast and got yelled at. When I dropped a clicker on
the floor or forgot my math notebook and got an "auto" while another girl
did not because she was better at math than me. I remember a math teacher
also telling us that [s]he believed the death penalty was a version of natural
selection. I remember having to stand for eight hours straight with no lunch
breaks for 8 years of my life. Standing [in] silence. Not being able to use the
bathroom so you hold your pee till it hurts in class. I can't even begin to com-
prehend the effect this had on my mental well-being. (July 7, 2020)

At EG, I had this white teacher that used to say how scary it was to teach black
kids and how we scare her! There was this dance teacher she used to call
students bums and curse them out and belittle them but when kids spoke up
nothing happened. (July 2, 2020)

I worked at RPLS for two years as a special education teacher. They hated
me. I always spoke up about how terribly they handled the special education
services and how they were disproportionately targeting kids with disabilities.
In both of my years, I received three letters of clarity, outlining how I was
"unprofessional" and "insubordinate." They tried to fire me numerous times.
I used to think something was wrong with me, but no they just did not like
people challenging their systems. I was asked for my opinion by the DSP and I
didn't like her idea and told her. She reported me to the DOO and principal
because she was offended. I was painted as the angry black woman within my
first month there. Everything I said was used against me. I told my DOO that
they were creating a "rap sheet" against me like I was a criminal. He was silent
because he knew that's exactly what was happening. My first INC loved me
and she was my saving grace. She battled for me and fought for me and called
LT on their crap. They pushed her out (this is a theme at Uncommon if you
know, you know) so I had nobody in my second year. We got new leadership
in year 2 so it was slightly better, but not much. The principal wants to be the
only voice for black women and attempts to silence other voices, especially
black women. I was subjected to the same treatment as year 1, but this time
I knew how to navigate the system. In year 1, I got the big boss involved and
reported and flagged everything to her so they couldn't bully me. No one was
holding LT accountable, so I had to. LT had a chip on their shoulder and they
could not predict my next move. It scared them so they kept giving me an unprofessional letter in an attempt to scare me into silence. It didn't work. I kept
advocating for my babies. I was willing and ready to lose my job doing what
was right. I had a 2nd job ready if and when they were to fire me. That's not
healthy. Always living on the edge like the means for your livelihood could be
taken from you over some asinine accusation that you're unprofessional when
in reality you are following IDEA and DESE's recommendations. I told our
principal that we were directly contributing to the school to prison pipeline
with our discipline policies and that I could not be complicit in that system
any longer. I still talk to my kiddos and their families. We were so close and I

miss them dearly. I do not miss that school and feel bad for kids subjected to that torment. I am proud of myself for not falling victim to the system and doing something different for kids. Even if the LT hated me for it. (July 2, 2020)

While these complaints are not peer-reviewed, it is important to listen to the voices of those implementing and impacting the techniques. These complaints are stunning and highlight the severe racial and disciplinary problems at Uncommon Schools, of which the whole foundation is Lemov's work.

CONCLUSION

While Lemovian teaching techniques have gained immense popularity, it is clear that they will not be successful with all students. As demonstrated in my literature review, Doug Lemov's teaching techniques are intrinsically problematic, as they do not address the needs of the most marginalized students. Colorblindness in schools does not address the experiences of students' lives. Many students may need a culturally-responsive approach. In considering what is successful, educators must confront the reality of trauma. We know that this has not been the case for the majority of schools due to disproportionate suspensions and expulsions for Black and Latinx students. Instead, we need more equitable approaches and root cause analysis, such as through multi-tiered systems of support. Teacher preparation programs must address systemic racism and its effects on not only the public education system but on Black and Latinx communities as well. Lemov did not address any of these crucial discussion points, nor did he supplement his techniques with peer-reviewed research, instead relying on test scores to back up his techniques. Yet Carnevale et al. (2019) shows how high-achieving early-childhood students born from into the lowest quartile of socioeconomic status have a significantly less chance of having a college education than children in the top quartile, demonstrating that test scores do not demonstrate mastery, but more so how to take a test and navigate a complex system. It is clear that while test scores are not irrelevant, they may not accurately demonstrate a student's intellectual capabilities, let alone whether teaching techniques benefitted them.

Lemov's work heavily promotes charter schools as well as the need to destroy the "achievement gap." This research addressed the problems in these arguments. First, charter schools have more autonomy to suspend or expel students that may not conform to strict, punitive behavioral expectations, such as Lemov's. This shows the techniques cannot work for all students in all schools. Secondly, Lemov did not support the validity of his techniques with any peer-reviewed research. Instead, he discussed closing the achievement gap and standardized test scores. As demonstrated in my research, standardized testing is problematic as is the notion of the achievement gap. The achievement depth is a better analysis as it addresses socioeconomic inequities. Thus, there is no conclusive proof that Lemovian techniques can be successful, let alone for the most marginalized students, including those with high behavioral needs.

The following chapter explores the next part of this study, in which the reader will learn about the methodology for assessing the effectiveness of Lemovian techniques. Teachers who had experience teaching in both charter and non-charter public schools completed a survey on the effectiveness of Lemov's techniques with their students. They were asked to evaluate Lemovian techniques, as well as their effectiveness on different tiers of students, as viewed through the framework of MTSS. Afterward, interviews were administered, and the results illuminated several topics, including teacher burnout, the techniques' lack of authenticity, and racial undercurrents of control in charter schools. The data presented are used to evaluate the effectiveness of Lemovian techniques and suggest more equitable approaches to better support Black and Latinx students.

REFERENCES

Alexander, N. N. (2016). Identity work in the classrooms: Successful learning in urban schools. *Multicultural Perspectives, 18*(4), 237–239. https://doi-org.neiulibrary.idm.oclc.org/10.1080/15210960.2016.1228350

Altonji, J. G., Huang, C.-I., & Taber, C. R. (2010). *Estimating the cream skimming effect of school choice* (NBER Working Paper No. 16579). https://www.nber.org/papers/w16579

Bell, D. A. (1980). Brown v. Board of Education and the interest convergence dilemma. *Harvard Law Review, 93*(3), 518–533.

Belser, C. T., Shillingford, M. A., & Joe, J. R. (2016). The ASCA model and a multi-tiered system of supports: A framework to support students of color with problem behavior. *Professional Counselor, 6*(3), 251–262.

Berger, E. (2019). Multi-tiered approaches to trauma-informed care in schools: A systematic review. *School Mental Health, 11*(4), 650–664.

Bernstein, N. (2014). *Burning down the house: The end of Juvenile prison*. The New Press.

blackatuncommon. [@blackatuncommon]. 2020. [Photographs]. Instagram. https://www.instagram.com/blackatuncommon/?hl=en

Bruhn, M. (2014). Challenging "waiting for superman." *Phi Delta Kappan, 95*(5), 47–51.

Candal, C. S. (2015). *Great teachers   are not born, they are made: Case study evidence from Massachusetts charters* (White Paper No. 130). Pioneer Institute for Public Policy Research. https://eric.ed.gov/?id=ED565732

Caraballo, L., Martinez, D. C., Paris, D., & Alim, H. S. (2020). Culturally sustaining pedagogies in the current moment: A conversation with Django Paris and H.

Samy Alim. *Journal of Adolescent & Adult Literacy, 63*(6), 697–701. https://doi
.org.neiulibrary.idm.oclc.org/10.1002/jaal.1059

Carmichael, D., Whitten, G., & Voloudakis, M. (2005). *Study of minority over-represen-
tation in the Texas Juvenile Justice System: Final report.* College Station, TX: Public
Policy Research Institute, Texas A&M University.

Carnevale, A. P., Fasules, M. L., Quinn, M. C., & Campbell, K. P. (2019a). *Born to win,
schooled to lose: Why equally talented students don't get equal chances to be all they can
be.* Georgetown University Center on Education and the Workforce. https://
1gyhoq479ufd3yna29x7ubjnwpengine.netdna-ssl.com/wp-content/uploads/
FR-Born_to_win-schooled_to_lose.pdf.

Carter, R. T. (2007). Racism & psychological and emotional injury: Recognizing and
assessing race-based traumatic stress. *The Counseling Psychologist, 35*(13), 13–
105. https://journals.sagepub.com/doi/abs/10.1177/0011000006292033

California Department of Education. (2018). *Multi tiered systems.* http://www.pent.
ca.gov/mtss.html

Coates, T. N. (2014). The case for reparations (Cover story). *Atlantic, 313*(5), 54–
71. https://www.theatlantic.com/magazine/archive/2014/06/the-case-for
-reparations/361631/

Cowan Pitre, C. (2014). Improving African American student outcomes: Understanding educational achievement and strategies to close opportunity gaps.
Western Journal of Black Studies, 38(4), 209–217. https://static1.squarespace
.com/static/52cf1070e4b048ae22d972b2/t/58b82d46a5790a60fdfce8eb/
1488465244758/Improving+African+American+Student+Outcomes+%28201
4%29.pdf

Darling-Hammond, L. (2010). *The flat world and education: How America's commitment
to equity will determine our future.* Teachers College.

Day-Vines, N. L., & Day-Hairston, B. O. (2005). Culturally congruent strategies for
addressing the behavioral needs of urban, African American male adolescents. *Professional School Counseling, 8*(3), 236–243.

DeAngelis, C. A., & Shakeel, M. D. (2017). Who is more free? A comparison of
the decision-making of private and public school principals. *Journal of School
Choice, 11*(3), 442–457, https://doi.org/10.1080/15582159.2017.1345235

Delgado R. (1989). Storytelling for oppositionalists and others: A plea for narrative. *Michigan Law Review, 87*(8), 2411–2441. https://www.jstor.org/stable/
1289308?seq=1

Delgado, R., & Stefancic, J. (2012). *Critical Race Theory: An introduction.* New York
University Press.

Dixson, A. D., & Ladson-Billings, G. (2017). Harambee: Pulling it all together. *Teachers College Record, 119*(1), 1–6. https://experts.illinois.edu/en/publications/
harambee-pulling-it-all-together-2

Egeberg, H. M., McConney, A., & Price, A. (2016). Classroom management and
national professional standards for teachers: A review of the literature on theory and practice. *Australian Journal of Teacher Education, 41*(7), 1–19. http://
ro.ecu.edu.au/ajte/vol41/iss7/1

Evnitskaya, N., & Berger, E. (2017). Learners' multimodal displays of willingness to
participate in classroom interaction in the L2 and CLIL contexts. *Classroom*

Discourse, 8(1), 71–94. https://www.tandfonline.com/doi/abs/10.1080/1946 3014.2016.1272062

Fallon, L., O'Keefe, B., & Sugai, G. (2012). Consideration of culture and context in school-wide positive behavior support: A review of current literature. *Journal of Positive Behavior Interventions, 14*(4), 209–219.

Fernandes, R., & Menezes-Filho, N. (2020). Charter schools, equity and efficiency in public education. *Education Economics, 28*(3), 275–290. https://www.tandfonline .com/doi/abs/10.1080/09645292.2020.1725959

Flouri, E., & Midouhas, E. (2016). School composition, family poverty and child behaviour. *Social Psychiatry & Psychiatric Epidemiology, 51*(6), 817–826. https:// link.springer.com/article/10.1007/s00127-016-1206-7

Fowler, D. (2011). School discipline feeds the pipeline to prison. *Phi Delta Kappan, 93*(2), 14–19. https://journals.sagepub.com/doi/abs/10.1177/00317217110 9300204

Fronius, T., Persson, H., Guckenburg, S., Hurley, N., & Petrosino, A. (2016). *Restorative justice in U.S. schools: A research review.* WestEd Justice and Prevention Research Center. https://eric.ed.gov/?id=ED596786

Grace, J. E., & Nelson, S. L. (2019). "Tryin' to survive": Black male students' understandings of the role of race and racism in the school-to-prison pipeline. *Leadership and Policy in Schools, 18*(4), 664–680.

Green, E. (2010, March 2). Building a better teacher. *The New York Times.* https:// www.nytimes.com/2010/03/07/magazine/07Teachers-t.html

Green, A. L., Maynard, D. K., & Stegenga, S. M. (2018). Common misconceptions of suspension: Ideas and alternatives for school leaders. *Psychology in the Schools, 55*(4), 419–428.

Gregory, A., Skiba, R., & Noguera, P. (2010). The achievement gap and the discipline gap: Two sides of the same coin? *Educational Researcher, 39*(1), 59–68. https://www.researchgate.net/publication/250183674_The_Achievement_ Gap_and_the_Discipline_Gap_Two_Sides_of_the_Same_Coin

Golann, J. W. (2015). The paradox of success at a no-excuses school. *Sociology of Education, 88*(2), 103–119. https://www.ncbi.nlm.nih.gov/pmc/articles/ PMC4877134/

Harris, C. (1993). Whiteness as property. *Harvard Law Review, 106*(8), 1707–1791. https://www.jstor.org/stable/1341787?seq=1

Holmes, V. R. (2017). *To Educate All Children (TEACH): Building effective teacher classroom management strategies in HISD schools, 2016–2017: Research Educational Program report.* Houston Independent School District. https://eric.ed.gov/ ?id=ED596673

Iyengar, N., Lewis-LaMonica, K., & Perigo, M. (2017). *The AUSL way: Moving from "good" to "truly excellent."* Bridgespan Group. https://eric.ed.gov/?id=ED582428

Jabbar, H., Chanin, J., Haynes, J., & Slaughter, S. (2020). Teacher power and the politics of union organizing in the charter sector. *Educational Policy, 34*(1), 211–238. https://journals.sagepub.com/doi/abs/10.1177/0895904819881776

Karanxha, Z. (2013). When the "dream" turns into a nightmare: Life and death of Voyager Charter School. *Educational Administration Quarterly, 49*(4), 576–609.

Kendall, F. (2012). *Understanding White privilege: Creating pathways to authentic relationships across race.* Routledge.

Kendi, I. X. (2019). *How to be an antiracist.* One World.

Kim, H., & Connelly, J. (2019). Preservice teachers' multicultural attitudes, intercultural sensitivity, and their multicultural teaching efficacy. *Educational Research Quarterly, 42*(4), 3–20.

Ladson-Billings, G. (2006). From the achievement gap to the education debt: Understanding achievement in U.S. schools. *Educational Researcher, 35*(7), 3–12. https://thrive.arizona.edu/sites/default/files/From%20the%20Achievement%20Gap%20to%20the%20Education%20Debt_Understanding%20Achievement%20in%20US%20Schools.pdf

Ladson-Billings, G. (2016). And then there is this thing called the curriculum: Organization, imagination, and mind. *Educational Researcher, 45*(2), 100–104. https://journals.sagepub.com/doi/10.3102/0013189X16639042

Lemov, D. (2010). *Teach like a champion: 49 techniques that put students on the path to college.* Joey Bass.

Lemov, D. (2015). *Teach like a champion 2.0: 62 techniques that put students on the path to college.* Joey Bass.

Marcucci, O. (2020). Implicit bias in the era of social desirability: Understanding antiblackness in rehabilitative and punitive school discipline. *Urban Review: Issues and Ideas in Public Education, 52*(1), 47–74.

McDonald, T. (2013). *Classroom management: Engaging students in learning* (2nd ed.). Oxford University Press.

Miron, G., & Nelson, C. (2002). *What's public about charter schools? Lessons learned about choice and accountability.* Corwin Press. https://eric.ed.gov/?id=ED467228

Mills, C. (1997). *The racial contract.* Cornell University Press.

Milner, H. R. (2012). Challenges in teacher education for urban education. *Urban Education, 47*(4), 700–705. https://doi-org.neiulibrary.idm.oclc.org/10.1177/0042085912452098

Munter, C., & Haines, C. (2019). "Students get what flows downward": District leaders' rationalizations of the standardized testing of children. *Educational Forum, 83*(2), 160–180. https://eric.ed.gov/?id=EJ1213453

Olsen, J. (2019). *An exploration of teacher retention in rural no excuse charter schools in the United States.* https://cdr.lib.unc.edu/concern/dissertations/qj72pc839

O'Neill, P. (2019). *Student discipline best practices for charter schools to employ.* National Center for Special Education in Charter Schools. https://eric.ed.gov/?id=ED601998

Osher, D., Moroney, D., & Williamson, S. (2018). *Creating safe, equitable, engaging schools: A comprehensive, evidence-based approach to supporting students.* Harvard Education Press.

Ponds, K. T. (2013). The trauma of racism: America's original Sin. *Reclaiming Children & Youth, 22*(2), 22–24. https://eric.ed.gov/?id=EJ1030317

Rozek, C. S., Hanselman, P., Feldman, R. C., Quast, E. A., Crawford, E. P., & Borman, G. D. (2015). *Inside the black box of self-affirmation: Which parts of affirmation exercises are critical for treatment efficacy?* Society for Research on Educational Effectiveness. https://eric.ed.gov/?id=ED562294

Skiba, R. J. (2014). The failure of zero tolerance. *Reclaiming Children and Youth, 22*(3), 27–33. https://eric.ed.gov/?id=EJ1038609

Skiba, R. J., Michael, R. S., Nardo, A. C., & Peterson, R. L. (2002). The color of discipline: Sources of racial and gender disproportionality in school punishment. *The Urban Review, 34*(4), 317–342.

Skinner, B. F. (1957). *Verbal behavior*. Appleton-Century-Crofts. https://psycnet.apa .org/record/2006-20887-000

Stovall, D. (2016). Out of adolescence and into adulthood. *Urban Education, 51*(3), 274–286. https://doi-org.neiulibrary.idm.oclc.org/10.1177/0042085915618718

Special Education Programs. (2003). *Identifying and treating attention deficit hyperactivity disorder: A resource for school and home, 2003*. American Institutes for Research. https://eric.ed.gov/?id=ED477481

Thompson, J. (2016). Eliminating zero tolerance policies in schools: Miami-Dade County Public Schools' approach. *Brigham Young University Education & Law Journal, 2016*(2), 325–349.

UncommonTruth. [@_theuncommontruth]. 2020. [Photographs]. Instragram. https:// www.instagram.com/_theuncommontruth/?hl=en

U.S. Department of Education, Office of Civil Rights. (2014). *Civil Rights data collection: Data snapshot: School discipline* (Issue Brief No. 1). https://ocrdata.ed .gov/assets/downloads/CRDC-School-Discipline-Snapshot.pdf

Verstegen, D. A. (2015). On doing an analysis of equity and closing the opportunity gap. *Education Policy Analysis Archives, 23*(41), n41.

Weinstein, C., Curran, M., & Tomlinson-Clarke, S. (2003). Culturally responsive classroom management: Awareness into action. *Theory Into Practice, 42*(4), 269–276. https://doi.org/10.1207/s15430421tip4204_2

White, B. R. (2016). *Laboratories of reform? Human resource management strategies in Illinois charter schools* (Policy Research: IERC 2016-1). Illinois Education Research Council. https://eric.ed.gov/?id=ED564421

Wilson, M. A. F., Yull, D. G., & Massey, S. G. (2020). Race and the politics of educational exclusion: Explaining the persistence of disproportionate disciplinary practices in an urban school district. *Race, Ethnicity and Education, 23*(1), 134–157. https://www.tandfonline.com/doi/abs/10.1080/13613324.2018.15 11535?journalCode=cree20

Woodworth, J. L., & Raymond, M. E. (2013). *Charter school growth and replication*. http://www.afscmeinfocenter.org/privatizationupdate/2013/03/charter -school-growth-and-replication.htm#.YjELOhBKhH1

Wormeli, R. (2016). Let's talk about racism in schools. *Educational Leadership, 74*(3), 16–22. http://www.ascd.org/publications/educational-leadership/nov16/vol74/ num03/Let's-Talk-about-Racism-in-Schools.aspx

CHAPTER 8

ASSESSING LEMOVIAN TECHNIQUES FOR SUPPORTING TRADITIONALLY MARGINALIZED STUDENTS AND SUGGESTIONS FOR MORE EQUITABLE PRACTICES IN SCHOOLS TO SUPPORT BLACK AND LATINX STUDENTS

Mike Friedberg
Northeastern Illinois University

Real education should consist of drawing the goodness and the best out of our own students.

—Cesar Chavez

Economic, Political and Legal Solutions to Critical Issues in Urban Education and Implications for Teacher Preparation
pages 137–161

This chapter studies teaching techniques popularized in *Teach Like a Champion* (Lemov, 2010, 2015). This research focuses on former charter school teachers who have applied (or attempted to apply) Lemovian techniques to students with high behavioral interventions in non-charter public schools. (For this research, we identify behavioral interventions through the MTSS framework [Belser et al., 2016].) The purpose is to evaluate the effectiveness (or lack thereof) of Lemovian techniques with all students in multiple learning environments. Because public charter schools intrinsically have more autonomy than non-charter public schools, it may be easier for the former to expel students who do not conform to their behavioral norms. This research seeks to determine if Lemovian techniques can successfully work in non-charter urban (Milner, 2012) public schools, with some scholars such as Gross (2016) documenting how charters have higher rates of expulsion over their non-charter counterparts, as well as best practices to reduce these inequities. In this chapter, "urban" is based on Milner's definition based on per capita population, not a race.

While this study contributes to the body of research on the effectiveness of Lemovian techniques found in the book *Teach Like a Champion* (Lemove, 2010, 2015), it could be improved by citing and referencing previous research. However, little peer-reviewed study on this teaching style exists. This study contributes to research on the effectiveness of these techniques. Another limitation present in this study was the sample size. Twenty participants are too small a sample to be able to present transferrable findings. Larger samples should be used in future studies.

Additionally, the study was completed without the help of Doug Lemov. There were attempts to contact Lemov for further clarification and misconceptions around the techniques, but they were not successful. Again, the intent of this study was rooted in objectivity with no goal of portraying his work either positively or negatively. An interview with Lemov could have clarified any misunderstandings. Future studies should involve the author of *Teach Like a Champion* (Lemov, 2010, 2015) in some way. They should also involve its critics, including former students and faculty of Uncommon Schools.

Finally, hearing from the perspectives of teachers in charter schools would be beneficial as well, particularly those who have made a conscious decision to stay in a charter school over several years. The original study was based on observing teachers who had been trained in Lemovian techniques applying them to Tier 2 and Tier 3 students and analyzing the effectiveness of these techniques. While obtaining informed consent from parents could present obstacles, it could help in identifying the effectiveness of teaching techniques. This type of study could provide more significant analysis and a more accurate perspective on supporting students with strong behavioral needs. Future research should also involve school board members and those in higher positions of authority. Multiple perspectives will provide better insights into this work.

How do teachers at charter schools and traditional public schools perceive and compare classroom management techniques for students with varying levels of behavioral needs? This was the guiding research question. For example, can a student with behavioral needs who refuses to commit to discipline techniques in *Teach Like a Champion* (Lemov, 2010, 2015) be successful in a non-charter public school? Could the behavior needs that exist in certain charter schools be because Lemovian techniques are implemented systemically and arguably too "one size fits all," or could it be due to other factors, such as high staff turnover rates? These secondary questions are within the framework of my guiding research question and what I sought to understand. Teachers who left charter schools to work in non-charter public schools were selected to participate to determine whether Lemovian techniques can work in varied environments.

To obtain the most accurate perspective, this study used a mixed-methods design using a quantitative survey and in-depth interviews. Twenty total participants completed the survey, and five of those participants also participated in a follow-up interview. The research participants include some of my current and former coworkers, as well as individuals identified through acquaintances in the education field. They were recruited either in person or through direct messaging after responding to a public social media post. The explanatory sequential research design was utilized (Creswell, 2015, p. 545).

RATIONALE

The rationale for using this form of mixed-methods research lies in the understanding that additional interviews could help further clarify the data extrapolated from the surveys. The survey included an initial set of questions with follow-up questions to be issued as necessary based on responses. In response to survey data analysis, I selected participants to interview so that they could clarify any possible misconceptions or false correlations. The purpose of asking my questions is centered on objectivity, as there is no intention of portraying Lemov in a positive or negative light.

METHODOLOGY

Background of Participants

All of the participants previously taught in charter schools and now teach in non-charter public schools within the Chicago Public Schools school district. All of the participants worked in charter schools that heavily promoted Lemov's work, and were all located on the south side of Chicago. All of the charter schools promoted Lemovian techniques as a means of student discipline. The purpose of interviewing these subjects was to see if teachers believed that these techniques could successfully work in noncharter public schools with Tier 2 and Tier 3 students. The findings of this study extrapolated data that can be used to inform the preparation of teachers in urban classrooms and better serve the needs of all students.

Administrative Procedures

The survey was administered via Google Forms, and all of the interviews were completed in person at a private location most convenient to the participant. All survey participants agreed to the terms of the consent form via Google Forms. All interview participants signed a paper copy of an additional consent form. Descriptive statistics were used to analyze the Likert scale surveys. The researcher is not a statistician and is limited in knowledge and training of more advanced methodology.

FINDINGS

Survey Findings

Twenty teachers completed the survey, the vast majority of them concluded that Lemovian techniques were ineffective, disproportionately so with Tier 2 and Tier 3 students.

The first set of questions in the survey assessed charter schools. First, teachers were asked about Tier 1 students. Again, these students should comprise about 80% of the classroom according to the MTSS framework (Belser et al., 2016) and should be students who generally do not have difficulty with listening and following teacher instructions. When asked about Tier 1 students, 50% of participants were neutral in stating the effectiveness of Lemov's techniques, while 40% either disagreed or strongly disagreed with their effectiveness for charter school students. When the teachers were asked about the effectiveness of the techniques with Tier 2 students, the results shifted dramatically, with 90% stating that they either disagreed or strongly disagreed that the techniques were effective. When presented with the statement that the techniques were effective with Tier 3 students, 90% of participants indicated that they either disagreed or strongly disagreed. Of this 90%, 70% strongly disagreed with the statement, as opposed to only 40% of the responses on the statement assessing Tier 2 students.

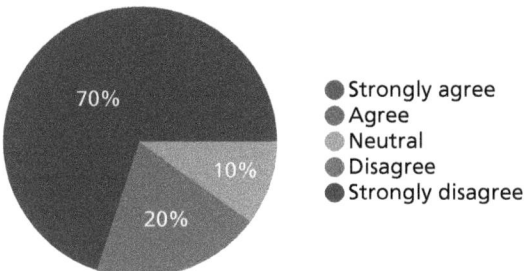

Figure 8.1 Statement: "Teach like a Champion behavioral techniques were effective for Tier 2 (approximately 5%) students at your previous charter school." (This question is based on the Likert scale. Please indicate the choice that best represents your opinion.)

The second portion of the survey presented participants with statements assessing the Lemovian techniques' effectiveness for students in their current non-charter public school. As illustrated in Figure 8.1, teachers had a variety of opinions on the effectiveness of the techniques with Tier 1 students in their current non-charter public schools. 20% were neutral on the statement that they were effective, while 40% strongly disagreed and 40% agreed. Figures 8.2 and 8.3 show similar results to how teachers perceive the lack of effectiveness of these techniques with Tier 2 and Tier 3 students. Figure 8.2 shows that 80% of participants either disagreed or strongly disagreed with the statement that the techniques could be effective with Tier 2 students in their current non-charter public schools, while only 10% agreed with the statement. Figure 8.3 applies the same statement to Tier 3 students, with 90% either disagreeing or strongly disagreeing with the statement, 60% of whom strongly disagreed. Notably, when asked about Tier 2 students, 10%

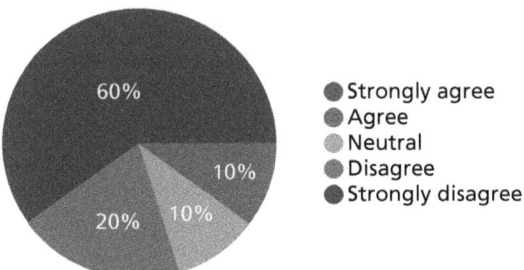

Figure 8.2 Statement: "*Teach like a Champion* behavioral techniques were effective for Tier 2 (approximately 80%) students at your current non-charter school." (This question is based on the Likert scale. Please indicate the choice that best represents your opinion.)

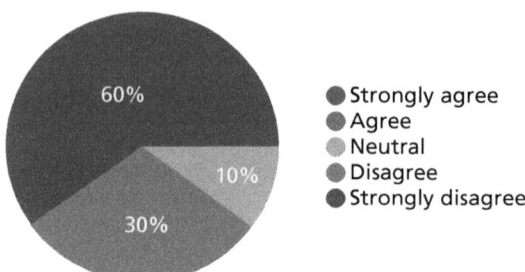

Figure 8.3 Statement: "Teach like a Champion behavioral techniques were effective for Tier 3 (approximately 5%) students at your current non-charter school." (This question is based on the Likert scale. Please indicate the choice that best represents your opinion.)

of participants were neutral to the statement and 10% agreed. When asked about Tier 3 students, 30% of participants stated that they disagreed with the statement (as identified in Figure 8.3), as opposed to 20% (as identified in Figure 8.2). Without further statistical analysis, this confirms the hypothesis that the Lemovian techniques could not be equally successful with Tier 2 and Tier 3 students. What is particularly illuminating is that the participants did not believe that the techniques could work with these students, even in charter environments. However, it should also be acknowledged that a significant number of participants did believe that the techniques could work with Tier 1 students. (10% of teachers "agreed" that the techniques could work with Tier 1 students in charter schools, and 40% of teachers "agreed" that the techniques could work with Tier 1 students in non-charter public schools.)

Conclusively, the majority of participants believed that Lemovian techniques could not be effective with Tier 2 and Tier 3 students in both charter and non-charter schools, which confirms the hypothesis that Lemovian techniques will not be effective with Tier 2 and Tier 3 students in non-charter public schools. Particularly eye-opening was how the participants also believed that these techniques could not be effective in non-charter public schools. Since these schools have less autonomy, it can be more difficult to suspend or expel a student if they do not conform to disciplinary expectations, leading to increasingly punitive disciplinary policies that have come under scrutiny (Zubrzycki et al., 2013). Participants expressed skepticism of Lemovian techniques with Tier 2 and Tier 3 students, in any environment.

Interview Findings

Interview questions were created after analyzing the survey results. An explanatory sequential research design was the research methodology used

(Creswell, 2015). This is a form of mixed methods research, where qualitative data is collected in one phase, and qualitative in a second. The purpose was to extrapolate data beyond the survey and to further rule out possible false assertions based on only quantitative data, which can have limitations. The interviews were coded for repetitive phrases and terminology. Three dominant themes emerged: rigidity in discipline systems in schools (with a focus on punitive disciplinary practices), teacher burnout and turnover rate, and racial implications in school disciplinary practices. Five participants, who are all referred to by pseudonyms, participated in face to face interviews.

Camille is a high school science teacher and ESL coordinator. She was born in Mexico City and came to the United States when she was 12. She is 49 years old and has taught for 16 years, 12 of those at her current school. Within her 4 other years of teaching, 1 was spent at a charter school and the other 3 were at non-charter public schools. She has a degree making her eligible to become an administrator but has not chosen to pursue it yet. She describes her classroom as an "invitation to inquiry." Camille has also worked with Chicago Public Schools in discussing the implementation of new standards into the scope and sequence for high school science teachers.

Ariana is a 28-year-old White woman who has been teaching for 6 years, 2 of them at charters. She teaches reading, writing, and social studies. She was a founding member of a charter school campus, which she left after 1 year. She has a strong belief in content literacy and works to promote "horizontal alignment," where teachers across a particular grade level collaborate on curriculum. For example, if students are learning about the industrial revolution in social studies, they might learn about its environmental consequences in science class. Ariana is also the winner of a Golden Apple award for excellence in teaching. She is a researcher and has published several studies, including one on how teachers should use pedagogy for English language learners with African American students, including, but not limited to, code switching and contrastive analysis.

Gabriel is a former teacher who now works in the science department for a public school system in a large metropolitan area. He is a 42-year-old African American male who spent 10 years in the classroom, and spent the past 4 years working in the science department, completing tasks including planning curriculum, professional development, and more. Before teaching for 1 year in a charter school, he was an engineer. He started his career in education by working with a partnership where engineers collaborate with schools. He enjoyed it so much that he stayed in the classroom. Gabriel also writes for a prominent education website.

Sandra has been teaching for 28 years in public schools, including 1 year at a charter. She also spent 4 years teaching in private Catholic schools. She is a 65-year-old White woman who teaches seventh-grade social studies. She grew up on Chicago's South Side, in a predominantly African American neighborhood.

Finally, Dina has been teaching for 16 years, including 2 years at a charter. She is a 49-year-old Latina who was born in the United States, while both of her parents were from Mexico. She has taught language arts and science. She describes herself as a "fighter for bilingual education and English language learners."

To know the demographics of students at the participants' schools, the researcher compiled the mean percentages of racial groups for both the previous charter schools where the participants had taught, as well as their current schools. In both school groups, nearly all of the student population was classified as low income. For the charter schools, 64% of the student population was Black, 27% was Latinx, 5% was White, and 4% was other. For the non-charter schools, 59% of the student population was Black, 39% was Latinx, 1% was White, and 1% was other. While the study is not ethnographic, it is important to acknowledge the context of student populations. Lemov's techniques are predominantly used in schools where the majority of students are of color. This begs an important question; if they are so effective, why are they not used in more affluent, White schools? My research is not trying to determine this, but it is important to acknowledge the racial and socioeconomic conditions of the schools where his techniques are used.

ANALYSIS

Ineffectiveness of Techniques and Inequities

The present study sought to investigate the effectiveness of Lemovian techniques on students that had fallen under Tier 2 and Tier 3 under the system of MTSS (Belser et al., 2016). While interviewing the participants, it became clear that they overwhelmingly believed that the techniques were ineffective with Tier 2 and Tier 3 students, both in non-charter public schools as well as public charter schools. There were mixed responses regarding whether the techniques could work with Tier 1 students in both environments. The participants seemed to agree that the techniques had the potential to work, and their effects varied depending on the student. Respondents continuously echoed that a restorative approach is necessary, particularly for Tier 2 and Tier 3 students to be successful.

While B. F. Skinner's (1957) verbal behavior and operant conditioning were used as one perspective, the primary theoretical lens was MTSS (Belser et al., 2016). Skinner repeatedly asserted how stimuli draw responses, and students are motivated by external factors such as rewards and consequences. The teachers in this study expressed that external factors (in this case, the Lemovian techniques) could not be effective with students with high behavioral needs. Belser et al.'s (2016) research specifically described how punitive discipline policies in schools mirror those used in prisons, and how these practices have disproportionately and negatively affected Black and Latinx students. The results from this study's surveys and interviews show that these students can be best supported with targeted interventions as opposed to strict, broad behavioral systems. Additionally, while teacher retention rates were not the focus of this study, the topic was mentioned often. Gabriel stated that charter schools have an "unrealistic, unmanageable, unsustainable workload," a sentiment echoed by other participants. The results from the interviews reveal that not only do classroom management and discipline problems lead to teacher burnout, but the excessive workload can also lead to low teacher retention in charter schools.

Finally, the racial implications of *Teach Like a Champion* (Lemov, 2010, 2015) came up repeatedly. While there is little peer-reviewed research on Lemovian techniques, one powerful blog post mentions the problematic racial components of the text (Treuhaft-Ali, 2016), which connects directly to how the participants responded during the interviews. After transcribing and coding the interviews, three dominant themes emerged. They are addressed in the following sections.

Broad Rigid Systems

Based on the survey responses, Lemovian techniques are too broad. This was the essential question of the research and the hypothesis proved to be correct. Indeed, teachers emphatically asserted that these techniques were ineffective and not individualized enough. Participants stated that the structures of charter schools were too all-encompassing and not tailored enough individually, particularly for students with behavioral needs. In response to the question, "Did you feel like the techniques were too broad, too one size fits all, with Tier 2 and Tier 3 kids?" Diana went into detail discussing a specific technique from the text called, *positive framing*, although at her charter school it was referred to it as *positive narration*:

> Yes definitely, but I felt like that with all of them. I'm thinking of positive narration. It felt disingenuous. It was very objective and just naming what we saw as kids were working independently. So the room was at level zero and I would say, "Jon picked up his pencil, I see Sarah has started writing, I see Jaunice has started in her notebook." In no way shape or form is that something I would do naturally...I don't narrate the whole group. I complement kids individually or in small group work. I feel that that public expression of observation wasn't genuine. I felt like I was doing it just to co-op other kids to start to work and you're putting a kid on display in perhaps a way they wouldn't want

to be. And not only that but picking up your pencil isn't something to be complemented. It's the baseline of what you do in a classroom. I thought it was condescending for what they were able to do. So no, I don't do that now. Students name in my classroom what they're proud of. Students share with their partners what's working for them and then they share it publicly with the classroom if they volunteer to do so. There's a lot more self-reflection, as opposed to me reflecting on them.

Sandra also discussed how the rigidity of the techniques felt inauthentic. At her charter school they were referred to as *signature strategies*:

It seems like they wanted us to script instruction. I hated it. It felt too "anti-signature" to me. It felt inauthentic, it felt forced. Not that there wasn't something in them that was worthwhile and something to be gleaned from them. But to have to use it rotely, as if the way it was scripted was the way everyone speaks, but to think that not every single student is not going to respond to every single strategy is demeaning to the individuality of our students. And also doesn't leave teachers a lot of room to explore what works for them and start to develop their teacher identity authentically. I felt like I was not allowed to figure out who I would be in the classroom. It felt very prescribed and that wasn't what I wanted to do.

Interviewees not only conveyed how the techniques were too broad but also how the disciplinary structure led to an increase in suspensions. This comment in particular illustrates how Gabriel believed that disciplinary systems can function, and how his particular charter school had an increasing number of suspensions because of it:

In my charter school, we had real common views about what constitutes a discipline issue. I think that that was admin and teachers, that was something we spent a lot of time on. We had a system: "This is what students can expect in every classroom." You have a warning, you have another warning and then we take a break, a third time we call home, a fourth time you spend time in another classroom, and then if it continues or if it's egregious it's an admin counsel. It felt like we had a system. That system leads to more suspensions than in my current school.

Gabriel was then asked if systems put in place could be beneficial if they were more restorative-based. He responded, "I do. I think it was too one-size-fits-all, but I think there was something great about a shared expectation between students and teachers. We spent a lot of time as a team working on them." It appeared that he believed systems can work, but the punitive nature of his previous charter school was not conducive to students' social-emotional learning. When asked if the strategies could work for Tier 1 students, Gabriel asserted the following:

Sure—the strategies could work for Tier 1 students. I think there was something in all of them that works. I don't think they were pulled out of thin air as this terrible thing. It's not that they didn't work at all. They were inauthentic, felt very prescribed, and we weren't given the freedom to make sense of our personality and our style and for the kids in front of us. And to even realize that some don't work and some don't feel natural—"This one I like, this one doesn't work for me." But we'd have to focus on certain strategies for a week. And you'd try it and you'd think, "I hate it," but you'd still have to do it.

In looking at Skinner's operant conditioning and verbal behavior (1957) as a theoretical framework, Gabriel's response illustrates how forcing teachers to implement these techniques was not only not successful for the students, but did not motivate the teachers either. The extrinsic motivation of being required to implement Lemovian techniques was inauthentic and did not make him want to use them, particularly the ones he found unsuccessful.

Teacher Retention Rates in Charter Schools

The rate of teacher turnover came up repeatedly with all of the interviewees. While some of this was expected as, in order to participate in the survey, the participants were all required to have left charter schools to teach in non-charter public schools, the emphasis on why the instructors left was illuminating. None of the original scripted questions centered around teacher burnout, yet all participants emphasized this as a reason they stopped teaching in charter schools. Camille noted, "While I learned a lot about my pedagogical reasoning and theoretical frameworks, it was impossible to have a life. I barely made it through the first year. It was beyond excessive. While I'm grateful for everything I learned, it's just not anything that can work in the long term."

Sandra elaborated on this sentiment:

I think that the lifestyle that a charter school has a teacher doing what is impossible for someone that wants to have a family. I was working 12-plus hour days regularly, plus I was working 10-plus hours most days, and then had a 45-minute commute every day. We couldn't even get a dog. My husband, we both worked at the same charter school. My husband then went to a CPS school, I went to a CPS school. Then we got a dog, and then we started to plan a family. Because it's just not feasible—the hours, plus the intensity of it. There's a lot of middle management. There's a lot of documentation. We had to turn in a lesson plan every day into a folder. We had to have an assessment every day. We had a 5-day folder that we had to put stuff in, and then the principal would collect it. Next week you'd do the same thing. It's unrealistic to maintain that type of . . . It's just insane. I also know somebody whose father is on the board of a charter school, and I was talking to him about how unrealistic it is, so he was talking to one of the principals at one of the schools. And he flat out told him, "My plan is not to keep teachers for the long term. I plan to mold you into how I want you to be, and if you leave after 2 years, I'll find somebody else to mold."

This last statement was particularly stunning. Many CEOs of charter networks are from non-educational backgrounds, such as business, and it is quite feasible that many of them have a similar "factory" mindset that this CEO echoed. This is problematic because, with a staff that is constantly rotating, it is impossible to create a positive school culture and climate where teachers will want to work for long periods. In contrast, other charter school networks seek strongly to implement strong, positive, school cultures with low staff turnover.

When asked if the classroom management issues that arose at charter schools contributed to teacher turnover, all the participants answered affirmatively to varying degrees, from, "It's quite possible" to, "Definitely." They all stressed that the burnout was caused by excessive workload and that the demands were not sustainable for long term praxis. Diana discussed how the lack of educators on the board contributed to this problem:

> I was working for a school in a network that was continuously looking to expand. I thought they were expanding before they were achieving real stability and success. It just always felt a bit unstable. I didn't think they were that concerned about the turnover. I don't want to speculate, but it seemed that the people at the board level had no education experience. They were bankers and attorneys. Their lens was the bottom line and the data, but nothing else. Not the daily teaching and learning, which, in my experience, isn't always reflected in a standardized test. Without experience in a school, I don't think they realized the full impact of turnover—on collegial morale, on students' trust levels. I don't think they were very introspective on the results of that turnover. I think that they were not very pragmatic. "What will we do because there's this turnover?" was not a question they were asking. And similarly, they were hiring inexperienced teachers, or young people straight out of Teach for America (TFA), and they could pay them very little money. So I think that they wanted to not have a lot of experienced teachers. And that wasn't true for everyone, there was also real inequitable salary distribution, and I think some people realized that and they jumped ship because they wanted to support themselves and their family. There was a high turnover rate because there was instability. They did not have a very reflective lens why the turnover was happening. Their response wasn't to fix the reasons why, it was just to create a curriculum that would support the turnover, so that was no longer enable for me.

Camille directly cited *Teach Like a Champion* (Lemov, 2010, 2015) and their techniques as her reason for leaving, particularly as the book became more popularized throughout the charter network:

I left the charter because they were moving away from the workshop approach to the one-size-fits-all model. Previously, students had a ton of time to collaborate and do independent practice and think for themselves, rather than "SLANT now," "Teacher does this—I do/We do/You do," "Do Now," "Back to me"—we didn't do any of that. I heard the whispers that it was gonna come to pass. Lemov started to be on all the shelves of the resource rooms throughout the network. I got out before I had to deal with that again.

Ariana added that she not only left because of the forcing of Lemovian techniques but also because of the charter network's desire for expansion as a priority over improving their current campuses:

The charter at first seemed very progressive and in line with my philosophy, but as they expanded I felt like they were trying to get control of the schools so they could focus on the new one, not develop this philosophy they had for the benefit of teaching and learning. I can't speak to other networks, but, at my school—it disgruntled a lot of teachers. Like, "Oh my God, you're opening up a new one when we're struggling with X, Y, and Z, that's what you're gonna give your attention to?!" And that was at both the networks that I worked at. It was a point of contention for teachers.

To follow up, I asked Ariana how many of her former coworkers still worked at the school. She responded, "The school that I was a founding member of 4 years ago, has no founding members anymore. As of its third year, there were only two." Connected to Ariana's sentiments, Gabriel highlighted how the lack of educational experience amongst the board members was frustrating because they did not understand pedagogy or best practices, but were only focused on data (standardized test scores):

Of course, I want my students to achieve and I put in 100% every day to reach that goal. But no one who has taught—and I don't care where they stand on the reform spectrum—no one will say that one day's test scores can always accurately reflect what the teacher has done for that year, let alone that day. One year I had 91% of my students meet or exceed their MAP goal. The next year I had 25%! That class had students with severe trauma and severe needs, and I got no help from my administration whatsoever. I would say that that year I worked even harder than the previous year! I worked tirelessly to help my students, but the scores didn't reflect that. And people who haven't taught don't get that. And charter boards often have people who have never taught and are clueless about theory and research, let alone best practices.

It is clear that for schools to be successful, they must have board members that are educators. Because this is not happening, there is a disconnect between administrators and teachers. If the people that compose school boards are only businesspeople, who focus solely on numbers but don't understand pedagogy, they will not be able to have a successful school or retain quality teachers.

Racism and Control

The only mentions of race in *Teach Like a Champion* (Lemov, 2010, 2015) discuss the disparities in standardized test scores between White students and students of color. The book does not explicitly focus on race or make any mentions of culturally relevant pedagogy or culturally responsive teaching. Teach for America (TFA) was mentioned by participants when discussing both teacher retention rates and the racial implications of working with the organization. Several of the participants argued that the program had profound racial implications. "It's disgusting," Diana noted, "They would never allow White kids to be guinea pigs for inexperienced teachers at affluent, White schools, so why is it acceptable for them to do this in Black and Brown schools? It's sick, and it's wrong."

Camille went further:

> They are explicitly using Black kids to improve their resumes. While I believe that many of them have good intentions, I don't think that's enough. In a world of police killing unarmed Black people, intentions are utterly meaningless. Every time this happens, the police apologists say, "Well, he had good intentions." But that cop's intentions aren't going to bring back that man's life. So while I do believe that most TFAs have good intentions, they mean nothing when they leave after 2 years. Many of them were often very open and honest that they were only in the program to get into law school or apply for the next program, which never had to do with education.

All of the interviewees mentioned the videos on the DVD that accompanies *Teach Like a Champion* (Lemov, 2010, 2015). The techniques demonstrated in the videos accompanying the text feature students of color being disciplined or redirected for minor infractions by teachers, often White. This raises multiple questions around race and whether Uncommon Schools are properly addressing these concerns, as well as the questionable racism in *Teach Like a Champion*. These implications may be completely unintentional, but the interviewees all stated that they were present and disturbing.

Multiple writers have strongly criticized the discipline techniques touted by Lemov, including them being rooted in the racial subordination of Black and Latinx students by White teachers. These criticisms are best synthesized by Layla Treuhaft-Ali (2016). She asserted that Lemov promotes "working-class behavioral norms through . . . order, uniformity, and obedience," which she points out to have been used to maintain class-based and racial hierarchies. Additionally, Treuhaft-Ali (2016) draws a comparison of White businessmen such as John Rockefeller funding the Hampton Institute, where Black teachers were trained in compliance and obedience. Similarly, contemporary White philanthropists fund charter schools that teach through nearly identical methods of compliance and obedience for Black students.

Camille asserted the following, referring to the "level zero" technique (an expectation that students are silent):

> There are racial undercurrents of control. I don't think it was intentional. I think I worked with really well-intentioned people, I do not doubt that. But I think for lack of a better term, they had been drinking the Kool-Aid for a very long time and they didn't know anything else. But to walk around, especially as a middle school teacher, telling students that they had to be at a level zero all the time and straight lines in the hallway—it's just developmentally inappropriate. It made me feel like a warden, not a teacher. Hundreds of times a day, to be telling kids to be at a level zero. Because it was the most unrealistic expectation for middle school students to be silent all day in the hallway. It felt very much like a control situation, rather than developing students' self-control. Because it could be at a level zero. But it could also be at a level five. They did struggle with a quiet conversation because they didn't have a lot of practice with it.

Treuhaft-Ali (2016) also pointed out that obedience is used as a form of control, and that it appears that through the *Teach Like a Champion* (Lemov, 2010, 2015) lens, critical thinking takes a backseat to submission to the teacher's authority. She analyzed the subtlety of Lemov's words and how there is an emphasis on submission and conformity to avoid democratic classrooms or even student choice. Arguably most striking is Lemov's application of the "broken window theory" to classrooms, where teachers are encouraged to give harsh consequences for small infractions. Outside of schools, these types of policies have led to mass incarceration for communities of color. However, the mentioning of this technique ("sweat the details," which insists teachers constantly redirect students for even the most minute mistakes) is notably absent in the second edition of the book, which was written after the deaths of Michael Brown and Eric Garner. While Lemov's text may not be explicitly racist, it implicitly is. These factors pose serious questions to the effectiveness of Lemov's (2010, 2015) techniques. It should also be noted that his text does not mention MTSS (Belser et al., 2016), trauma-informed pedagogy, or restorative practices. This is important because it implies that not only are these factors not essential for student success but that Lemov techniques are all a school needs to be successful.

Participants also reflected on their race and pedagogical framework. "I wasn't taught this way. If I were a student, I know that if I had gotten detention for not 'tracking the speaker' or not doing 'SLANT' I would have shut down," Sandra noted. She then made a personal connection with the hiring practices of the network and how her White family members are treated in school in comparison to students in her previous charter school:

> I think that too speaks to—they were a network that was also looking to hire young and creative teachers that were very, very similar. It felt disrespectful to the students of color, the students who are marginalized in so many ways, that we were serving, that we were doing it in another way. It was just another way to marginalize. We're going to treat them as others because I certainly never had "signature strategies" when I was in school. I have nieces and nephews in school. I'm White, they're White. No one is telling them to SLANT or put their feet in a certain way, or narrating positively that they're picking their pencil up. Some of the strategies felt condescending to me.

In discussing one school's approach, Sandra repeatedly emphasized the administration's need to control Black students through being constantly silent ("level zero"):

> The students in the class were collaborative, but they had to be at a complete level zero everywhere outside of the classroom, which is bizarre in my opinion because we had common transitions. So no one in the hallway was learning when we were transitioning, so whom were we being level zero for other than to display control? I've also noticed that when I give students more autonomy and choice without threats of punishment, they are more likely to be successful. My high needs Black and Hispanic students often do best without extrinsic motivation. I am trying to do more project-based learning and create a more student-centered classroom.

In comparison, operant conditioning and verbal behavior demonstrate that while some students can work well under extremely strict conditions, it may produce an adverse reaction in others, particularly Tier 2 and Tier 3 students (Skinner, 1957). We are also confronted with the question of why Black and Latinx students are often forced to be silent and behave in "punitive" manners (in the words of Gabriel) at school when their White peers are not. (There appears to be little to no evidence that Lemovian techniques are used in more affluent, White schools.) The interviews in this study should offer important notes for all administrators: Schools that use Lemovian techniques cannot be successful without flexibility. They may also need an increase in restorative practices, along with an acute, reflective racial lens that ensures there is not a disproportionate rate of disciplinary consequences for Black and or Latinx students. In addition, they should promote a school focus on retaining quality teachers. The latter will require giving teachers autonomy to develop their classrooms as they see fit, and a manageable workload.

DISCUSSION

The intent of this study was not to promote or repudiate the work of Doug Lemov. Through both the quantitative surveys and the qualitative interviews, it became clear that the participants overwhelmingly believed that while some of the techniques could work with some students, they were overall too broad and could not work for all students, particularly those with behavioral needs. It cannot be ignored that Lemovian techniques have become popularized in charter schools. Their proponents argue that their autonomy has the potential to lead to academic success. It should be noted that every charter network is unique, and it is overly simplistic to make broad statements about every charter school. However, the majority of the participants stated that the strengths and successes of their charter schools were far outweighed by punitive disciplinary practices and an increase in detentions, suspensions, and expulsions. For example, participants repeatedly asserted that one of the largest charter school networks in Chicago also was the quickest to expel students for minor infractions. As a result, those students either returned to their neighborhood non-charter public school or to one of the charter school networks that had less punitive disciplinary practices.

The autonomy of charter schools is a double-edged sword. While it can create a new vision for education, it also can lead to easier dismissal of students who do not conform to that vision, and to the disenfranchisement of said students. In this research, the disenfranchised students were defined as Tier 2 and Tier 3 students according to MTSS. Again, when we discuss behaviors in these tiers, it is important to not blame the student but to realize that many teachers lack cultural knowledge and responsiveness in their practice, and may be unable to recognize the potential manifestation of trauma (Caraballo et al., 2020; Flouri & Midouhas, 2016). While Lemov repeatedly used the phrase "high expectations" throughout the text, this leads us to ask, how should those expectations look for students that do not conform to strict, arguably punitive, behavioral expectations? The text does not attempt to answer this essential question. Is this reason Lemov did not address this because in the charter school network he directs, it is presumably easier to expel a student who does not conform to the expectations? The absence of addressing students who have severe challenges with meeting such behavioral expectations is glaring. Indeed, educators should reflect on how typical behavioral systems, both in charter and non-charter public schools, have failed to meet the needs of all students, including marginalized racial groups.

Part of ensuring the success of these students will involve more research on trauma-influenced pedagogy. Jennings (2019) demonstrates how traumatic experiences (particularly those linked to poverty) affect student behavior. Why was this research not acknowledged by Lemov? One might believe that this would be an "excuse" and lead against the "no excuses" model popularized in charter schools. However, research demonstrates the failures of this approach (Golann, 2015). Furthermore, while teachers should reflect on how the consequences of disciplinary systems of cause and effect work on students (Skinner, 1957), administrators should also consider how forcing these techniques on teachers who do not believe in them can have detrimental effects on the teachers, including their retention rates. As demonstrated previously, many participants in this study did not believe in the Lemovian techniques because of what they perceived as racial elements of control disproportionately harming Black and Latinx students.

Lemov repeatedly discussed the "achievement gap" between White students and students of color. (Again, it is important to challenge the concept of the "achievement gap," but to view it as the opportunity gap [Cowen-Pitre, 2014] or "educational debt" [Ladson-Billings, 2006], which harms Black and Latinx students [Bernstein, 2014].) If we truly seek to have increased rates of standardized test scores for students of color, we must acknowledge that punitive, rigid systems and techniques may not only not work with these students; they may be detrimental to them. School boards, administrators, counselors, and teachers must understand that these techniques may not work for all students or even a majority of them.

In fact, in providing appropriate academic and social-emotional support to students with severe behavioral needs, it must be recognized that "traditional" classroom techniques may not work at all. While Lemov did not explicitly assert otherwise, the absence of discussion of interventions for behavioral needs, diverse learners, culturally relevant pedagogy, and student trauma appears to suggest that the techniques should work universally. He did not mention cultural responsiveness, nor are his techniques culturally responsive. Students of color may not display an engagement similarly to their White peers. Forcing students to behave and respond in a particular manner is intrinsically racist.

Additionally, those promoting Lemov's techniques must recognize the teacher sustainability within the schools in which they are promoted, as well as their racial implications of control, however unintentional they may be. Ignoring these factors is not only doing a disservice to educators but more importantly to the students they serve. These techniques are harmful to students of color. Especially for students with behavioral needs, schools must do better. As both the literature and the participants in this study illustrate, classroom management cannot be rote but must be tailored to the students, both in charter and non-charter schools. Only an approach that takes the factors discussed into consideration will truly be successful, especially for students classified as Tier 2 and Tier 3.

Consequently, the results of this study have implications for how teachers working in urban environments should be trained. Educators must learn to adopt a lens of antiracism and constantly reflect on their actions. In *How to be an Antiracist* (2019), Dr. Ibram X. Kendi argued that instead of using the term "racist" as a pejorative, we need to objectively look at our actions as either segregationist, assimilationist, or antiracist. Lemov used a colorblind approach, except for discussing test scores by race. Kendi argued that no one ever arrives at truly becoming an antiracist, but that we must constantly strive to be, in order to create the most equitable world. In searching for teacher preparation programs throughout the United States, I could not find one that uses a theoretical framework such as Kendi's, despite mission and vision statements with repeated words like "equity."

Truly, equity cannot be a buzzword. To create more equitable outcomes, teachers must be trained through a lens of antiracism and constantly be reflective of their actions. Lemovian techniques are not rooted in antiracism. It could be argued that some of the techniques are rooted in assimilation, if not racism, as no evidence suggests students of color will benefit from being forced to behave in carceral-like conditions in school. Preservice teachers should be not only trained through a theoretical framework of antiracism but also work with professors who model reflective practices in challenging racist and assimilationist policies and their effects in schools. Preservice teachers should be able to analyze how Lemovian techniques are not rooted in antiracism, and be shown alternative antiracist teaching techniques.

Furthermore, teacher training programs must be extensive, and not the brief seminars of programs like TFA. Properly teaching students from marginalized communities will require immense preparation. TFA students spend six weeks training to work in urban schools. We must ask ourselves, would this be acceptable in more affluent White communities? They would not, as TFA does not exist in their schools. The respondents discussed their frustrations with working with TFA, supporting research of its criticisms (Turner et al., 2018). In the interviews, the respondents repeatedly asserted that the TFA teachers were mainly trained in Lemovian techniques. Aspiring educators should instead opt for more rigorous, extensive colleges of education, especially when working with Black and Latinx students in communities disproportionately affected by poverty through systemic racism.

Additionally, preservice teachers should not be presented with Lemov's work, but research-based techniques. Teachers must have better training in research methodology, to question the validity of data promoting specific teaching methodology. Undergraduate students should have more rigorous training in such methods to understand the effectiveness of certain studies. Professors should strive to present best practices in the most objective terms possible. While it would be impossible to root out all bias in academia, if aspiring teachers are better trained in research methodology, they can question studies about teaching techniques such as Lemov's. They can better understand how data can be manipulated to promote teaching methods, or how strong methodology can be used to correctly analyze best practices in schools. Preservice teachers trained in research methodology can assess the strengths and flaws in studies, including teaching techniques, to adequately prepare themselves for the classroom.

Equally important, teachers must be shown that certain techniques are too broad and may be ineffective with Black and Latinx students, including by communicating with current teachers. Beyond Lemov, there is a range of literature about best practices for classroom management and empathy (Sorakin et al., 2020), behavioral interventions (Little & Akin-Little, 2019), and restorative practices (Manassah et al., 2018). Teacher preparation programs should create collaborative networks with pre-service and in-service educators to discuss best practices, including differentiating classroom management practices and teaching techniques. Preservice teachers should learn about classroom management strategies that are successful in urban schools.

Finally, preservice educators must be trained in behavioral interventions and restorative practices. While it is difficult to find current research on how embedded these components are in contemporary teacher training programs, all of the participants interviewed explained that not only were they not trained in these areas, but they felt their classroom management preparation in college was neither based on culturally relevant pedagogy or best practices. Instead, they all stated that the traditional punitive teaching and classroom management techniques, including Lemov's, exacerbated gaps in success with students with high behavioral needs. Preservice teachers should be shown how interventions work, MTSS teams operate, and MTSS success stories. MTSS is ideal because analyzing the root causes of behaviors can lead to identifying problems and creating effective solutions to benefit a student's social-emotional growth. In contrast, Lemov's techniques make no mention of the social-emotional state of students and how they might lead to certain behaviors.

Preservice teachers should also have professors who can model restorative practices and talking circles, and be able to share their experiences using such activities. A significant problem with many teacher education programs is that many White professors are disconnected from contemporary classrooms (Harris et al., 2020). Adopting antiracist suggestions and acknowledging whiteness in these programs would prepare preservice teachers to meet the needs of Black and Latinx students, and those who have been marginalized by traditional, punitive discipline with racial undercurrents of control. Taking these steps in teacher training programs will create better-prepared teachers to meet the needs of all students with tangible action to create equitable outcomes, benefitting all students. Once this happens, "equity" will no longer be an abstract concept, but we will be closer to it as a reality for all learners.

SUGGESTIONS FOR FUTURE RESEARCH

Future research should focus on teaching techniques with the intersections of multiple fields, such as culturally relevant pedagogy. Identifying culturally-relevant teaching techniques could help create more conducive learning environments for Black and Latinx students. MTSS and teaching techniques should be researched together. Identifying techniques that could be used as interventions, such as helping off-task students get back on track, could help support these learners. Scholars should examine how restorative practices and trauma-informed pedagogy can be synchronously used with teaching techniques to create schools that are holistic and benefit the whole child. This, coupled with disproportionate rates of suspension and expulsion for Black students, should be critically examined as schools work to end these inequities so Black children can learn freely without being criminalized. As discussed in my research, the myth of the "achievement gap" needs to be not only challenged, but also examined as far as whether, and to what extent, certain teaching techniques can develop intellectual growth. Lemov claimed they could but provided no research or methodology to prove so.

Additionally, while teacher retention rates and charter school expansion were not the focus of this study, they must be examined as well. As the interviews showed, some participants felt that their previous charter school networks were too focused on expansion and not on developing a strong curriculum or building community and relationships with students. Participants viewed these "signature strategies," as one participant's school referred to them, as rote, mechanical, and not differentiated enough to support all learners. Researchers should work to identify how charter schools can succeed and retain teachers.

I used an explanatory sequential research design (Creswell, 2015) for this study and recommend it be used for researching all of the topics listed above. While it is not a universal method for educational research, drawing on both qualitative and quantitative data in multiple phases can produce a more holistic picture of a given situation. My research would not have been complete without both the information from the Likert scale surveys as well as the interviews. Lemov's work proves that quantitative data alone is insufficient. Similarly, qualitative observations of the techniques included in the DVDs also do not paint a whole picture. A mixed-methods approach is best and an explanatory sequential research design should be used as the methodology for investigating the topics listed above.

Researchers should interview students from charter and non-charter public schools that have used Lemovian techniques, and assess the students' perspective of their effectiveness (or lack thereof). It is also important to understand the perspectives of current teachers who have stayed in charter schools and believe in Lemovian techniques. Finally, research should be done based on classroom observations, whether they be Lemovian techniques or interventions based on MTSS. After the behavioral technique or behavioral intervention is administered, the researcher could record the student's response, and whether the targeted behavior begins to change for the student.

I advocate for researching a diversity of topics for several reasons. First, there is a lack of peer-reviewed research on teaching techniques. While a plethora of scholarly work can be found in the field of classroom management, much of it is vague and theoretical. There needs to be more research rooted in the praxis of day-to-day pedagogical work. This will be complex and will require teachers to be trained in techniques, with researchers observing them interacting with students and recording students' responses. Doing so will require informed consent from parents, as well for schools to buy into the importance of this work. I am not naive to the challenges that this research will pose. It will take a challenging, long-term, pragmatic approach. Yet as Lemov's work proves, it is unequivocally necessary to do so. Repudiating standardized test scores as validity for the success of teaching methods is essential.

REFERENCES

Bernstein, N. (2014). *Burning down the house: The end of Juvenile prison.* The New Press.

Belser, C. T., Shillingford, M.A., & Joe, J. R. (2016). The ASCA Model and a multi-tiered system of supports: A framework to support students of color with problem behavior. *Professional Counselor, 6*(3), 251–262. https://files.eric.ed.gov/fulltext/EJ1115903.pdf

Caraballo, L., Martinez, D. C., Paris, D., & Alim, H. S. (2020). Culturally sustaining pedagogies in the current moment: A conversation with Django Paris and H. Samy Alim. *Journal of Adolescent & Adult Literacy, 63*(6), 697–701. https://ila.onlinelibrary.wiley.com/doi/epdf/10.1002/jaal.1059

Cowan Pitre, C. (2014). Improving African American student outcomes: Understanding educational achievement and strategies to close opportunity gaps. *Western Journal of Black Studies, 38*(4), 209–217. https://static1.squarespace.com/static/52cf1070e4b048ae22d972b2/t/58b82d46a5790a60fdfce8eb/1488465244758/Improving+African+American+Student+Outcomes+%282014%29.pdf

Cresswell, J. W. (2015). *Planning, conducting, and evaluating quantitative and qualitative research* (5th ed.). Pearson.

Flouri, E., & Midouhas, E. (2016). School composition, family poverty and child behaviour. *Social Psychiatry & Psychiatric Epidemiology, 51*(6), 817–826. https://doi-org.neiulibrary.idm.oclc.org/10.1007/s00127-016-1206-7

Golann, J. W. (2015). The paradox of success at a no-excuses school. *Sociology of Education, 88*(2), 103–119. https://www.ncbi.nlm.nih.gov/pmc/articles/PMC4877134/

Gross, B., Tuchman, S., & Yatsko, S. (2016). *Grappling with discipline in autonomous schools: New approaches from D.C. and New Orleans.* Center on Reinventing Public Education. https://files.eric.ed.gov/fulltext/ED566659.pdf

Harris, B. G., Hayes, C., & Smith, D. T. (2020). Not a "who done it" mystery: On how Whiteness sabotages equity aims in teacher preparation programs. *Urban Review: Issues and Ideas in Public Education, 52*(1), 198–213. https://link .springer.com/article/10.1007/s11256-019-00524-3

Jennings, P. A. (2019). Teaching in a trauma-sensitive classroom: What educators can do to support students. *American Educator, 43*(2), 12–17. https://eric .ed.gov/?id=EJ1218755

Kendi, I. X. (2019). *How to be an antiracist.* One World.

Ladson-Billings, G. (2006). From the achievement gap to the education debt: Understanding achievement in U.S. schools. *Educational Researcher, 35*(7), 3–12.

Lemov, D. (2010). *Teach like a champion: 49 techniques that put students on the path to college.* Joey Bass.

Lemov, D. (2015). *Teach like a champion 2.0: 62 techniques that put students on the path to college.* Joey Bass.

Little, S. G., & Akin-Little, A. (2019). *Behavioral interventions in schools: Evidence-based positive strategies*(2nd ed.). APA Books.

Manassah, T., Roderick, T., & Gregory, A. (2018). A promising path toward equity: Restorative circles develop relationships, build community, and bridge differences. *Learning Professional, 39*(4), 36–40. https://learningforward.org/ journal/august-2018-vol-39-no-4/a-promising-path-toward-equity

Milner, H. R. (2012). Challenges in teacher education for urban education. *Urban Education, 47*(4), 700–705. https://doi-org.neiulibrary.idm.oclc.org/10.1177/ 0042085912452098

Skinner, B. F. (1957). *Verbal behavior.* Appleton-Century-Crofts. https://doi.org/10 .1037/11256-000

Sorakin Balli, Y., Basari, S., & Guldal Kan, S. (2020). The relation between classroom management skills and empathic tendencies of high school teachers' classroom management skills and empathic tendencies. *Cypriot Journal of Educational Sciences, 15*(1), 144–152. https://www.researchgate.net/ publication/339686307_The_relation_between_classroom_management_ skills_and_empathic_tendencies_of_high_school_teachers_high_school_ teachers'_classroom_management_skills_and_empathic_tendencies

Treuhaft-Ali, L. (2016). *The power of pedagogy: Why we shouldn't teach like champions.* https://citiessuburbsschoolchoice.wordpress.com/2016/05/07/the-power -of-pedagogy-why-we-shouldnt-teach-like-champions/

Turner, H., Ncube, M., Turner, A., Boruch, R., & Ibekwe, N. (2018). *What are the effects of Teach for America on math, English language arts, and science outcomes of K–12 students in the USA?* Campbell Collaboration. https://eric.ed.gov/?id =ED586250

Zubrzycki, J., Cavanagh, S., & McNeil, M. (2013). Charter schools' discipline policies face scrutiny. *Education Week, 32*(21), 1–16. https://eric.ed.gov/?id=EJ1007542

CHAPTER 9

MINDFULNESS PRACTICES AND HIP-HOP THERAPY FOR MARGINALIZED YOUTH

Torie Wheatley
The University of North Carolina at Charlotte

> *How you gone win if you ain't right within?*
> —Lauryn Hill

In the United States, Black adolescents are pushed out of the education system, incarcerated at higher rates, and live in fear of being victims of police brutality. These factors are fueled by systemic racism, and are triggers that greatly affect the psyche of targeted youth (Bonnie et al., 2014). Emerging studies evaluate the effectiveness of mindfulness-based stress reduction (MBSR) practices and the implementation of hip-hop therapy (HHT) for marginalized youth, to promote improved mental health, self and communal awareness, and overall well-being. MBSR techniques incorporate practices such as yoga, deep breathing, and meditation, which are proven to have health and academic benefits. HHT is a culturally relevant practice that utilizes rap music, bibliotherapy (poetry therapy), and music therapy to attain the goal of creating a better sense of self and community, and of

Economic, Political and Legal Solutions to Critical Issues in Urban Education   pages 161–173
and Implications for Teacher Preparation
Copyright © 2022 by Information Age Publishing
www.infoagepub.com
All rights of reproduction in any form reserved.

understanding diverse perspectives (Tyson, 2002). MBSR and HHT provide holistic interventions that support mental health and self-awareness in educational spaces.

Research reveals that mental health and educational disparities are factors that greatly impact marginalized youth, classified as justice-involved youth, young adults aging out of foster care, disabled youth, teen parents, homeless or impoverished youth, youth pushed out exhibiting by schools for behavioral challenges, sexual minorities, immigrants, youth with disabilities, and others impacted by systemic racism and other external factors (Bonnie et al., 2014). In urban areas, the demographic of marginalized youth are disproportionately Black and Brown.

Due to the Covid-19 pandemic, mental health and educational disparities are becoming magnified concerns for educational stakeholders. The pandemic may have increased long-term adverse consequences on youth; additional vulnerability factors include developmental age, current educational status, having special needs, pre-existing mental health conditions, being economically underprivileged, and child/parent being quarantined due to infection or fear of infection (Singh et al., 2020). With much research revealing the need for holistic interventions and alternatives for mental health awareness and rehabilitation practices, mindfulness-based techniques and culturally relevant therapy including HHT are emerging as effective practices for marginalized youth.

The term "mindfulness" is explained as an awareness of the here and now, as well as the ability to internally conceptualize the importance of being in the present (Kielty et al., 2017). Although mindfulness practices have been around for centuries, recent studies have explored how these practices promote mental health, self and communal awareness, and overall well-being for marginalized youth (Allen, 2005). Mindfulness-based intervention is often intertwined with the term MBSR, which focuses on utilizing mindfulness practices to reduce the mental challenges of societal and personal stressors. MBSR practices include, but are not limited to, yoga, deep-breathing techniques, and meditation.

Examples of positive implementation of mindfulness practices can be seen at Robert W. Coleman Elementary school in Baltimore, Maryland, which had a high detention rate before the implementation of mindfulness practices like deep-breathing (Bloom, 2016). Several pieces of research have revealed that meditation can help suppress, reduce, or cure health concerns like chronic pain, reverse some components of cardiovascular disease, reduce epileptic seizures, and lower rates of substance abuse (Wisner et al., 2010). Mindfulness is connected to hip-hop because music is a form of therapy that has listeners focused on the here and now while being attuned with the words and sound. Hip-hop influences also make listeners and appreciators of the genre reflect on personal connections and systemic ills that are exposed by the rawness of many lyricists. HHT is the implementation and integration of hip-hop music, narratives, and the arts, which are rooted in hip-hop pedagogy and culture (Tyson, 2002). Hip-hop is a "term used to describe the collective experiences, modes of thinking, and epistemologies of urban youth" (Love, 2014).

In this chapter, hip-hop refers to the multiple subgenres and extensions of the genre, including Rap. HHT aims to merge mental health initiatives and culturally relevant concepts in hip-hop to build a sense of identity and cognitive support to help with emotional development (Tyson, 2002). Research suggests that hip-hop based curricula can help foster communal and self-knowledge, and raise critical consciousness (Love, 2016). With the implementation of both practices, positive outcomes for marginalized youth can manifest in their academics and self-management. This chapter highlights the benefits of mindfulness practices and HHT as holistic methods to promote positive effects for marginalized youth, which can be implemented in the classroom to support mental health and self-awareness. The presented information should influence teacher preparation by providing future educators with techniques to promote social emotional learning in urban educational settings.

LITERATURE REVIEW

Mindfulness-Based Stress Reduction

Marginalized youth are impacted by outside factors and experience social exclusion, a concept denoting the economic, social, political, racial and ethnic, and cultural marginalization experienced by specific groups of people because of social forces such as poverty, discrimination, violence and trauma, disenfranchisement, and dislocation (Bonnie et al., 2014). Educational sectors often dismiss the oppressive forces that can restrict the equity of marginalized youth. Educational institutions and educators often misunderstand or dismiss the ways in which racist, heterogeneous, Eurocentric ideologies affect marginalized students, and even profit from these students' vulnerabilities. Oppressive circumstances that marginalized youth encounter further validate the need for holistic, culturally relevant interventions that can be utilized in educational and rehabilitation centers.

Without proper intervention in facilities that interact with youth during the most crucial times of their development, lasting health effects in addition to pre-existing trauma can greatly affect students at the latter stages of their life. National data reveal that 50% of all lifetime mental illnesses develop by age 14 and 75% develop by age 24, and that 1 in 6 U.S. youth aged 6–17 experience a mental health disorder each year. Suicide is the second leading cause of death among people aged 10–34 (National Alliance on Mental Illness, 2019). External stressors that affect the mental well-being of marginalized youth include poverty, failing educational systems, exposure to the community and interpersonal violence, all of which can lead to chronic physical health concerns including hypertension, obesity, anxiety, aggression, and depression (Sibinga et al., 2011; Singh et al., 2020).

Research on mindfulness-based stress reduction (MBSR) practices has shown benefits in quality of life, alleviation of adverse physical symptoms, and decreased psychologic distress (Sibinga et al., 2011). Mindfulness techniques for marginalized youth can alleviate the stress of the following factors: poverty, stress, failing educational systems, exposure to community violence, and interpersonal violence (Sibinga et al., 2011). Two million youth are arrested each year in the United States, and 70% of them have a mental health condition (Hammond, 2007). These hindrances negatively affect the academic success of urban students in conjunction with mental health concerns. Experts in the field revealed that mindfulness-based interventions help students to gain academic and psychosocial strengths, improve self-regulation, as well as coping abilities (Gould et al., 2012).

The cognitive benefits of MBSR for adolescents include increased self-esteem, improvements in emotional intelligence, increased feeling of well-being, reduction in behavioral problems, decreased anxiety, decrease in blood pressure and heart rate, improvements in sleep behavior, increased internal locus of control, and improved school climate. They also reduce behaviors associated with attention-deficit hyperactivity disorder (ADHD; Gould et al., 2012). The health benefits are even more extensive and impressive.

Hip-Hop Therapy and the H.Y.P.E.

Dr. Adia Winfrey created the H.Y.P.E. (Healing Young People thru Empowerment) program, inspired by the HHT work of Dr. Edgar Tyson that centered around at-risk Black males to help them better develop their behavioral and social skills. HHT provides an outlet for youth to analyze specific hip-hop lyrics that engage and encourage self-reflection, agency, and regulation of emotions, which are essential components of mindfulness. From hip-hop music and culture emerged hip-hop pedagogy and therapy. HHT consists of specific art from therapy, including spoken word poetry, film and theater, music, and other expressive arts (Tyson, 2002). The implementation of HHT is a recent trend in culturally relevant practices, which produces positive relationship building and self-awareness, as well as expression. HHT can be used with any group of youth, although according to Allen (2005), it helps if they have a familiarity with hip-hop genres and culture. HHT first begins with gauging the interest of youth in hip-hop music and culture, and building their understanding of how it connects with their intersectionalities (Allen, 2005).

THEORETICAL FRAMEWORK

Hip-hop in education and therapy is used to discuss complex topics, such as systemic racism and mental health awareness, that greatly impact marginalized communities. Hip-hop extends beyond the classroom via the concept of collectivism, integrating lived experiences, and encouraging counternarratives that reflect resilience and expose oppressive forces. Hip-hop is becoming, in a sense, the universal language of youth because it provides them with representation and a space to express what is repressed. According to Robinson et al. (2017), recent studies that explore the utilization of HHT for health behavior interventions have not discussed their theoretical frameworks in detail. However, doing so would provide greater validity or stronger support for HHT practices. This study employs social cognitive theory, which suggests that behavior is a function of personal and environmental factors (Robinson et al., 2017). By connecting culturally relevant social emotional learning with hip-hop, students are allowed to engage in an intervention that encourages reflection through counternarratives and lived experiences. Hip-hop based education and therapy discusses culture and social capital as they relate to the experiences of African American and Latinx urban students (Adjapong, 2017; Emdin, 2010).

LITERATURE ANALYSIS

Research on mindfulness-based intervention and HHT is evolving in the field of urban education, supporting their utilization as alternatives to Eurocentric interventions for marginalized youth. In 2016 The Holistic Life Foundation in Baltimore, Maryland started implementing the use of mindfulness practices for at-risk youth (*Mindfulness Education, Yoga Meditation*, 2016). Holistic Life collaborated with Coleman Elementary school to provide mindfulness interventions for the students, including yoga, meditation, and deep breathing techniques. Overall, the program reduced detention and suspension rates, as well as improved students' abilities to self-assess and regulate. According to former Coleman Elementary student Janasia Brown, she has noticed the benefits in her academics with an increased GPA of 3.8, as improvements in her family life. After leaving Coleman, Brown continued to practice MBSR from fourth through ninth grade (George, 2016). Mindfulness practices are also transferable skills that can create generational change. As a result of the mindfulness benefits, Janasia has also taught her mother and younger brother the same techniques that she has been utilizing throughout her academic journey (George, 2016).

In another study, researchers used subjects ages 13–20 years old to test the outcome of mindfulness with students with severe health, cognitive, and social limitations (Gould et al., 2012). The result of the study showed a significant reduction in hostility, general discomfort, and emotional discomfort. Other practitioners of MBSR revealed that there were perceived improvements in interpersonal relationships, school achievement, and physical health, along with fewer conflicts and reduced stress (Sibinga et al., 2011).

Tyson (2002) created the platform for HHT to be used in individual or group settings for 11 at-risk youth Black and Latinx males and one female in a residential facility in Miami. There is a pretest and posttest given to participants to evaluate their progress. The following step is implemented when hip-hop therapist are implementing the intervention: (a) complete an assessment, (b) plan "icebreaker activities," (c) establish HHT group guidelines, (d) assemble materials and resources, (e) prepare, (f) establish HHT 24 learning objectives, (g) set goals, (h) encourage journal writing, (i) facilitate discussion, (j) intervene, and (k) facilitate a closing activity (Winfrey, 2009). The study revealed positive outcomes of self-efficacy. Winfrey used HHT to construct a program for at-risk males, to educate the participants about their diagnoses, help them constructively handle "strong emotions," improve their racial identity development, teach anger management techniques, encourage accountability, augment and enhance personal growth, and finally, increase appropriate behavior (Winfrey, 2009). The program entitled "Healing Young People thru Empowerment" (H.Y.P.E.) is a 12-session program designed for Black males with emotional behavior disorder (EBD) labels, whose primary diagnoses include disruptive behavior disorders such as conduct disorder and oppositional defiant disorder (Winfrey, 2009). The intention of the program is to provide culturally relevant alternatives and support racial identity, as well as to encourage group collaboration and vulnerability. The program utilizes HHT, rap therapy, relational-development model, and interpersonal cognitive problem-solving (ICPS). The program began with sessions that address issues relevant to what the participants have experienced. The lessons used the relational-development model and were guided by nigrescence theory, which focuses on understanding one's Black racial identity, which was coined by Cross (2000) and implemented in the Cross model (Vandiver et al., 2001).

DISCUSSION

Culturally Responsive Alternatives

HHT creates a safe space for youth to express themselves. Group discussion is centered around analyzing hip-hop songs that address challenging real-life topics, combining creative expression with mindfulness techniques (yoga, deep-breathing, journal reflections). The merging of the two practices also provides culturally relevant alternatives from traditional Eurocentric therapy or disciplinary methods that can further harm Black and Brown students. Both practices also require teachers to gain an understanding of their students' situations and the correlation to mental well-being. Research reveals that the integration of holistic methods such as yoga and deep breathing can produce positive cognitive and health outcomes for marginalized youth. Simple practices including deep breathing and meditation do not require teachers to have additional certification to practice in the classroom. For teacher preparation programs, it is important for educators to become practitioners of MBSR to implement social emotional learning skills. Teachers can start by becoming aware of how to conduct basic mindfulness practices within the classroom and make a consistent routine.

Sense of Self, Community, and Vulnerability

Analysis of the given research reveals how the implementation of MBSR and HHT promote a better awareness of self and closer community/peer connections for participants. By utilizing hip-hop based concepts, marginalized youth that identify with the genre have the opportunity to relate their lived experiences with that of the music genre which can serve as a reflective lens on reality. Teachers must be mindful to create a safe space and welcoming environment for all students to evaluate their mental well-being and encourage growth and dialogue while understanding the power of counter-narratives of Black and Brown voices. Allowing vulnerability, the assessment of counternarratives, and the examination of lived experiences through the lens of hip-hop music, are all important components in HHT. hip-hop music in itself reflects vulnerability with one's emotions and the respect of others who are listening to that vulnerability. Teachers must emphasize the importance of vulnerability, as well as the need to listen to multiple perspectives. Additionally, HHP could also be extended with mindfulness practices.

Understanding of Hip-Hop Culture

Educators should conduct research on hip-hop culture and how it contributes to students' experiences. Understanding the cultural and historical context of hip-hop music is a crucial foundation for starting dialogue that addresses and promotes self- reflection while in a vulnerable atmosphere. It is imperative for educators to be facilitators of cultural exchange for students to grow an understanding and awareness of other perspectives.

RECOMMENDATIONS

Practicing MBSR and HHT as SEL

For the appropriate implementation of mindfulness-based stress reduction practice and HHT, educational stakeholders such as counselors and teachers should familiarize themselves with the practices and content before implementation. It is important for educators to also integrate some practices of MBSR in their personal routine for social emotional growth within students and practitioners. During times of mental unrest, it is critical for students and teachers to take into consideration their mental well-being. By making MBSR practices and HHT a component of social emotional learning (SEL), students will be gaining skills that can help them cope with stressors of the outside world, thus being equipped with a lasting life skill of self-regulation. For mindfulness practices, meditation should typically be two 10-minute sessions; one in the morning and one in the evening to receive the full benefits of meditation and mindfulness healing (Gould et al., 2012).

Simultaneous Use of MSBR and HHT

Practitioners should also consider implementing MSBR and HHT simultaneously to promote self-awareness and community within the classroom by allowing creative expression of emotions and the acceptance of diverse perspectives. There is minimal research on the use of HHT during Covid-19 due to the newness of the pandemic in research. HHT includes mental health practices including culturally relevant group therapy that analyzes, reflects, and shares thoughts relating to hip-hop lyrics, culture, and reality. Reflection through journaling, authentic conversations, and expressing triumph through trials by creating rap songs as journal entries.

LIMITATIONS OF STUDY

Despite the extensive research on hip-hop, therapy, and mindfulness, several limitations are presented in the study. The first limitation is utilizing secondary data sets and being restricted to using previous studies. Because HHT is a relatively new approach, academic research is limited regarding its application. The studies are not inclusive of today's hip-hop culture and aesthetics, and much of the research focuses on the negative commercialized perspective of "rap" music, rather than the full range of arts within the umbrella of hip-hop. Just as education evolves, so do the aesthetics of hip-hop, and thus their abilities to be combined; academia needs to be more inclusive of what is considered research-worthy. The goal is to bring relevance into practice and make education student-centered, which is a cornerstone of hip-hop pedagogy. It is vital to not discredit HHT, or the cultures by which youth are influenced. Instead, educational stakeholders should pull from students' previous knowledge of hip-hop and hip-hop perspectives as a way of displaying to students the value of multiple perspectives and empathy for marginalized people.

Another limitation of the study is that HHT is modeled for those within the field of counseling, although it is recommended for educational stakeholders, including teachers and staff. There is little research on specific instructions or procedures on how HHT can be implemented in an academic setting that can create the same lasting effects as in a counseling group session. The gap in the research revealed that there is not a multidisciplinary approach for all educational stakeholders to utilize for marginalized youth.

CONCLUSION

The benefits of HHT and mindfulness practices are proven interventions that produce promising outcomes for marginalized youth. Culturally relevant interventions such as HTT, along with mindfulness-based activities, allow for a safe, creative space that encourages healing through vulnerability. Such a space can be an alternative to the stigmas of counseling and therapy amongst marginalized communities. The innovative implementation of both practices together can create a transformative change that can prepare youth to self-regulate, advocate, properly communicate and take priority in their overall well-being. Extending the interventions into the classroom can potentially become an effective asset to equity and trust in mental health for marginalized communities.

REFERENCES

Adjapong, E. S. (2017). Bridging theory and practice in the urban science classroom: A framework for hip-hop pedagogy in STEM. *Critical Education, 8*(15).

Allen, N. (2005). Exploring hip-hop therapy with high-risk youth. *Praxis, 5,* 30–36.

Bloom, D. (2016, November 4). *Instead of detention, these students get meditation.* CNN. https://edition.cnn.com/2016/11/04/health/meditation-in-schools -baltimore/index.html

Bonnie, R. J., Stroud, C., & Breiner, H. (Eds.O. (2014). *Investing in the health and well-being of young adults.* The National Academies Press.

Cross, S. E., Bacon, P. L., & Morris, M. L. (2000). The relational-interdependent self-construal and relationships. *Journal of Personality and Social Psychology, 78*(4), 791–808.

Emdin, C. (2010). Affiliation and alienation: Hip-hop, rap, and urban science education. *Journal of Curriculum Studies, 42*(1), 1–25.

George, D. S. (2016, November 13). How mindfulness practices are changing an inner-city school. *Washington Post.* https://www.washingtonpost.com/local/ education/how-mindfulness-practices-are-changing-an-inner-city-school/201 6/11/13/7b4a274a-a833-11e6-ba59-a7d93165c6d4_story.html

Gould, L. F., Dariotis, J. K., Mendelson, T., & Greenberg, M. T. (2012). A school based mindfulness intervention for urban youth: Exploring moderators of intervention effects. *Journal of Community Psychology, 40*(8), 968–982. https:// doi.org/10.1002/jcop.21505

Hammond, S. (2007). *Mental health needs of juvenile offenders.* https://www.ncsl.org/ print/health/Mental_health_needsojuvenileoffendres.pdf

Kielty, M. L., Gilligan, T. D., & Staton, A. R. (2017). Whole-school approaches to incorporating mindfulness-based interventions: Supporting the capacity for optimal functioning in school settings. *Childhood Education, 93*(2), 128–135. https://doi.org/10.1080/00094056.2017.1300491

Love, B. L. (2014). What is hip-hop-based education doing in nice fields such as early childhood and elementary education? *Urban Education, 50*(1), 106–131. https://doi.org/10.1177/004208591456318

Love, B. L. (2016). Complex personhood of hip hop & the sensibilities of the culture that fosters knowledge of self & self-determination. *Equity & Excellence in Education, 49*(4), 414–427.

Mindfulness Education, Yoga Meditation. (2016). Holistic Life Foundation. https:// hlfinc.org/

National Alliance on Mental Illness. (2019). *Mental health by the numbers.* https:// www.nami.org/mhstats

Robinson, C., Seaman, E. L., Montgomery, L., & Winfrey, A. (2017). A review of hip hop-based interventions for health literacy, health behaviors, and mental health. *Journal of Racial and Ethnic Health Disparities, 5*(3), 468–484. https:// doi.org/10.1007/s40615-017-0389-2

Sibinga, E. M. S., Kerrigan, D., Stewart, M., Johnson, K., Magyari, T., & Ellen, J. M. (2011). Mindfulness-based stress reduction for urban youth. *The Journal of Alternative and Complementary Medicine, 17*(3), 213–218. https://doi.org/ 10.1089/acm.2009.0605

Singh, S., Roy, D., Sinha, K., Parveen, S., Sharma, G., & Joshi, G. (2020). Impact of COVID-19 and lockdown on mental health of children and adolescents: A narrative review with recommendations. *Psychiatry Research, 293*, 113429. https://doi.org/10.1016/j.psychres.2020.113429

Tyson, E. H. (2002). Hip hop therapy: An exploratory study of a rap music intervention with at-risk and delinquent youth. *Journal of Poetry Therapy, 15*(3), 131–144. https://doi.org/10.1023/a:1019795911358

Vandiver, B. J., Fhagen-Smith, P. E., Cokley, K. O., Cross, W. E., & Worrell, F. C. (2001). Cross's nigrescence model: From theory to scale to theory. *Journal of Multicultural Counseling and Development, 29*(3), 174–200. https://doi.org/10.1002/j.2161-1912.2001.tb00516.x

Winfrey, A. (2009). *H.Y.P.E- Healing Young People Thru Empowerment: A hip hop therapy program for Black teenage boys*. African American Images.

Wisner, B. L., Jones, B., & Gwin, D. (2010). School-based meditation practices for adolescents: A resource for strengthening self-regulation, emotional coping, and self-esteem. *Children & Schools, 32*(3), 150–159.

CHAPTER 10

MAKING SUCCESS

A Legal Solution for Teachers and Students in Alternative Schools

Abby F. Holland
Wingate University

*I've heard of nothing coming from nothing, but I've never heard
of absolutely nothing coming from hard work.*

—Uzo Aduba

In the United States, nearly 8% of the teaching force leaves the profession annually, and only about one in three exiting teachers reenters the classroom (Sutcher et al., 2019). High-need schools, which disproportionately serve students with disabilities or other obstacles to learning, encounter 50% more turnover than average (Haynes, 2014; Ingersoll et al., 2014). Enrollment in teacher education programs fell 35% between 2009 and 2014, and in the 2017–2018 academic year, 109,000 teaching positions were left unfilled by certified educators (Sutcher et al., 2019). Sutcher et al. (2016) suggested that policy decisions to address teacher shortages tend to involve either making teaching a more attractive career or lowering standards for teacher qualification. As the latter solution deemphasizes student

Economic, Political and Legal Solutions to Critical Issues in Urban Education   pages 173–191
and Implications for Teacher Preparation
Copyright © 2022 by Information Age Publishing
www.infoagepub.com
173

achievement, this chapter proposes legal action that could both lead to a fresh approach toward teacher preparation and change outcomes for the most vulnerable students. Eliminating standardized testing requirements for students who attend school in alternative settings and instead allowing them to produce artifacts of learning, is a possible solution in the search for a positive change in K–12 education. An environment of teacher trust (as opposed to accountability) could make teaching in high-need schools an attractive option, and thereby increase the supply of qualified teachers.

Johnson (2017) offered a reminder of a quote attributed to Albert Einstein: "The definition of insanity is doing the same thing over and over again but expecting different results" (p. 19). Regardless of the accuracy of the quote, it serves as an appropriate framework to rethink how testing requirements may not best serve students who are already cast out of regular classrooms, or teachers who work alongside them. The discussion unfolds in four parts, focusing on the following questions:

1. What are the federal testing requirements for K–12 students?
2. Which students attend schools in alternative settings, and why?
3. What replaces standardized testing, and why are student-created artifacts a viable option?
4. What are the implications for teacher preparation?

THE STATE OF STANDARDIZED TESTING

Rury (2013) identified the standards movement in education as beginning in the 1990s. A decline in manufacturing jobs diminished the need for vocational education, and a growing demand for a tech-savvy workforce led to more students pursuing higher education. For the first time, academic curricula were no longer reserved for an elite minority. All students were expected to achieve academically, and the standards movement arose in response. The premise of the standards movement is to align course objectives to standardized tests, "so that reliable estimates could be made of what children were learning and of how well schools were fulfilling their instructional mission" (Rury, 2013, p. 225). The result was a new educational climate, in which student test scores measured the effectiveness of teachers and schools.

Standards-based schooling, despite its emphasis on test preparation that may do little for a child's education, continued to receive public support in the new millennium (Rury, 2013). Shortly after taking office, President George W. Bush signed the No Child Left Behind Act of 2001 (NCLB). According to Hursh (2007), NCLB (2001) required that 95% of students in Grades 3–8 and students in high school complete standardized assessments in math and reading. Students also completed annual science testing beginning in the 2007–2008 school year. Each state was required to submit to the federal government a plan for student assessment and how adequate yearly progress would be determined. Schools that failed to meet adequate yearly progress would be identified as such. Each state also had to allow the National Assessment of Educational Progress (NAEP) to administer standardized tests to a sample population from each state for the purposes of comparing data across the states.

Hursch (2007) argued that NCLB (2001) proposed a narrow view of knowledge and research. The act upheld an assumption that standards are unquestioningly objective and appropriate, and standardized tests are a viable way to assess student learning. The language used in NCLB documents alluded to distrust of teachers' ability to select course materials and measure learning. The *Parents' Guide to NCLB* (U.S. Department of Education, 2003), addressed what NCLB can do to "prevent bad or untested programs in the classroom" (p. 18). The answer began with, "too many schools have experimented with lessons and materials that have proven to be ineffective—at the expense of their students" (p. 19). NCLB provided federal support to implement curricula "that have been demonstrated to be effective through rigorous scientific research" (p. 19). According to the *Parents' Guide to NCLB*, approaches to learning require the same kind of experimental study used to determine the effectiveness of medication and therapy. Hursch claimed the actual result of NCLB was a narrowing of curricula that made it difficult for teachers to connect their lessons to students' interests and lives outside of school. NCLB expired in 2015, and was replaced with the Every Student Succeeds Act (ESSA; Camera, 2015).

Beachum (2018) explained that ESSA reduces federal oversight and gives more control to states and local school districts. However, states must still submit accountability plans to the federal government, and testing requirements by grade level have not changed. Under ESSA, 95% of students must undergo state testing, and no more than 1% of students with severe cognitive disabilities can be exempt (Russo, 2016). Leaders in individual states are free to develop standards for each grade level. The standards, however, can be Common Core (Beachum, 2018). According to the Association for Supervision and Curriculum Development (Lavenia et al., 2019), as of 2019, all but three states adopted Common Core Standards. ESSA also provides grant funds to school districts that experiment with paying teachers and administrative staff for performance (Aspen Education & Society Program & Council of Chief State School Officers, 2016). Therefore, teachers and other school leaders can receive financial incentives for improving test scores. While measuring trends in test scores is an efficient means to assess achievement, Hursh's (2007) claims could identify why the nation is suffering from a teacher shortage. Federally mandated standards push aside personalized learning, and curricula based on state or Common Core Standards may not meet the needs of marginalized students.

ALTERNATIVE SCHOOLING

The most recent data from the National Center for Educational Statistics show 645,500 children and youth are enrolled in an alternative school or program for at-risk students (Carver & Lewis, 2010). According to Carver and Lewis, reasons for alternative placement can include poor grades, truancy, challenging behavior, or pregnancy. Of the 645,000 students, 90,300 receive special education services. Among students who qualify for special education services, those with emotional and behavioral disabilities (EBD) are most likely to be removed from the regular setting. (Office of Special Education and Rehabilitation Service, 2017). Among the 350,000 students in the United States that receive special education services for EBD, 17% attend school in a separate setting. For the purposes of this chapter, the term alternative schools is used to describe both disciplinary alternative schools, and special public schools exclusively for students with EBD.

Frank (2019) explained that alternative schools for at-risk students vary widely in purpose, population, and impact on student achievement. Data that describe this population as a whole are limited, although students tend to be of minority background, of low socioeconomic status, and do not thrive in a regular setting. Concerning students diagnosed with EBD, Kern (2015) stated, "this group fares worse than any other disability group along almost any dimension we can consider" (p. 24). On average they perform two grade levels behind their peers in reading, math, and writing (Gage et al., 2014), and more than 75% fail one course or more (Wagner & Cameto, 2004). Unfavorable outcomes include an approximate 50% graduation rate, and high rates of arrest (VanAcker, 2004; Wagner et al., 2005). Kern explained that students with EBD encounter high rates of exclusionary school discipline for behaviors that harm self and others, including substance abuse, weapon-related incidents, and physical violence.

According to Maggin et al. (2016), disparate outcomes for students with EBD do not happen in isolation. Farmer et al. (2016) explained that youth development happens in a web of behavioral, biophysical, cognitive, psychological, and sociological variables. Problems functioning in one area of school, such as academics, behavior, or relationships, can affect another. Chen et al. (2015) reported that students with EBD are more likely to live in out-of-home placement (e.g., foster care or group home) compared to students with other disabilities. As every student with EBD presents unique struggles and abilities to function, Maggin et al. suggested individualized interventions that respond to students' unique needs.

Attempting to standardize students who have unique challenges could exacerbate stressors, which, according to Frank (2019), could include chronic school failure, depression, anxiety, aggression, disruptive classroom behavior, and involvement in the juvenile justice system. Removing these students from regular schooling, but subjecting them to the same testing requirements, resembles Einstein's definition of insanity. Students who transfer to alternative schools often carry a history of negative interactions with teachers and other school leaders (Loutzenheiser, 2002). An impersonal test does not invite interpersonal relationships and could perpetuate feelings of school failure.

A 2018 study of these schools revealed that their test scores were comparatively lower. A large school district in the southeastern United States features both a special school for students with EBD, and a disciplinary alternative school. At the first school, only 10% of the students scored at grade level or above on the state math assessments, compared to 40% district wide. Less than 20% of the same group scored grade level proficient or better in English language arts, compared to 45% across the district. The other alternative school fared about the same, with only about 8% of the students at grade-level proficiency in math, and 9% in English language arts (North Carolina School Report Cards, 2019). Instead of publishing test data that suggest these schools are failing, school systems could allow students to create personalized artifacts of learning, thereby producing a different outcome and disrupting a cycle of failure.

ALTERNATIVES TO STANDARDIZED TESTS

Blomberg and Waldo (date, as cited in Pane & Rocco, 2014) noted that students in alternative environments benefit from learning strategies that are nontraditional, motivational, immediately responsive, and sensitive to social factors. Statistics can show achievement disproportionality among criminalized and behaviorally/emotionally disabled students, but the means to eliminate the gap is not often discussed in academic literature (Pane & Rocco, 2014). Merely eliminating the statistics through test exemptions does not solve the problem either. Alternative means to demonstrate learning that tap students' interests and strengths can cease deficit thinking and create a more positive working environment for teachers.

Gruen (2018) discussed the positive implications of classroom makerspaces. Through creating a meaningful product in lieu of taking a test, students alter the way they participate in a learning environment. Instead of focusing on one test score, students focus on process, growing, and pruning. This shift allows students to speak aloud about what they are doing, assume leadership roles in the classroom, and feel accomplished. In Gruen's words, "Building confidence in this way may make learners more willing to take risks and increase their opportunities to learn instead of feeling defeated by failure and shying away from participating in learning" (p. 135).

Classroom Makerspaces

Learning by making is not new. The idea traces back to Deweyan progressive education, in which the purpose of schooling is to engage students in interdisciplinary projects that are connected to their everyday lives (Martinez & Stager, 2013). In *Democracy and Education*, Dewey (1916) asserted that "education is not an affair of 'telling' and being told but an active and constructive process" (p. 38). In *Experience and Education*, Dewey (1938/1986) explained the teacher's role is not to connect course material to students and enforce discipline, but to supply appropriate learning experiences that pave ground for subsequent experiences. As a progressive educator, Dewey believed learning should be enjoyable and incorporate students' natural curiosity. Progressive schools were intended to be places of liberation and self-expression, not order and restraint (Rury, 2013).

Rury (2013) explained how progressive education fell out of favor in the mid-20th century, particularly among public school teachers working with large groups of students. Student learning through practical experience demands a great amount of attention to individual students, and some teachers found that students learning in progressive environments often lacked basic skills in spelling and memorizing historical facts. At the time, parents commonly believed children needed to be controlled, and frowned upon student self-expression. Teachers were supposed to command strict authority and instill factual knowledge. As today's alternative schools generally offer smaller class sizes and more individualized attention than traditional schools, they could serve as incubators for bringing back progressive learning. Students in alternative schools often suffer from negative experiences with teachers and cycles of failure; allowing them to follow their natural curiosity and focus on process instead of product may produce a different outcome.

Deweyan progressive education focused on learning through experience and building democratic community (Rury, 2013). The theoretical framework behind 21st century makerspaces adds a layer of Papertian constructionism, the idea that learning happens particularly well when students engage in constructing a meaningful and shareable artifact, which could take the form of a sculpture, machine, song, or computer program (Harel & Papert, 1991). Most recently, Dougherty (2012) coined the term *maker movement*. Halverson and Sheridan (2014) defined constructionism as the theory of learning that frames the maker movement's focus on problem solving and working with objects. Makerspaces, environments equipped with tools for making, are often set up in libraries and museums (Somanath et al., 2016). Dougherty admitted hesitancy in bringing the maker movement into schools with the current focus on testing and accountability (Corcoran, 2015). Other researchers promoted its value as a foundation for classroom learning and sought a balance between formal and informal learning (Martinez & Stager, 2013; Peppler & Bender, 2013).

Martin (2015) explained that there is not yet a solid definition of *making*. He borrowed from a collection of conceptions to define making as "a class of activities focused on designing, building, modifying, and/or repurposing material objects, for playful or useful ends, oriented toward making a 'product' of some sort that can be used, interacted with, or demonstrated" (p. 31). According to the author, community and mindset are just as important as the use of objects. Maker communities can include clubs, online social network sites, and classrooms. The community aspect of making allows sharing of ideas, support, troubleshooting, and finding an interested audience.

Martin (2015) outlined the maker mindset as having four facets: (a) playful, (b) asset- and growth-oriented, (c) failure positive, and (d) collaborative. According to Dougherty (2013), the essence of making is experimental play. Martin described a playful environment as intrinsically motivating, and one that invites persistence when working through challenges. Dougherty argued that the maker mindset is a growth mindset that assumes anyone can learn the skills needed to make things. Making is free from an imposed "this skill is an area for improvement" attitude, as not everyone needs to learn how to knit, weld, or code. Makers are free to nurture their talents, find new ones, or walk away when a new skill does not meet the intended purpose. Martin explained that failure is not a positive term in traditional schooling; in making, however, failure leads to overcoming obstacles, better understanding of a problem, and learning to become more adaptive. According to Scardamalia and Bereiter (2006), collaboration creates a knowledge-building community that works collectively to create and share knowledge. This differs from a traditional classroom, where the goal is to learn pre-planned and pre-existing knowledge better and faster than one's peers. Collaboration within a maker mindset, however, is non-competitive.

As stated, students in alternative environments benefit from strategies for learning that are nontraditional, motivational, and immediately responsive. A standardized test offers none of those. When students make artifacts of learning, however, it allows historically struggling students to assume leadership roles, gain problem-solving skills, and become more adaptive. Currently there is a paucity of research that suggests students in alternative schools would benefit from maker-based learning in lieu of standardized testing. The few studies that do exist (Cavallo, et al., 2004; Gruen, 2018; Somanath et al., 2016; Stager, 2005, 2013) present data that sheds new light on alternative schools with show promise.

Constructionist Learning in a Juvenile Detention Center

Stager (2013), working with Seymour Papert, designed the Constructionist Learning Laboratory (CLL) at the Maine Youth Center (MYC), a "troubled" (p. 487) juvenile detention center. Angus King, then Governor of Maine, looked to Papert to create a model of what learning could look like in the future. At that time Amnesty International along with former inmates accused the MYC, accused the organization of torturing students. King, then governor of Maine, recognized Einstein's definition of insanity and understood that education of at-risk youth needed change. He looked to Papert to create a model of what learning could look like in the future, and subsequently freed the CLL of all state curricular and testing requirements.

According to Stager (2013), instead of mastering course objectives to pass a standardized test, the CLL emphasized direct experience, hands-on projects, tinkering, and invention. There was no grouping by age, grade level, or (dis)ability, and no dividing time by academic subject. Teachers limited direct instruction to one or two minutes. Instead, they spent instructional time circulating, joining student project teams, and assisting students in problem-solving. The author explained that the teachers did not engage in coercive practices and students often assumed an instructional role, thus confronting the power dynamics found in traditional classrooms. Students engaged in "extraordinary learning-by-making" (p. 490) such as building classical guitars, producing a radio documentary, raising caterpillars, and exchanging written correspondence with authors. During the 3-year project, not one student was removed from the classroom for disciplinary reasons. Among the students who participated in Stager's project, the recidivism rate plummeted from over 70% to 14%.

Alternative School Enrichment

In a similar experiment, Somanath et al. (2016) worked alongside students with EBD in an enrichment program for students attending an alternative school in Canada. The authors reported that most of the students lived with foster families or in group homes. The students' life experiences, including abuse and trauma, contributed to the risk of dropping out of school. Somanath et al. (2016) found that the opportunity to be creative motivated the students, as creativity is "a feeling which lacks in other aspects of their lives, which are heavily monitored, regulated and surveilled" (p. 155).

Somanath et al. (2016) also found that merely placing students in a room with technology equipment and/or art supplies does not engage them. During the first phase of the project, the authors intended to teach the basics of circuitry and coding, and offered a choice of projects including making an

LED bookmark, simple video game, or animation. The students quickly lost interest when the task was not meaningful to their lives, and instead surfed YouTube and chatted. During the second phase, however, students completed real-world or abstract building tasks including making a windshield wiper, elevator, and sun blinds. Supporting Dewey's argument for meaningful experiences, the students communicated that completing a project for the sole purpose of acquiring a skill was not good enough, but that they would persist through a project that was personally relevant. Personal relevance allowed them to build problem-solving skills and improve skills for subsequent projects, which supports what Stager (2013) called technology ecology, in which one experience begins a spiral of subsequent experiences.

Composition Making in a GED Center

Gruen (2018) shared the experience of integrating making into a high school equivalency classroom. Although she did not mention that a disability could lead to students dropping out, the fact is that only half of students with EBD graduate from high school (U.S. Department of Education, 2014). Gruen explained that the only two pathways to a high school diploma are finishing high school or passing an equivalency exam. Therefore, GED classes center around mastery of test content, with a focus on memorization. Gruen's (2018) study took place in a composition makerspace for adult learners, with a purpose to redefine "what counts as learning" (p. 134). She explained that in a composition makerspace, students engage in various genres of written composition, including blogs, videos, and podcasts.

Gruen (2018) found that participants appreciated a failure-positive environment where they were allowed to make mistakes. She explained that in a traditional environment, where success is measured by a standardized test score, the learning process can be sabotaged. These environments create a high cost of failure; as a result, students shut themselves off from making progress. Although Gruen's participants were adult learners, her claim is relevant to a younger student population in which more than 75% fail at least one course (Wagner & Cameto, 2004). Because the composition makerspace was a low-stakes environment that encouraged tinkering and correcting mistakes, students were willing to explore different technologies and styles of writing. Unfortunately, none of Gruen's (2018) participants passed the writing portion of the GED exam. However, she reported that Illinois and other states are considering alternative methods to passing a high school equivalency exam. Gruen concluded that future studies could examine how to assess mastery of basic skills in a classroom makerspace.

IMPLICATIONS FOR THE TEACHER SHORTAGE

Kohn (2000) reported that many teachers leave the profession due to the pressure of high-stakes testing. In a 2015 survey of 212 teachers, Thibodeaux et al. (2015) found that most participants affirmed that the pressure of standardized testing leads to teacher burnout. As high-need schools experience the most teacher turnover (Haynes, 2014; Ingersoll et al., 2014), allowing students in alternative schools to complete artifacts for learning instead of taking tests could ease the problem.

García and Weiss (2019) noted the teacher shortage is dire. Cognizant of being of limited supply, qualified teachers have options concerning where they want to work, and they are more likely to flock toward schools that provide better support and working conditions. Factors that contribute to less-desirable work conditions include a lack of autonomy, teaching to the test, and behavioral problems. Giving back autonomy and allowing teachers to create student-centered classrooms is likely to slow down the revolving door of teachers leaving the profession. If standardized testing disappears, so can teaching to the test. As students are often placed in alternative settings as a result of behavioral problems, the challenge for teachers does not magically disappear in the new setting. Sufficient teacher preparation to work with such students, however, could be part of the solution.

IMPLICATIONS FOR TEACHER PREPARATION

Refine the Role

Buttner et al. (2016) and Mihalas et al. (2009) suggested that teacher preparation programs do not sufficiently emphasize the need to create a nurturing and inclusive environment to work effectively with students with EBD. Multiple studies (Buttner et al., 2016; Cook et al., 2007; Willmann & Seeliger, 2017) suggested that students who display symptoms of EBD, including non-compliance and aggression, are among the most challenging students to instruct. According to Orasti and Causton-Theoharis (2013), teachers tend to label the students, rather than their disabilities, as the challenge. Instead of perceiving the outward display of their disabilities as a need that requires intervention, teachers often consider the students themselves to be problematic individuals who should be removed from the classroom. Kern (2015) suggested teachers often believe their purpose is to teach academics, not socially appropriate behavior. They may blame parents for students' lack of behavioral control instead of acknowledging a disability. The result is an acclivity to move these students to restrictive placements, including self-contained classrooms and alternative schools.

Garwood and Van Loan (2018) pinpointed caring, along with learning to separate the student from the disability, as important components of preparing teachers to work with students with EBD. However, according to Graziano et al. (2007), students with EBD can act impulsively, and mistakenly dismiss their classmates' and teachers' feelings, leading to social isolation and difficulty forming relationships. Lowenthal (2001) explained that many students with EBD lack functional relationships with adults and could disregard teachers' attempts to form them, even if they do desire connection with others. Therefore, teacher preparation should focus on learning to connect "with all students, not just those who display *good behavior*" (Garwood & Van Loan, 2018, p. 12, emphasis in original).

Cavallo et al. (2004) described the learning curve they experienced when staffing teachers in the CLL. They reported that their first teacher was affable and supportive, but viewed his primary role as keeping the students out of trouble. He did not engage in their projects or offer mentoring. A new teacher arrived after the first 9-week session, Sue Finch. Finch had no science or technical background, but engaged with the students' projects and taught herself computer programming. She organized work plans for each student and reviewed them with the students daily. Finch created new projects and challenges for the students and seldom called on the research team for help. The authors said, "This was the exact manner in which we challenged the students and how their attitude changed once they overcame the obstacles and achieved their objectives" (p. 119). In *Invent to Learn*, Martinez and Stager (2013) offered the same strategy for teachers. In the classroom, teachers should pause before intervening and determine if it is possible to bestow power and agency to the learner.

Rethink Learning

Stager (2005) contextualized productive learning as "an environment and set of experiences that would lead students to construct knowledge through the act of engaging in long-term personally meaningful project work" (p. 3). To successfully change outcomes for students in alternative schools through eliminating testing requirements means giving less credence to any kind of assessment. In Stager's words:

> This represents a radical departure from the mainstream educational community in an age when assessment and externally determined outcomes drive nearly everything that happens in schools. The CLL celebrated and valued that which students found interesting. Educational success was not measured by a rubric, quiz, or test. Student learning was represented by a desire to learn more, an ability to share knowledge with another person or inherent in a project artifact containing evidence of mastery. The fundamental belief

that knowledge is the consequence of experience laid a foundation for the construction of a context for productive learning. (p. 3)

Rethink Making

Blikstein and Worsley (2016), in an effort to steer the maker movement back to its progressive and constructionist roots, examined maker culture and its potential impact in schools. The authors intended to reframe maker culture to meet the needs of diverse populations. Halverson and Sheridan (2014) asserted that making, with cultural ties to hacking and robotics, can be perceived as an activity for nerdy White males. Blikstein and Worsley claimed the cultural roots of making can take a firm hold, unless diverse communities involved in the maker movement prioritize "research, equity, pluralism, and powerful ideas" (p. 76). The authors noted that hundreds of schools have makerspaces, but they are concentrated in affluent communities, where schools possess a more valuable resource than financial support: flexibility. In their words:

> Rather than equipment funding, what is increasingly setting those affluent schools apart is their freedom to experiment with more advanced, project-based pedagogies, rethink the curriculum, sometimes deviate from it, promote interdisciplinary projects, and provide proper facilitation and support. To truly make a difference, these opportunities need to be present in *all* schools rather than just the most affluent ones. (p. 76)

Concerning discourse, Vossoughi et al. (2015) warned that "advancing making as an alternative to standardized, test-centric education without also confronting discourses of failure, persistence, and grit risks replicating deficit views of students" (p. 216). The authors promoted educators who present imperfect samples of artifacts to spark discussion about different ways to solve a problem. This values ideas over results, and views problems as a learning opportunity, rather than something to avoid. The authors cited Martinez and Stager (2013), who asserted that finding what works and discarding what does not is not failure, but learning. However, they also cited Martin (2015), who noted that since some students and schools are consistently labeled as failures, the term is difficult to reframe.

Vossoughi et al. (2015) implored educators to develop sensitivity to the ways injustices can emerge in a making environment. The authors reported observations of teachers giving students make-based activities as a reward for good behavior. This can invoke attitudes of ability grouping and tracking. Further, researchers noted what happened when teachers observed students off task: They received more directed assistance and fewer "opportunities for authorship" (p. 217) compared to others. As a potential solution, Vossoughi et al. suggested that teachers engage in ongoing reflection and action to confront their deficit ideologies. This reflection begins in teacher preparation.

CONCLUSION

In the search for legal, political, and economic solutions to problems in urban education, changing testing legislation for K–12 students in alternative schools is a possible option. As the country experiences a shortage of teachers and students entering teacher preparation programs, it is time to consider how high-stakes testing impacts working conditions for teachers and the well-being of students. As students in alternative schools already suffer from a history of school failure and could benefit from more personalized learning, a school environment based on creative problem-solving and collaboration is a solution. Freeing teachers from teaching to a test and allowing students to explore their natural interests could make teaching a more attractive and satisfying career. Doing the same thing and expecting a different result is insanity. It is time for a change.

REFERENCES

Aspen Education & Society Program, & Council of Chief State School Officers. (2016). *Advancing equity through ESSA: Strategies for state leaders.* https://files .eric.ed.gov/fulltext/ED577041.pdf

Beachum, F. D. (2018). The Every Student Succeeds Act and multicultural education: A critical race theory analysis. *Teachers College Record, 120*(3), 1–18. http://www.tcrecord.org/library/content.asp?contentid=22339

Blikstein, P., & Worsley, M. (2016). Children are not hackers: Building a culture of powerful ideas, deep learning, and equity in the maker movement. In K. Peppler, E. R. Halverson, & Y. B. Kafai (Eds.), *Makeology: Makerspaces as learning environments, volume 1* (pp. 64–79). Routledge.

Buttner, S., Pjil, S. J., Bijstra, J., & E. van den Bosch, E. (2016). Personality traits of expert teachers of students with EBD: Clarifying a teacher's x-factor. *International Journal of Inclusive Education, 20*(6), 569–587. https://doi.org/10.1080/13603116.2015.1100222

Camera, L. (2015, December 9). No Child Left Behind Act has finally been left behind. *U.S. News and World Report.* https://www.usnews.com/news/articles/2015/12/09/congress-replaces-no-child-left-behind-shifts-power-to-states

Carver, P. R., & Lewis, L. (2010). *Alternative schools and programs for public school students at risk of educational failure: 2007–08* (NCES 2010–026). U.S. Department of Education, National Center for Education Statistics.

Cavallo, D., Papert, S., & Stager, G. (2004, June). Climbing to understanding: Lessons from an experiential learning environment for adjudicated youth. In *Proceedings of the 6th international conference on learning sciences* (pp. 113 –120).

International Society of the Learning Sciences. https://dl.acm.org/citation .cfm?id=1149138

Chen, C. C., Culhane, D. P., Metraux, S., Park, Y. M., & Venable, J. (2015). The heterogeneity of truancy among urban middle school students: A latent class growth analysis. *Journal of Child and Family Studies, 25*, 1066–1075. https://doi .org/10.1007/s10826-015-0295-3

Cook, B. G., Cameron, D. L., & Tankersley, M. (2007). Inclusive teachers' attitudinal ratings of their students with disabilities. *The Journal of Special Education, 40*(4), 230–238. https://doi.org/10.1177/00224669070400040401

Corcoran, B. (2015). *Dale Dougherty, father of the maker movement talks about breaking rules, erasers & building a learning culture.* EdSurge. https://www.edsurge .com/news/2015-05-27-dale-dougherty-father-of-the-maker-movement-talks -about-breaking-rules-erasers-building-a-learning-culture

Dewey, J. (1916). *Democracy and education.* The Free Press.

Dewey, J. (1986). Experience and education. *The Educational Forum, 50*(3), 241–252. https://doi.org/10.1080/00131728609335764 (Originally published 1938)

Dougherty, D. (2012). The maker movement. *Innovations, 7*(3), 11–14. https:// www.mitpressjournals.org/doi/pdf/10.1162/INOV_a_00135

Farmer, T. W., Gatzke-Kopp, L. M., Lee, D. L., Dawes, M., & Talbott, E. (2016). Research and policy on disability: Linking special education to developmental science. *Policy Insights From the Behavioral and Brain Sciences, 3*(1), 138–145. https://doi.org/10.1177/2372732215624217

Frank, J. (2019). Establishing empirical benchmarks for disciplinary infractions in alternative school settings: Findings from a national sample. *Preventing School Failure: Alternative Education for Children and Youth, 63*(3), 242–253. https:// doi.org/10.1080/1045988X.2019.1579166

Gage, N., Wilson, J., & MacSuga-Gage, A. (2014). Writing performance of students with Emotional and/or behavioral disabilities. *Behavioral Disorders, 40*(1), 3–14. https://doi.org/10.17988/0198 -7429-40.1.3

García, E., & Weiss, E. (2019). *The teacher shortage is real, large, and growing, and worse than we thought.* Economic Policy Institute. https://www.epi.org/publication/ the-teacher-shortage-is-real-large-and-growing-and-worse-than-we-thought -the-first-report-in-the-perfect-storm-in-the-teacher-labor-market-series/

Garwood, J. D., & Van Loan, C. L. (2018). Pre-service educators' dispositions toward inclusive practices for students with emotional and behavioural difficulties. *International Journal of Inclusive Education, 40*(1), 1–16. https://doi.org/10.1080/ 13603116.2018.1447614

Graziano, P. A., Reavis, R. D., Keane, S. P., & Calkins, S. D. (2007). The role of emotion regulation in children's early academic success. *Journal of School Psychology, 45*(1), 3–19. https://doi.org/10.1016/j.jsp.2006.09.002

Gruen, R. (2018). Authoring self: GED students transforming their identities in a composition makerspace. *Literacy research: Theory, method, and practice, 67*(1), 131–146. https://doi.org/10.1177/2381336918787197

Halverson, E. R., & Sheridan, K. M. (2014). The maker movement in education. *Harvard Educational Review, 84*(4), 495–504. https://doi.org/10.17763/haer.84.4 .34j1g68140382063

Harel, I., & Papert, S. (1991). *Constructionism.* Ablex.

Haynes, M. (2014). *On the path to equity: Improving the effectiveness of beginning teachers*. Alliance for Excellent Education. https://all4ed.org/reports-factsheets/path-to-equity/

Hursh, D. (2007). Exacerbating inequality: The failed promise of the No Child Left Behind Act. *Race, Ethnicity and Education, 10*(3), 295–308. https://doi.org/10.1080/13613320701503264

Ingersoll, R., Merrill, L., & Stuckey, D. (2014). *Seven trends: The transformation of the teaching force* (CPRE Report # RR-80). Consortium for Policy Research in Education.

Johnson, C. (2017). Reflective practice. *Teaching Business & Economics, 21*(1), 19–22. https://search.proquest.com/docview/2213054132/abstract/98260FB517F242E6PQ/1?accountid=14605

Kern, L. (2015). Addressing the needs of students with social, emotional, and behavioral problems: Reflections and visions. *Remedial and Special Education, 36*(1), 24–27.

Kohn, A. (2000). Standardized testing and its victims. *Education Week, 20*(4), 46–47. https://www.alfiekohn.org/article/standardized-testing-victims/

Lavenia, M., Cohen-Vogel, L., & Lang, L. B. (2015). The Common Core State Standards initiative: An event history analysis of state adoption. *American Journal of Education, 121*(2), 145–182.

Loutzenheiser, L. W. (2002). Being seen and heard: Listening to young women in alternative schools. *Anthropology & Education Quarterly, 33*(4), 441–464. https://doi.org/10.1525/aeq.2002.33.4.441

Lowenthal, B. (2001). Teacher strategies and interventions for maltreated children. *Early Child Development and Care, 168*(1), 1–15. https://doi.org/10.1080/0300443011680101

Maggin, D. M., Wehby, J. H., Farmer, T. W., & Brooks, D. S. (2016). Intensive interventions for students with emotional and behavioral disorders: Issues, theory, and future directions. *Journal of Emotional and Behavioral Disorders, 24*(3), 127–137. https://doi.org/10.1177/1063426616661498

Martin, L. (2015). The promise of the maker movement for education. *Journal of Pre-College Engineering Education Research, 5*(1), Article 4. https://doi.org/10.7771/2157-9288.1099

Martinez, S., & Stager, G. (2013). *Invent to learn*. Constructing Modern Knowledge Press.

Mihalas, S., Morse, W. C., Allsop, D. H., & McHatton, P. A. (2009). Cultivating caring relationships between teachers and secondary students with emotional and behavioral disorders. *Remedial and Special Education 30*(2), 108–125. https://doi.org/10.1177/0741932508315950

North Carolina School Report Cards. (2019). https://ncreports.ondemand.sas.com/src/

Office of Special Education and Rehabilitation Services, U.S. Department of Education. (2017). *39th annual report to congress on the implementation of the Individuals with Disabilities Education Act, 2017*. https://sites.ed.gov/idea/2017-annual-report-to-congress-on-the-individuals-with-disabilities-education-act/

Orasti, F. T., & Causton-Theoharis, J. (2013). Challenging control: Inclusive teachers' and teaching assistants' discourse on students with challenging behaviour. *International Journal of Inclusive Education, 17*(5), 507–525. https://doi .org/10.1080/13603116.2012.689016

Pane, D. M., & Rocco, T. S. (2014). *Transforming the school-to-prison pipeline*. Sense Publishers.

Peppler, K., & Bender, S. (2013). Maker movement spreads innovation one project at a time. *The Phi Delta Kappan, 95*(3)3, 22–27. https://doi.org/10.1177/ 003172171309500306

Russo, C. (2016). An overview of the Every Student Succeeds Act. *Educational Leadership Faculty Publications, 82*(3), 189. https://ecommons.udayton.edu/eda _fac_pub/189

Rury, J. (2013). *Education and social change: Contours in the history of American schooling* (4th ed.). Routledge.

Somanath, S., Morrison, L., Hughes, J., Sharlin, E., & Sousa, M. C. (2016, February). Engaging 'at-risk' students through maker culture activities. In *Proceedings of the TEI'16: Tenth international conference on tangible, embedded, and embodied interaction* (pp. 150–158). ACM. http://utouch.cpsc.ucalgary.ca/docs/Engaging AtRiskStudents-TEI2015.pdf

Stager, G. (2005, August 28–31). *Papertian constructionism and the design of productive contexts for learning* [Paper presentation]. EuroLogo X. http://www.stager .org/articles/eurologo2005.pdf

Stager, G. (2013, June 24–27). *Papert's prison Fab Lab: Implications for the maker movement and education design* [Paper presentation]. IDC. https://www.makers empire.com/wp-content/uploads/2018/02/Paperts-Prison-Fab-Lab -Implications-for-the-maker-movement-and-education-design-Stager-13.pdf

Sutcher, L., Darling-Hammond, L., & Carver-Thomas, D. (2016). *A coming crisis in teaching? Teacher supply, demand, and shortages in the U.S.* Learning Policy Institute. https://learningpolicyinstitute.org/product/coming-crisis-teaching

Sutcher, L., Darling-Hammond, L., & Carver-Thomas, D. (2019). Understanding teacher shortages: An analysis of teacher supply and demand in the United States. *Education Policy Archives, 27*(15), 1–40. http://dx.doi.org/10.14507/ epaa.27.3696

Thibodeaux, A. K., Labat, M. B., Lee, D. E., & Labat, C. A. (2015). The effects of leadership And high-stakes testing on teacher retention. *Academy of Educational Leadership Journal, 19*(1), 227–249.

U.S. Department of Education. (2003). *No Child Left Behind: A parents' guide.* https:// www2.ed.gov/parents/academic/involve/nclbguide/parentsguide.pdf

U.S. Department of Education. (2014). *The 36th annual report to congress on the implementation of the "Individuals With Disabilities Education Act."* https://eric.ed .gov/?q=title%3a(%22annual+report+to+congress%22+AND+%22individuals +with+disabilities%22)+NOT+title%3a(%22assistative+technology+act%22+ OR+programs)&id=ED557419

VanAcker, R. (2004). Current status of public education and likely future directions for students With emotional and behavioral disorders. In L. M. Bullock & R. A. Gable (Eds.), *Quality personnel preparation in emotional/behavioral disorders: Current perspectives and future directions* (pp. 79–93). Institute for Behavioral and Learning Differences.

Wagner, M., & Cameto, R. (2004). *The characteristics, experiences, and outcomes of youth with emotional disturbances: A report from the National Longitudinal Transition Study-2.* National Center on Secondary Education and Transition. https://eric.ed.gov/?id=ED484283

Wagner, M., Kutash, K., Duchnowski, A. J., Epstein, M. H., & Sumi, W. C. (2005). The children and youth we serve: A national picture of the characteristics of students with emotional disturbances receiving special education. *Journal of Emotional and Behavior Disorders, 13*(2), 79–96. https://doi.org/10.1177/10634266050130020201

Willmann, M., & Seeliger, G. M. (2017). SEBD inclusion research synthesis: A content analysis of research themes and methods in empirical studies. *Emotional and Behavioural Difficulties 22*(2), 142–161. https://doi.org/10.1080/13632752.2016.1255441

CHAPTER 11

AFTERWORD

This book has illustrated problems and solutions in urban education through the lens of teacher preparation and education. Authors presented innovative and culturally relevant ideas to ensure all children, especially marginalized Black and Brown children, receive an equitable education. All students, especially Black and Brown students who have been histori- cally marginalized, deserve equitable access to a quality education which has been systemically denied to them due to racism which has pervaded the power structures that keep poor people poor and rich people rich (Royce, 2009). As such, the critical race theory woven throughout this book remind- ed us how racism plays an integral and permanent place in our society, allowing for the least qualified teachers to teach the most vulnerable stu- dents. Furthermore, the African American Pedagogical Excellence (AAPE) reinforces the need to prepare a majority White middle-class monolingual female workforce using techniques best illustrated from their Black female counterparts (Acosta et al., 2018).

Teacher preparation is a matter of equity and can be used as a tool for social justice. It appears that inexperienced, uncertified teachers are disproportionally affecting majority-minority schools and communities with economically disadvantaged students. As a result, Black and Brown economically disadvantaged students are provided with fewer opportuni- ties, hence the opportunity gap widens with every school year the student has with an unqualified, unprepared teacher. This can lead to discipline

Economic, Political and Legal Solutions to Critical Issues in Urban Education   pages 191–196
and Implications for Teacher Preparation
Copyright © 2022 by Information Age Publishing
www.infoagepub.com
All rights of reproduction in any form reserved.

disproportionality (Butler et al., 2012), school push out (Tuck, 2012), and eventually contribute to the school-to-prison pipeline (Pane & Rocco, 2014). Every child deserves equitable access to quality education; as such, an interdisciplinary approach is needed to make sure teachers are prepared not only professionally, but mentally. Identifying economic, political, and legal solutions to some of these major concerns can create an environment where teachers are set up for success and all students gain equitable access to quality education. Community involvement is also key to maintaining sustainable solutions to urban education.

SOLUTIONS TOWARD A MORE EXPERIENCED WORKFORCE

States should create laws that determine the percentage of new teachers at low-income underperforming schools. If the school is categorized as "low performing" or primarily serves economically disadvantaged youth, laws should be established so that a new teacher would not be allowed to teach there alone until their third year of teaching. Teachers with less than 3 years of experience are often placed in schools with a higher percentage of students of color and higher in poverty. According to Sass et al. (2012), the average effectiveness of teachers in high poverty schools is, in general, less than teachers in other schools, and there is significantly greater variation in teacher quality among high poverty schools. A legal approach to this concern can become a viable option.

To provide students of all economic levels and ethnicities equitable access to highly qualified teachers, the least experienced teachers are not suitable to educate students with the highest need. This measure can also be coupled with economic incentives to provide long-term sustainable solutions. Primarily, the U.S. tax system needs to be restructured so all communities have equitable access to fully fund their school regardless of the community or tax base. This would ensure that a child's zip code does not determine their access to quality education. Educational models that are substandard for economically privileged children should never be acceptable for Black and Brown children and children in under-resourced communities (Lafer, 2014). Secondly, teachers who teach in the highest needs schools should be paid more. This would incentivize higher needs schools while creating a compensation model that would allow the teacher the means to provide additional support and resources to their students.

States should also create laws that provide provisional licensure to teachers with 3 years or less experience. Similar to restrictions for a new medical professional, a teacher should not be allowed to teach alone until after the third year. New teachers, as in many successful school systems, should co-teach with an experienced teacher to gain the skills necessary to become an effective educator. Once that provisional time is complete, they will be eligible for a full license. This would dramatically increase the need for mentor teachers in schools with a higher percentage of teachers with less than 3 years of experience. Over time, with the constant support of a mentor teacher, the new teacher will grow in their pedagogical practices, as well as content knowledge, to become a highly effective teacher. Soon this highly effective teacher will be ready to mentor a new teacher and recreate similar results. This has the potential to positively influence teacher retention, reduce teacher stress and burnout, and create a new cyclical teacher pipeline to support a continuous flow of teachers into the school systems. Teacher education programs are doing a disservice to the community, school, and students through expediting teacher education. Learning takes time, and teacher preparation programs must change the practice of releasing under-developed, novice teachers directly into their own classrooms.

SOLUTIONS USING CLINICAL EXPERIENCES AND DIVERSIFYING OF TEACHER FORCE

Very simply, clinical student teaching should be paid. According to the National Education Association (NEA) report on Ranking of States 2018 and Estimates of School Statistics 2019 report, in 2017–2018, the average salary for a teacher in North Carolina is $52,850 and the National average is $60,477 (National Education Association, n.d.). The average school debt for teachers who entered the field in 2018 is $29,200 (Friedman, 2020). To decrease the potential of this debt, an economic solution is to pay student teachers. Solutions that provide student teachers funding through their clinical experience are needed, especially for under-resourced teachers to navigate a system originally designed for the elite. Paying teachers during their required clinical experience would narrow the opportunity gap for those of various economic backgrounds who want to pursue a career in education. Providing paid student teaching opportunities would increase the economic and ethnic diversity of teacher applicants which would ultimately create better outcomes for diverse students. To overcome this issue in urban education, becoming a teacher should not be an economic sacrifice, but a career that can help individuals build wealth.

SOLUTIONS FOR TEACHERS AND MENTAL HEALTH

As this book has illustrated, teacher burnout influences teacher retention, and the experiences of first-year teachers can be particularly stressful (Orfield et al., 2016). Economic and legislative methods should be considered to provide solutions to this problem. Schools should not only fully staff counselors for students, but provide in-house mental health services for teachers and staff. If the school is a place where traumatic experiences occur (Howard, 2016), it should also be a place where healing can occur. Research has shown that under-resourced schools tend to need the most access to mental health services. However, for this solution to be sustainable, society must simultaneously address the systemic root causes of stress and trauma when supporting the mental health needs of students and teachers. Solutions to this issue are especially needed in the wake of COVID-19, which has exacerbated and uncovered the stress and anxiety teachers and students experience at home. An interdisciplinary approach is needed for this solution to manifest, including stakeholders, policymakers, and healthcare professionals.

SOLUTIONS FOR TEACHERS IN ALTERNATIVE SCHOOLS

When identifying legal, political, and economic solutions to issues in urban education, accountability is critical. In the United States, there is a shortage of highly qualified teachers. This book explained how seeking various methods of teacher accountability can be a sustainable solution for educators in alternative schools. This includes the depersonalized curriculum, exposing the opportunity gaps based on summative assessments, and discontinuing biased merit pay which negatively affects teachers who educate vulnerable students. Historically, Black and Brown students in alternative school settings have been marginalized, yet can benefit from personalized learning (Pane et al., 2015) and culturally relevant teaching (Ladson-Billings, 1992). However, it takes a community effort to embrace alternative ways of supporting teachers and educating students. Communities must unpack systemic inequities that poison the root of educating Black and Brown youth. School communities must become more culturally competent, more inclusive, and more supportive of ethnically, linguistically, and culturally diverse students. Educators must also learn, through ongoing professional development, how to create a brave, caring classroom where all students can achieve. Teaching in an alternative school setting is not a punishment, but an opportunity for culturally relevant teaching practices to thrive and for students to find sustainable success, including tools to re-enter their home school using personalized learning strategies.

SOLUTIONS TO INCREASE STUDENT ACHIEVEMENT

Economic, political, and legal solutions to urban education that center on teacher preparation include discontinuing privatization practices often used in education. The cancer of systemic racial oppression masked as school privatization has infiltrated America since long before *Brown v. Board of Education*. Similar to the Hippocratic oath of the medical profession, stakeholders have an ethical obligation to Black and Brown children, especially in urban schools. School boards, parents, and community members must be made aware of the toxicity of school privatization and its predatory contractors across the nation, particularly in communities of color in which an influx of charter schools has taken root. Privatization must no longer be used as a tool to further widen the opportunity gap for marginalized students of color.

Every child, regardless of race, class, or privilege, deserves equitable access to a high-quality education. Historically in the United States, the economically disadvantaged Black and Brown students are not given the same educational access as those who have wealth. This has resulted in a disproportioned number of unqualified inexperienced teachers flooding low-income school communities. As a matter of equity, this needs to change. Solutions include staffing schools in a way that ensures that all children have access to prepared, experienced teachers. States and school districts must dismantle racist systems and implement strategies that address multiple problems simultaneously (Almy & Theokas, 2010). However, we cannot ask teachers to carry the burden of changing urban education on their own. We also cannot evaluate a teacher's success in the classroom solely on their student's test scores. Solutions must be centered on creating teaching environments in which such change is not their only responsibility, but the responsibility of the entire learning community. Implementing policies, taking legal action, and incorporating an economic approach can all solve issues in urban education through the lens of teacher preparation.

REFERENCES

Acosta, M. M., Foster, M., & Houchen, D. F. (2018). "Why seek the living among the dead?" African American pedagogical excellence: Exemplar practice for teacher education. *Journal of Teacher Education, 69*(4), 341–353. https://doi.org/10.1177/0022487118761881

Almy, S., & Theokas, C. (2010). *Not prepared for class: High-poverty schools continue to have fewer in-field teachers.* Education Trust. https://eric.ed.gov/?id=ED543217

Butler, B. R., Lewis, C. W., Moore, J. L., III, & Scott, M. E. (2012). Assessing the odds: Disproportional discipline practices and implications for educational stakeholders. *The Journal of Negro Education, 81*(1), 11–24. https://doi.org/10.7709/jnegroeducation.81.1.0011

Friedman, Z. (2020, February 3). Student loan debt statistics in 2020: A record $1.6 trillion. *Forbes.* https://www.forbes.com/sites/zackfriedman/2020/02/03/student-loan-debt-statistics/

Howard, T. C. (2016). Why Black lives (and minds) matter: Race, freedom schools & the quest for educational equity. *The Journal of Negro Education, 85*(2), 101–113. https://doi.org/10.7709/jnegroeducation.85.2.0101

Ladson-Billings, G. (1992). Reading between the lines and beyond the pages: A culturally relevant approach to literacy teaching. *Theory Into Practice, 31*(4), 312–320. https://doi.org/10.1080/00405849209543558

Lafer, G. (2014). *Do poor kids deserve lower-quality education than rich kids? Evaluating school privatization proposals in Milwaukee, Wisconsin* (EPI Briefing Paper #375). Economic Policy Institute. https://eric.ed.gov/?id=ED558116

National Education Association. (n.d.). *National Education Association releases annual rankings & estimates report.* https://www.nea.org/research-publications

Orfield, G., Ee, J., Frankenberg, E., & Siegel-Hawley, G. (2016). *"Brown" at 62: School segregation by race, poverty and state.* Civil Rights Project- Proyecto Derechos Civiles. https://eric.ed.gov/?id=ED565900

Pane, D. M., & Rocco, T. S. (2014). *Transforming the school-to-prison pipeline: Lessons from the classroom.* Springer Science & Business Media.

Pane, J. F., Steiner, E. D., Baird, M. D., & Hamilton, L. S. (2015). *Continued progress: promising evidence on personalized learning.* RAND Corporation. https://doi.org/10.7249/RR1365

Royce, E. C. (2009). *Poverty and power: The problem of structural inequality.* Rowman & Littlefield.

Sass, T. R., Hannaway, J., Xu, Z., Figlio, D. N., & Feng, L. (2012). Value added of teachers in high-poverty schools and lower poverty schools. *Journal of Urban Economics, 72*(2), 104–122. https://doi.org/10.1016/j.jue.2012.04.004

Tuck, E. (2012). *Urban youth and school pushout: Gateways, get-aways, and the GED.* Routledge.